FLAT OUT UNCONSTITUTIONAL

A. M. Perez

CONTENTS

FLAT OUT UNCONSTITUTIONAL

Chapter 1 Power

POWER DOESN'T IMPLY AUTHORITY

- The Constitution[1] neither lives nor breathes.
- The 10th Amendment[2]: Enumerated powers
- The 9th Amendment[3]: Rights need not be enumerated.
- God, not government, grants rights.
- Federal handouts are bribes.
- The Constitution stands in the way of power, which is why it is constantly under attack.

What does the United States Federal Government do that is flat out unconstitutional? Well, as hard as it is to believe, almost everything. The U.S. Constitution gave almost zero domestic power to the federal government, leaving any governing of our day to day lives to individual states. Since the founding and particularly in the

---

[1] See pages 232-248

[2] See page 251

[3] See page 251

last century, the Federal Government has been usurping more and more power without the slightest bit of authority to do so.

When I decided to write my thoughts down I wasn't sure where to start. If it were up to me, every class given on the Constitution would start at the end of the Bill of Rights[4], Amendment 10[5], so that seems as good a place as any. If you can understand the 10th Amendment the rest of the Constitution is easy to understand. It simply says what it says.

The Constitution is no more living and breathing than any contract, mortgage, insurance policy or any other document. If documents could be interpreted to say whatever you want them to say at a whim, why write them down? Our Founding Fathers wrote the Constitution in plain English that anyone could understand. It wasn't a mystery to be decoded as time went on. They gave us a method to amend the Constitution if We the People decide we want some changes. Conservatives are content with reading the Constitution, but liberals have to interpret it, because it simply doesn't say what they want it to say. The Founders wrote the Constitution in a way that is easy for any layman to understand. I will attempt to do the same, keeping this simple.

The 10th Amendment of the Constitution is very basic. "The powers not delegated to the United States by the Constitution, nor prohibited by it to the States, are reserved to the States respectively, or to the people." What is hard to understand about that? If a power is not delegated to the United States in the Constitution, they don't have it. Known as enumerated powers, federal powers must be specified and listed. If the Constitution doesn't say they can do something, they can't. Period. Those powers are reserved to the States or the people, unless of course, as the 10th Amendment says, the Constitution prohibits that particular power.

Simplified: The Federal Government doesn't have a power unless the Constitution says it does. States and the people have every power not given directly to the Federal Government unless specifically

---

[4] See pages 249-251

[5] See page 251

prohibited. The powers that are specified as federal are very few, especially domestic powers. The Federal Government acts as a single voice for all of the states on international matters and therefore is granted most of the power in international matters.

With the 10th Amendment in mind it is easy to ask yourself if anything is constitutional or not. If the Federal Government does something or passes a law, does the Constitution specify that they can? If a state passes a law does the Constitution say they can't? People attend law schools for years to learn how to ignore the 10th Amendment.

The 9th Amendment[6] is less often cited, but goes hand in hand with the 10th. It ensures that the Constitution doesn't have to enumerate rights. "The enumeration in the Constitution, of certain rights, shall not be construed to deny or disparage others retained by the people." Keep in mind, our Founders told us that our rights are given to us by God. They are unalienable. The Constitution and the Bill of Rights merely protects some of our rights. The 9th Amendment makes it clear that we have rights whether the Constitution lists them or not, the exact opposite of federal powers, which must be listed.

What did the Founders mean by our rights being given by God? Well, first of all, they weren't taking credit for giving them to us and were founding our country on the basis that our rights were inherent. If they claimed our rights were given by government then they could also be taken by government. In The Declaration of Independence they used the word "unalienable" to describe our rights. They chose words wisely and this word has a very specific meaning, which is that our rights are unable to be given or taken. So even if you are not religious, your rights are absolute and government cannot revoke them.

Government doesn't have to revoke rights if you don't know you have them. If We the People are ignorant of our rights or unwilling to protect them ourselves, they are not worth the parchment they are written on.

---

[6] See page 251

It is very important that we understand these basic concepts regarding enumerated federal powers and the rights of the States and the People, or it will be too easy to accept the premise that we are ruled by the Federal Government. Nothing could be further from the truth. The Federal Government is supposed to answer to us. The states are supposed to govern themselves like separate countries with their own governments and laws, with the Federal Government authorized to wield only those domestic powers which protect our shared rights and ensure fair trade and free movement among the states. International powers of the Federal Government are far more broad and are the core of what unites the states.

The Federal Government is split into three branches, the Executive, Legislative, and Judiciary. Each branch has its responsibilities and enumerated powers in the Constitution. All three are responsible for egregious usurpations of power and they get away with it because the vast majority of Americans are ignorant of the Constitution, their rights, and the limitations placed on the Federal Government. It is assumed by the majority of Americans, and constantly portrayed in our education system and by most of the main stream media, that Congress can simply pass any law they want as long as they get a majority vote and the President signs the bill. This is entirely wrong. This is the modern, common practice, and is why we have so many unconstitutional laws, but it is wrong.

It is true that Congress legislates and when they pass a bill and the President signs it, it becomes law. It is not true that they are allowed to legislate on anything they like. Remember their enumerated powers. Everything Congress has the authority to legislate on can be found in Article 1, Section 8[7] of the Constitution. It's a very specific list of things, very few of which are domestic.

With regard to any federal law, determining its constitutionality is as easy as looking in Article 1, Section 8 for permission for Congress to legislate on that topic. I will refer to Article 1, Section 8 quite often, as it is probably the most violated section of the Constitution by our Federal Government. Article 1, Section 8 is fantastic. It lays out all of the powers Congress needs to secure our freedom, conduct

---

[7] See page 237

foreign diplomacy, lay tariffs, and declare war. There is much more for such a short section, but key to the American citizen at home are the domestic powers, which are to regulate commerce among states, coin money, establish post offices and post roads, promote science and art and protect intellectual property with patents. Domestically, that's about it.

In that short list of domestic powers it's easy to see why Congress was powerless to legislate a ban on alcohol, leaving it to the states to ratify the 18th Amendment[8] to the Constitution to outlaw liquor sales. Where did Congress get the authority to outlaw marijuana or other intoxicating substances? They didn't. They have no such authority. The 10th Amendment makes it clear that it is a state issue unless you cross an international border with drugs or perhaps mail them from your local Post Office.

Does this mean I support drug use? Of course not. I think it's stupid. We are free to be stupid if we like without the intervention of Congress. The states on the other hand have far more authority to outlaw substance use and abuse, as we see today in dry counties across the country. The 21st Amendment[9] negated the 18th Amendment making alcohol legal again, right? Not really. The 21st Amendment doesn't say, "Alcohol consumption is a right and hereby legal." The 21st just repeals the 18th, making it irrelevant at a federal level once more. So dry counties and cities have outlawed liquor on their own, perfectly legally and without violating the Constitution.

Some people will point out that the 21st Amendment has three clauses and that while the first clause merely negates the 18th Amendment, the other two grant more federal power to control alcohol. Well, not exactly. The second clause really only allows the Federal Government to control international importation of alcohol, a power they really already had. The third clause is nothing more than a waste of space, as it only says that the 21st Amendment isn't legal unless it is ratified. Well, that is an obvious fact regarding any constitutional amendment.

---

[8] See page 256

[9] See page 258

Over the course of several years Congress has become more brazen. They prey on our sense of morality to justify passing laws they have no authority to pass and which should be left to the states. They want any speaking out against it to appear as support for the bad behavior rather than the condemnation of Federal Government overreach that it is. Libertarians are commonly accused of wanting to legalize abhorrent behavior, which is usually not the case at all. This isn't what constitutional conservatives want either, but we are met with questions like, "How dare you want to legalize X, Y or Z?" We just don't want the Federal Government involved where it is not authorized to be. States are more than capable of legislating for themselves. Every state has different laws and consequences, even for murder. They should have no problem deciding a legal drinking age for themselves.

Before Congress was totally corrupt and were still aware of at least some of their limitations they were pressured to raise the legal age to consume alcohol, but they realized they had no authority to do so. How did they solve this problem? With bribes of course. They bribed the states with interstate highway funding and all 50 states eventually took the bribes and raised the drinking age to 21. Did this solve any problems? Not really. It merely made criminals out of previously law abiding citizens and filled more jails. This is costly for the states in housing inmates and in the loss of alcohol tax revenue from 18-20 year old citizens.

It should also be noted that Congress established the Highway Trust Fund in 1956 to pay for highway projects, using their power to establish post roads. We pay a tax when we purchase gasoline to pay for this. Congress then bribes the states with this revenue they are already obligated to spend. It's ludicrous.

Congress bribes more than just states. They bribe the people and businesses with unconstitutional wealth redistribution. Whether it's welfare or food stamps for individuals or subsidies for corporations, it's all unconstitutional and is outright bribery. People who rely on welfare, food stamps, HUD housing and any other meager handouts that the Federal Government gives them, are going to continue voting for the party who gives it to them. The same party which has systematically taken over the education programs these people also rely on. No one knows or cares that their handouts are unconstitutional as long as the check rolls in. The system has become so institutionalized that it seems cruel to cut these people off of these programs.

The names of these programs are designed to deceive. It is no coincidence that the Welfare Program is called "Welfare." That made it easy to claim it was constitutional, by pointing at the general welfare clause, which was never intended to be an individual welfare clause. The Founding Fathers never meant for the Federal Government to help people out of financial difficulty or they would have said so. By naming the program "Welfare" the Constitution was effectively amended by amending the dictionary.

The socialists in Congress who were peddling food stamps to bribe their voters came to the realization that the program had become a stigma. Some people were embarrassed to pull out a book of "Food Coupons" to pay for their groceries. To make it more glamorous they renamed the program The Supplemental Nutrition Assistance Program (SNAP), so it would sound appealing and gave the recipients an innocuous looking debit card. Now the deadbeats could blend in with those who they had effectively stolen from, the hard working, over taxed producers. More than 1 in 7 Americans are now on the SNAP program, unconstitutionally stealing from their neighbors. This is deplorable and unnecessary. If government assistance were truly needed, it should be left to the states that actually have the constitutional authority to create such programs and also can't print more money when they need it, so have to maintain stricter financial restraint. States can't afford the waste and fraud that take place in the Federal Government entitlement programs.

Every single federal entitlement program is unconstitutional, but we've been conditioned to consider it cruel to suggest that. WIC, Medicare, Obamacare, and even Social Security are all unconstitutional. They should all be cut off immediately, with the exception of Social Security which should allow those above a certain age who have paid into it all of their lives to get what they paid for and then wean the rest of those who are younger off of the program. We always hear that there will be riots in the streets if we cut off the handouts. That is tacit admission that we're no longer a republic, but rather a mob rule. Sure, there will be a little pain in the beginning, but the cessation of handouts should coincide with equal cuts in taxes, so the money is not taken from the private market any longer. This would result in a hiring boom across the country like we have never seen.

Bribing companies with subsidies and bailouts are just as unconstitutional as redistributing wealth to individuals, except that the Federal Government is able to get more bang for their bribery dollars. The Troubled Asset Relief Program (TARP) has taken corporate bailouts to an all new level with over half a billion dollars given to Solyndra just in time for them to go bankrupt. General Motors was stolen from the bondholders and given to the United Auto Workers Union along with a check for 11 billion dollars. The Federal Government claims to be getting paid back, but it's all a money shell game with bribes and kickbacks going both ways, all on the backs of the tax payers.

None of this is what our Founders envisioned when they ratified the Constitution. Article 2, Section 4[10] forbids bribery and demands impeachment for all Civil Officers of the United States who take part in it. Bribery is rampant and has bought both power and silence. Power for those in government and silence from the masses who won't let go of their government teat long enough to learn how wrong it is.

There is no one left to speak out. There is no one who can put a stop to it. The silence has grown so deafening and the power has grown so great that the Federal Government doesn't even bother trying to hide its unconstitutional actions anymore. Anyone who could possibly do anything about it is on the take. Laws which the Federal Government once knew better than to pass or at least underhandedly bribed and blackmailed states into passing for them, are second nature for them to pass in Congress today. Today Congress would have no problem passing a national drinking age, because they no longer have any regard for the Constitution or compelling reason to act like they do.

We even have Executive Order legislation from the Oval office, with no mention of Executive Orders in the Constitution. Few question them and when they do, they are chastised by the masses of

---

[10] See page 242

dumbed down Americans who don't know any better. When the President of the United States tried to create a treaty with the enemy nation of Iran in direct violation of Article 2 Section 2 Clause 2[11], by calling it an Executive Agreement, 47 Senators wrote a letter to Iran, truthfully saying that it won't be binding. The media and the ignorant, drooling, socialist sycophants on the left attacked the Senators with accusations of treason.

Our government has become lawless while continuing to burden Americans with more unconstitutional laws. Given any recent, domestic, federal law, if asked whether or not it is constitutional, it is almost a sure bet that it is not. You can pick almost any law, look for it's authorization in Article 1, Section 8[12] and you will almost certainly not find it.

The Constitution is under attack from all sides and the attacks are perpetuated by the Federal Government itself. By using the unconstitutional Department of Education to infiltrate our schools and brainwash the public, they have created huge contingencies of socialist groups who actually demand the Federal Government curtail our rights. Mass media craves the power and celebrity they obtain by being in cahoots with the Federal Government. They cover up for and even glamorize the unconstitutional encroachments on our liberty.

With the enormous increase in unemployment in the last few years, we have all seen the media call it Funemployment and run stories about how happy everyone is to have so much free time on their hands to spend with family and taking part in wonderful, fun activities! With terrorism and infrequent but highly publicized firearms accidents or murders, the media has also been advancing the trade of freedom for false security. When people are demanding that the citizenry disarm in favor of a police state, there is definitely something very wrong. We've seen this scenario play out in other countries throughout history and it always ends badly.

---

[11] See page 241

[12] See page 237

America has begun to wake up. The Tea Party, which started off as a fiscally concerned group of citizens, has started reading the Constitution, something they were never required to do in school. They are growing in numbers, albeit slowly, but more importantly they are increasing their knowledge. There is a newfound thirst for knowledge among many who were once complacent.

All of the answers to our problems are in the Constitution. There is still a lot that we as conservatives, Tea Partiers, and Constitutionalists need to learn and accept. We have to come to a realization as a group that the left does not play fair. Things like voter fraud are real. The left takes advantage of our trusting nature. We are afraid to make any accusations that will get us labeled as a conspiracy theorist or a "phobe" of some kind. It's time to take the gloves off and start questioning and scrutinizing with steadfast vigor.

Chapter 2   Arms

"SHALL NOT BE INFRINGED" ACTUALLY MEANS "SHALL NOT BE INFRINGED"

- There is no such thing as a Constitutional gun control law.
- Felons are unconstitutionally classified as 2nd class citizens. The mentally ill are next.
- Gun registration and background checks are unconstitutional.
- Militias are necessary. People have rights.
- $50,000,000 can buy a fake grass roots campaign.
- British Gun Control sparked the Revolutionary War.

Perhaps the most unconstitutional laws across the country are gun control laws. Whether a federal, state, or local law, every gun control law is unconstitutional. Yes, every single one. Our 2nd Amendment[13] right to bear arms is the most important right we have

---

[13] See page 250

and the one which secures all others, which makes it the primary target of all leftists. Throughout history, one of the early steps to control a populace with tyranny is to disarm the public.

While the number is debated, there are said to be about 20,000 gun control laws across the country. That there is no exact count and accuracy of the number of gun control laws is not the point. One unconstitutional law is enough to cause concern.

The left has done a very good job over the years of indoctrinating the general public into accepting slow encroachments on our freedom through the principle of institutionalization. The left will demand a yard, so that we compromise by giving an inch. That's a win for the left and a loss for the Constitution. Every compromise is a win for the left. Over time that inch becomes institutionalized, so that it almost seems ludicrous to question it any longer. The left demands another yard and accepts another inch in compromise. The cycle never ends except that lately we are compromising with feet rather than inches.

The Gun Control Act of 1968 (GCA) was a direct assault on the 2nd Amendment and does many things, all of which are unconstitutional. It infringes on the 2nd Amendment right to keep and bear arms and Congress had no enumerated authority to legislate on the subject. One of the most egregious things the GCA did was to ban felons from owning firearms. We are talking about ex-felons really, although many will jump at the chance to point out that they are legally still referred to as felons. These are people who have committed a felony, whether it was violent or not, then served their sentence, paid their debt to society and are freed. Once free they are now informally classified as 2nd class citizens. They lose their 2nd Amendment right and for the rest of their lives are unable to legally protect themselves or their families.

Because over 40 years have gone by since felons have had targeted rights revoked, people have forgotten that there were ever arguments against it. This unconstitutional law is now institutionalized with little chance of being repealed. Prior to 1968 it was unthinkable to create 2nd class citizens of felons, but due to the magic of institutionalization it is now unthinkable to a majority for felons to have their constitutional rights restored.

Now the mentally ill are targeted to become 2nd Class citizens, beginning with our veterans who suffer from PTSD after serving our country with honor. Don't underestimate the intentions the left has for the millions of children being pumped full of Ritalin today as a growing segment of our population considered to be mentally ill.

Now it almost sounds crazy to allow felons or mentally ill people to maintain the rights that all Americans cherish even though the truly dangerous ones don't follow the law anyway. At least one recent court case in Louisiana has tried to take on this issue, so there may yet be hope.

It is very important to understand the 2nd Amendment and why the Founding Fathers put so much importance on it. It is actually the first amendment in the Bill of Rights[14] to guarantee rights at all, unlike the 1st Amendment, which only limits Congress, something most people are unaware of. The 2nd Amendment clearly limits all levels of government from infringing by not specifying Congress.

"A well regulated militia, being necessary to the security of a free State, the right of the people to keep and bear arms, shall not be infringed." This one sentence brings out a lot of reading comprehension issues among liberals. They redefine the word "regulated" and miss the comma after the word "State" in a willful effort to imply a mandated membership in a militia for the 2nd Amendment right to apply.

The word "regulated" has become synonymous with government ruled, whereas the true meaning at the time the Bill of Rights was written was well trained and in good working order. The meaning of the word regulated doesn't matter. Liberals want to focus on that in order to take attention away from the fact that it is the right of the people, the 2nd Amendment guarantees, not the right of the militia. The 2nd Amendment is clearly about the right of the People to both keep and bear arms. It also says that right shall not be infringed.

The 2nd Amendment doesn't say, "...shall not be infringed, unless..." There is absolutely no reason to infringe and no government power with the authority to infringe. Having no

---

[14] See pages 249-251

authority doesn't stop the government at all levels from wielding power unconstitutionally and infringing anyway. We have laws which infringe on our bearing of arms in many states, cities, federal buildings, courthouses, Post Offices, airports, parks, and numerous other places. Every one of these infringements is unconstitutional.

Since there is no reason given in the 2nd Amendment where infringement of the right is acceptable, there is no reason for the right to be revoked. This means there is no reason for a background check to be performed when purchasing a firearm. What are they checking for? There is nothing they can check for that they can constitutionally use against you to prevent you from making the purchase. Well, they are checking for your status as an ex-felon for one thing, an unconstitutional infringement. Perhaps the ex-felons of America should unite and abdicate their 16th Amendment[15] right to pay income tax until all of their rights are lawfully restored.

Background checks also violate the 4th Amendment[16] right not to be searched and your 5th Amendment[17] right not to incriminate oneself. The violation of 2nd Amendment rights has tentacles which reach out and violate so many more of our rights and threaten to violate them all.

Every state law which requires you to register a gun is unconstitutional. Again, it is a violation of your 2nd and 4th Amendment rights. The state of Connecticut is the latest to have passed a law requiring the registration of certain types of weapons. The residents of Connecticut have declined to comply and the police have declined to enforce it. The people of Connecticut deserve to be applauded in their defiance of this unconstitutional and tyrannical demand.

While the right to bear arms is very important in providing us with the self defense we deserve in our every day lives, the Founding Fathers did not include the 2nd Amendment in the Bill of Rights as a

---

[15] See page 255

[16] See page 250

[17] See page 250

means of self defense. They purposely did not clarify which arms we have the right to bear, because they understood that technology advances and wanted the people to be able to arm themselves with the best arms of the day. They told us why.

This is where the attention should be given to the word "militia" in the 2nd Amendment. This is where reading comprehension is required. The first part of the 2nd Amendment is the prefatory clause. Consider that a reason for what follows. "A well regulated militia, being necessary to the security of a free State." This is the reason for the operative clause, "the right of the people to keep and bear arms, shall not be infringed."

It is very clear that we have a right guaranteed to the people and a reason for it. That reason is not self defense. Self defense is a given. The 2nd Amendment says that the people have the right to keep and bear arms so that they can secure a free State. The word "free" was included purposefully. It is not to secure The State. It is to secure a free State. This is why the oaths to protect and defend the Constitution mention all enemies foreign and domestic.

The founders fought a revolution. They went up against their own government, which had the most powerful military in the world at the time. The 2nd Amendment provides the people with the ability to maintain freedom whether that means fighting a foreign country or their own tyrannical government. To suggest that the founders would want the Federal Government to be better armed than the people is ludicrous.

When reminded of this, liberals will counter with something such as, "So people should be able to have nukes?" They never have a counter argument if you suggest they simply amend the Constitution to outlaw private nuclear arms ownership. If they should be banned in private hands, then surely amending the Constitution to do it legitimately will be easy to do.

Those on the left who want to control the people understand what the 2nd Amendment means very well. That is why they hate it so much. They abhor the restriction it puts on government by empowering the people. They misrepresent their understanding of the 2nd Amendment in an attempt to convince the people to disarm. Radical fear mongering groups have been lobbying the government and businesses for years to infringe on our right to bear arms. The same leftists who are responsible for the murder of 54 million babies in the womb, 1/7th of the American population, claim to be concerned about the safety of children in their misleading ad campaigns designed with the end goal to disarm the people. Dead children are their favorite props.

The latest group of fanatics to crop up with the support of $50,000,000 of Michael Bloomberg's bankroll, is Moms Demand Action for Gun Sense in America. They run around targeting businesses with the claims that their small, ragtag group will boycott them if they don't ban guns from their premises. They have wasted millions of dollars for lip service from a few company executives but have not been winning any of their battles outright.

Many businesses will make a statement agreeing that guns are bad, but they will follow local laws, which is usually all it takes for Moms Demand to go away and declare victory where there is none. Roughly 57,000 businesses, such as Kroger have told Moms Demand to take a hike with no uncertain terms. In Kroger's case this resulted in huge mobs of 5 Moms at a time storming Kroger stores to deliver petitions with 300,000 signatures on them demanding Kroger ban guns. Kroger continues to throw the Moms Demand groups off of their property.

While monitoring the group Moms Demand fairly closely over the past year or so, I have never seen any indication of a petition being passed around, so there is no evidence that these 300,000 signatures are valid. The group is notorious for lying in their ads. They claim to be a grass roots organization, but with Bloomberg financing, nothing could be further from the truth. Liberals have to lie in order to convince the public that there is something to be alarmed about and give up some freedom in exchange for security.

It is no surprise that where mass shootings occur, guns aren't allowed. Whether it be a gun free theater, gun free school, or gun free military base such as Ft. Hood, mass shooters go where the guns aren't allowed. These mass shootings are more propaganda for Moms Demand to use to push their agenda. The more gun free zones they can create, the better their chances for having another mass shooting to use as evidence that we need more gun free zones. It's a vicious and nefarious cycle that must stop.

The people have realized this to a large extent and it has started to come to a stop. In the last few years gun control laws across the country have been repealed, thrown out in court, and legislatively negated by less restrictive laws, even in Missouri where it took overriding a veto. Surprisingly the 9th Circuit court has forced the state of California to start giving out concealed carry permits. While having a permit to exercise a right is still unconstitutional, it's a step in the right direction from the point California started from, which was a policy of refusing all concealed carry permit applications. Now they must approve them, unless of course you are an ex-felon. They still hang onto that unconstitutional rights infringement.

The 2nd Amendment wins have been numerous lately. Washington D.C. lost the Supreme Court case of Heller vs. DC. and must now allow gun ownership. Georgia now allows guns almost anywhere. The Supreme Court has forced Illinois, like California, to start handing out concealed carry permits. Missouri just began allowing open carry of guns for anyone and teachers to be armed. Where the left has passed one unconstitutional law after another over the past several years, the one area the right has been gaining ground is on the 2nd Amendment, the most important area of all.

The 2nd Amendment is the greatest sentence in the entire Constitution. Nothing else in the Constitution is worth the parchment it is written on without the 2nd Amendment to enforce it. America has become the greatest nation on the face of the earth because of the 2nd Amendment. We avoided an attack on the mainland of the United States from Japan, because the Japanese were afraid of the number of arms the civilians had.

In sheer numbers, the American people are armed to the teeth. No one knows how many guns are in private hands. Estimates of the number of guns in the hands of the entire U.S. military, federal agencies, and all police departments combined are only 4-5 million. Estimates of the number of guns in private American citizen hands range between 300-500 million. Regardless of the precise number, the American people hold more guns than the rest of the entire world and all militaries of the world combined. We are a very well armed people and there is nothing anyone is going to do about it.

Being well armed is the American way. Our Revolutionary War started over British attempts at gun control. We are taught that it was all about taxation, but that was an issue for many years by the time the Revolutionary War started. The British advance in May 1775, to confiscate our weapons stores in Concord, Massachusetts is what sparked the "Shot heard round the world."

Our country was founded on the rejection of gun control and the most important way to keep our republic intact is to continue to stave off all attempts at gun control. We are a nation of guns. That's who we are and why America achieved more in 200 years than all of the rest of the countries of the world have achieved in thousands of years. Freedom like the world had never seen, ensured by the right to bear arms, unleashed the human spirit to motivate unparalleled innovation. Without the ability to protect yourself, you are not free.

When confronted with any law that infringes on your right to bear arms, question it. If it disarms you, it is unconstitutional. If it requires you to apply for government permission or report information to government in any way, it is unconstitutional. Permits, registration, gun free zones, even not being allowed to carry a gun on domestic flights, is all unconstitutional and all of these laws are relatively new, but just old enough to have become institutionalized and therefore have the impression of being reasonable.

It is past the time where we need to go on offense and instead of defending our rights from those who would infringe on them by passing unconstitutional gun control laws, we need to attack the unconstitutional laws that are in place and fight to repeal them. We have been making strides, but we need to increase our education on the subject and our fervor in the fight. We have been pushing back, but that isn't good enough. We have to push ahead. The difference is an offensive rather than defensive position.

No right is more important than the right to bear arms. While we can hope and pray that the right never becomes a necessary means to an end, it is our last best hope to defeat tyranny.

Chapter 3
Unconstitutional Federal Agencies

REGULATIONS ARE NOT LAW

- ATF Director resigned over unconstitutional attempt to ban ammo.
- Department of Education indoctrinates your youths.
- The TSA strips you of your 1st, 2nd, 4th, 5th, 9th, and 10th Amendment rights[18].
- States and Capitalism do a better job than the FDA.
- Obama said, "electricity rates would necessarily skyrocket."
- Bundy Ranch: 2nd Amendment meets Tyranny.
- Free housing, safety, and security aren't rights.

---

[18] See pages 249-251

Probably worse than any unconstitutional laws are unconstitutional agencies. The Federal Government has created a vast number of agencies, which the American people have to answer to as rulers, yet they have no constitutional authority to rule over us.

Rather than trying to pass laws that will not pass constitutional muster, the Federal Government found it easier to set up agencies that will create regulations that we are forced to follow as if they are laws. This is very convenient for our elected representatives. An agency can create a regulation you don't like, but are beholden to follow without it reflecting negatively on your congressman, so you will reelect him.

The list of unconstitutional agencies is almost as long as the list of agencies as a whole. Any federal agency which regulates anyone not within the direct chain of command of the agency is unconstitutional. The DoD (Department of Defense) is constitutional, because all DoD regulations apply only to people who are voluntarily a part of the DoD.

The Constitution provides legislative power to Congress and even then, only in very specific areas found in Article 1, Section 8[19]. Almost every federal agency we have is outside of the scope of any authorized legislative subject covered in Article 1, section 8. Not only has Congress passed off their legislative powers to agencies that should not exist, they have granted them legislative powers in areas that are not part of the federal jurisdiction. Federal agencies act as legislators as well as the judge and jury as to whether you violate their commands. Ask yourself why Obama is arming these agencies? They can't pass laws, yet they enforce their regulations as if they are laws.

Choose any federal agency you like. Ask yourself if what they do is covered in Article 1, Section 8. Chances are, the answer is no. Even if the answer is yes, the Constitution doesn't allow Congress to pass its responsibilities to an agency which regulates the people. They are required to pass laws and be held accountable for their votes.

---

[19] See page 237

Does Article 1, Section 8 allow federal legislation in the area of environmental protection? No. Congress can make no environmental protection law. So why do we have the Environmental Protection Agency (EPA)? The EPA is an unconstitutional agency.

The EPA attacks businesses and costs them huge sums of money in what can be compared to a huge mob protection racket. If you comply with EPA demands and pay them fees and fines, they may back off. If you don't, they will ruin you. The EPA has confiscated land by claiming ditches are protected wetlands. The EPA has its tendrils in every company in the US. They are a huge extortion racket and the best way, but most unlikely way to put a stop to them is a universal denial of their authority. The people have been dumbed down and scared into compliance.

The 18th Amendment[20] outlaws alcohol. Congress used to know they had no authority to write any law they wanted and the states ratified the 18th Amendment. The 21st Amendment[21] repealed it. Now there is zero federal authority over alcohol in the Constitution. The Constitution doesn't mention tobacco. The 2nd Amendment[22] is clear that the right to keep and bear arms shall not be infringed. So, what is the purpose of the Alcohol, Tobacco, and Firearms (ATF) agency? Why do they exist? They are flat out unconstitutional.

Not one of their alphabet letters is even remotely a federal concern. Why do they have any power? They certainly have no authority to wield any power. All alcohol, tobacco, and firearms manufacturers and retailers should ignore them. If they actually ignored the ATF in mass, there is nothing the bogus ATF could do about it.

This was recently proven when 80,000 people responded to the ATF regarding their attempt to ban M855 .223 caliber ammunition for the popular AR15, which resulted in the resignation of the ATF

---

[20] See page 256

[21] See page 258

[22] See page 250

director, B. Todd Jones. Word got out about the backdoor ban before it happened and the people spoke out and won! Resist them! It works. They should not exist and are quite possibly the most unconstitutional of all unconstitutional agencies. Fear of the ATF is why each individual company complies. Each individual company should organize with all other companies against the ATF. Liberals love unions. They should love this idea.

Why is there a Department of Education (DOE)? It's unconstitutional. Try to find education in Article 1, Section 8. You won't find it. Education is not a constitutionally enumerated power for the federal government to control. The reason there is a DOE is because if the government can control what you know and don't know, they can get away with doing anything they want in any other arena. If they determine what you can know or what you can't know, they own you.

The DOE is the most evil of all unconstitutional agencies and should be disbanded immediately. The DOE bribes states and local school systems into accepting their curriculums. They offer money in exchange for their authority, when in fact they have no authority, only unconstitutional power. The DOE ensures that schools are politically correct. Every liberal agenda from evolution to Common Core is enforced while religious morals are forbidden. The DOE is the largest cult leader in America. Brainwashing is their bread and butter.

In the words of Eric Holder when explaining how to coerce the people into hating guns, "We just have to be repetitive about this. It's not enough to have a catchy ad on a Monday and then only do it every Monday. We have to do this every day of the week and just really brainwash people into thinking about guns in a vastly different way."

It doesn't matter which domestic agency you choose, if it is one that controls you or any other American citizen in some way, it is unconstitutional. The Patriot Act gave us a few more unconstitutional agencies, such as the TSA. What is constitutional about the TSA? Nothing.

The TSA violates our 4th Amendment[23] rights by searching us and seizing our property on a daily basis. They have no warrant with our name on it or probable cause to suspect us of a crime, as the 4th Amendment requires.

The TSA asks us questions which violate our 5th Amendment rights[24] and they are blatant revokers of our 2nd Amendment right.[25] Our 1st, 9th, and 10th Amendment[26] rights are also violated. Say the wrong thing and you won't make your flight. The mere existence of the TSA as a federal agency negates any rights the states or the people have according to the 9th and 10th amendments. No agency strips more rights at one time than the TSA.

The federal government does have authority to control aspects of international travel, but not domestic. Disregarding the arguments of private property rights over 2nd Amendment rights, it would be vastly different if airline companies were refusing arms on their planes and were responsible for their own security check points. We would have the opportunity to fly on a gun free plane or choose another airline company and spend our money on a flight that doesn't violate our rights and allows us to fly armed. The decision would be made by consumers.

What is the most constitutional thing about the FDA? Nothing! They sure do make a lot of decisions though and nothing in the Constitution allows anyone to make decisions regarding the food we buy or sell. I've heard it all. The FDA protects us! How could we trust the food we eat if the FDA wasn't there to protect us? I guess you would have to ask the humans who lived for thousands of years before us.

It is doubtful that a company which sold poisonous food would last long in a free market. It is in every food company's best interest to sell things that are desired. Poison is not desired. Every state

---

[23] See page 250

[24] See page 250

[25] See page 250

[26] See pages 249, 251

already regulates every type of product sold within their own agencies. These are completely constitutional, because Amendment 10 gives states the right to control things that the federal government has no authority to control.

People suggest that it is too difficult for companies to comply with 50 different state regulations as opposed to a single federal agency, but they already do. They just have the federal agency to comply with as well, making it 51. Removing the federal regulations decreases the number from 51 to 50. It only decreases the burden on companies. This is without considering the 200+ different countries in the world that most food companies have to answer to as well. The FDA has nothing to do with your Big Mac in Germany.

The FDA has a history of failure. They don't seem to be proven to be very protective, but they continue their existence due to their promise of protecting us. They are useless, unconstitutional and it is time to shut them down.

I can't find the word "energy" in the Constitution. Why is there a Department of Energy (the other DOE)? It's not the Federal Government's business where we get our energy. The Federal Government has purposely increased the cost of energy to consumers. In the words of Barack Hussein Obama, "electricity rates would necessarily skyrocket."

We have given too much power to a Federal Government, which doesn't have the authority and they only use that power to strangle the people in political nooses. Affordable energy is one of the major contributors to the wealth and prosperity that America has achieved. To stifle this should be labeled as treasonous. When states regulate power companies and energy exploration, such as the state of Alaska, the people are more likely to benefit than they are with unconstitutional federal agencies in control who seemingly answer to no one.

The Bureau of Land Management is perplexing. They are responsible for regulating all sorts of activities that Americans, who are supposedly free, take part in as well as the land they do it on. They meddle with everything from hunting, gold mining, hiking, camping, fishing, and pretty much anything you can think of doing in the wilds of America where you would hope to be left alone.

Most recently they became famous for running off with their tails between their legs when faced down by a militia exercising their 2nd Amendment rights at Bundy Ranch. The Bundy Ranch face off was between an American citizen backed by militia and an unconstitutional federal agency, which sent in militarily equipped police in order to enforce an unconstitutional fee being imposed on the last of the ranchers left in the area that the BLM hadn't bankrupted.

It was later exposed to be a Senator Harry Reid backed land grab scandal in an effort to lease the land to foreign Chinese green energy companies. This is a fantastic example as to why the Constitution does not grant authority to the Federal Government to legislate and mete out justices via federal agencies. Even the activities the BLM regulates are unconstitutional for Congress to legislate anything about. There is no constitutionally enumerated authority for charging a citizen grazing fees. The Bundy Ranch stand off showed us how the 2nd Amendment can be applied to halt federal tyranny without firing a single shot.

Not one word in the Constitution gives any reason to suggest that the Federal Government has any authority over housing. Nothing about The Department of Housing and Urban Development (HUD) is constitutional. Responsible for countless hundreds of billions of dollars in unconstitutional wasteful spending, this agency seems to have one purpose, to perpetuate and increase poverty.

Pushed and expanded almost entirely by Democrats, they provide free (tax payer funded) housing to the same people dumbed down by the Department of Education. This is effectively a bribe for democrat votes. As with all federal entitlements, these unconstitutional bribes to vote democrat are paid for almost solely by hard working republicans. We pay to bribe others to vote against our interests. This is a brilliant strategy of the left and one that needs to be exposed more publicly for what it is. The largest slumlord in the country is the Department of Housing and Urban Development.

Occupational Safety and Health (OSHA) is in tight competition with the EPA for which unconstitutional agency can regulate companies to death more effectively. We all want safety in the work place, but how much freedom should we have to relinquish to federal agencies to keep from hurting ourselves? None.

Every state is capable of regulating work place safety in a far more cost effective and less restrictive manner. The number of regulations that every company has to comply with from OSHA are impossible to keep up with. They regulate everything from the number of inches a handrail has to be from the floor to how often you must inspect ladders. I am not certain what is supposed to make you an expert ladder inspector, but even if you have one that you only use once per year, you had better inspect and label it every 3 months.

The micromanaging agency of all agencies is OSHA. Companies are forced to hire entire Environmental Safety and Health (ES&H) departments filled with staff in order to comply with OSHA regulations. The enormous cost of this requirement gets passed on to the consumer.

Employees are forced to waste valuable time in periodic safety training classes that have little to do with their jobs. Perhaps we all want our secretaries to know the dangers of confined spaces while using an acetylene torch. We all probably feel better knowing our dentists are trained to be careful of slips, trips and falls while working on scaffolds.

Unlike state agencies, which have limited budgets, a federal agency like OSHA can become bloated beyond all reason with almost unlimited funding. Common sense goes right out the window when it becomes more profitable and powerful for an agency to micromanage every aspect of our daily working lives or the businesses we own.

Probably the best trick OSHA ever pulled off was scaring every business into doing OSHA's job for them. If you were to flat out ignore OSHA, chances are you would never see an OSHA agent in your entire life. The internal ES&H departments within each company have gleefully taken on the roles of enforcing all of the OSHA regulations, so OSHA doesn't have to. Fear is the catalyst that produced this anomaly: fear that a government agent will knock on your door.

Covering the cost of OSHA extortion has become an institutionalized part of the price of doing business. OSHA has only been around since the Nixon administration, but that's long enough for the victims of the Department of Education to forget that it's unconstitutional.

The Department of Homeland Security, on its face, should be a perfectly constitutional agency. If it were actually concerned with homeland security and if we didn't have a military already responsible for our homeland security, then there may be a purpose for it. If our Customs and Border Protection agency was doing its job, there would be no need for a Department of Homeland Security. Unfortunately the only people the DHS seem to be concerned with are Americans.

Barack Hussein Obama said, "We cannot continue to rely on our military in order to achieve the national security objectives that we've set. We've got to have a civilian national security force that's just as powerful, just as strong, just as well funded." Really? We cannot rely on our military? When it comes to foreign threats, that's why we have a military.

No, the DHS is not concerned in the slightest with foreign threats regardless of what they tell us. They have set up border checkpoints inside the American borders as far as 100 miles from any border. These checkpoints stop Americans while driving, otherwise freely, on American roads in the middle of America. They question the people they stop as if they are crossing a border. They want to see your papers. These check points are not even close to being constitutional and even they know it.

If stopped at one of these check points, refuse to answer any question. Refuse to show any paper or ID. Refuse everything. Do not pull over into the secondary line when ordered to. Continue to ask if you are being detained and if you are free to go. It is none of their business what your name is, where you are headed, what your nationality is or anything else they want to know. Ignore every word that comes out of their mouths until they answer your question about being free to go with an affirmative. You won't have to wait too long. They harass, but they know they have no authority to force you to comply. It's all part of an elaborate conditioning system, straight from the Nazi playbook.

The DHS has been buying up thousands of guns and billions of rounds of ammo. Why? So far they haven't shown any interest in protecting the homeland from a foreign threat. Who are they planning on shooting?

The key thing to understand about most federal agencies is that they are in fact unconstitutional. The transfer of powers that are constitutionally enumerated to the three branches of government to agencies that are not accountable and not elected is unconstitutional in and of itself. The fact that their directives involve issues which are not constitutionally enumerated matters for federal involvement only compound the unconstitutionality of these agencies. Your safety, outdoor activities, and the food you eat are not the Federal Government's business.

The fact that they have to create such enormous agencies to enforce all of this unconstitutionality tells us two very important things. Elected representatives don't have time to do it themselves as the Constitution requires and they don't want to be personally held accountable for the actions of these agencies. Having unconstitutional agencies do their dirty work insulates them from criticism and political retribution.

Chapter 4 Not Everything is a Right

RIGHTS THAT DO NOT EXIST

- Feeling safe is not a right.
- Liberals want us to disarm, so government can keep us safe.
- If you vote for a nanny/police state, you might get it.
- Health care is not a right.
- There is no right to vote granted by the Constitution.
- Young people are not well informed voters.
- It would not be unconstitutional to forbid federal entitlement recipients to vote

The left has a favorite tactic for making arguments by establishing a false premise. They use this method most effectively by creating rights which do not exist and then begin their argument from that point rather than having to argue whether or not that right even exists. Many rights don't exist, but are assumed to exist by many because of repeatedly establishing them by false premises. A few examples are the right to security or safety, right to health care and the right to vote. There are a lot more fake rights that liberals hang their arguments on, but these three seem to come up the most in recent years.

In almost every gun control argument the liberal will eventually make the claim that they have a right to feel safe if they are in a restaurant and not to feel threatened by the sight of someone openly carrying a gun. There is no constitutional right to feel safe. Your safety is your own concern and not something anyone else can provide. A constitutional right trumps warm and fuzzy feelings every time and that is all one has to say to these liberal namby pambies.

Simply dismiss their right to feel safe and don't try to explain why they should feel safer with armed citizens around. Don't point out all of the statistics which prove that more guns equate to less crime. That is a debate you will never win, because you are more than likely talking with someone who has been thoroughly brain washed and who will never listen to logic. Just tell them they have no right to feel safe and it is up to them to provide for their own safety. Suggest they buy their own gun. This usually sends them into a frantic tizzy fit where they start getting vulgar and comparing the need for guns to be a compensation for poor male endowment and claiming they don't need a gun to take care of themselves. This only exposes their original claim of feeling unsafe as a lie. A person can't be afraid and confident that they can take care of themselves at the same time.

A large part of the objective to convince us that we have a right to security and safety is to increase the police state. Recent events have illustrated exactly what happens when we demand a police state and then get what we ask for. Liberals have been demanding more of a police state for decades and all the while fighting to disarm American citizens. The standoff at Bundy Ranch and the protests over the death of Mike Brown in Ferguson, Missouri stand in stark contrast to one another in showing how people react to the police state when it shows up.

Unconstitutional BLM law enforcement officers showed up at the Bundy Ranch and demanded unconstitutional fees be paid, basically at the end of a barrel. They began rustling and slaughtering cattle that belonged to the Bundy Ranch. Militia from all around the country mobilized and went to Bundy Ranch to stand against the BLM. We the People took a stand and the federal police state backed off with their tail between their legs. These people neither asked for the police state, nor tolerated it.

The residents of Ferguson, Missouri are a completely different type of people. Many of the ones involved in the protests and looting following the shooting of Mike Brown live lives of dependency on government. They accept their welfare bribes to vote democrat and march to the polls in lock step. Whether they know it or not, which is debatable, these people have been voting for a nanny state and police state for the entirety of their adult lives. Then when they riot, loot stores, and throw molotov cocktails, basically acting like a bunch of savage heathens, they are surprised when the police state they voted for comes down on them. Unlike the militia who showed up at Bundy Ranch, it doesn't even dawn on the residents of Ferguson that they could make a stand. They are too busy rioting and looting to really do much more than whine about it.

Truthfully though, the police reaction in Ferguson was far more constitutional than that of the BLM at Bundy Ranch. First of all it was in reaction to actual crime being committed by mobs of people, and the police were a state, not a federal agency, answerable to no one. That said, the later U.S. Justice Department involvement in the issue was unconstitutional. Their investigation of racism in the Missouri police forces and digging for hate crimes is unconstitutional. The entire concept of a federal hate crime is unconstitutional.

The lesson to be learned by comparing these two events isn't really why police action was taken, although that is important. The real lesson is the response of the people to the police action. One group who votes against a police state, dealt with an unconstitutional federal police encroachment in a dignified, yet unyielding manner. The other group, who votes for a police state, is shocked when it arrives and responds by crying and throwing the race card around. Ironically, the same liberals that whined about the police state showing up in Ferguson were condemning the people at Bundy Ranch for not submitting to the police state there.

The fake right to health care is another favorite of liberals. They like to claim that health care or even being healthy is a human right. They love lumping anything they want into the category of human rights. It sounds catchy and makes you look like the bad guy if you oppose anything labeled a human right.

Liberals in power want government controlled health care, because then they own you. The liberal sheep in their flock are just fed the talking points about health care being a human right and taught to use insults and name calling against anyone who would deny it. The sheep believe Obamacare is free health care for all, but those in power know that it is the key to regulating and controlling almost anything we do.

Once the government has a stake in covering our health care, then any risks we may take can be deemed too costly for the government or even made criminal. Freedom is lost. Things like smoking, eating bacon, mountain climbing, children sledding or on a playground are dangerous, so such lifestyles can be targeted with taxes, fees, or fines. The riskier they classify our lifestyle, the more we have to pay. This will inevitably lead to bans on activities that people enjoy.

The fight over Obamacare is not over yet. The latest false premise to be pushed on us is that the Supreme Court has declared Obamacare to be constitutional. Nothing could be further from the truth and as a matter of fact, their decision that Obamacare is a tax should have been the final nail in Obamacare's coffin, because that made it a revenue raising bill. All revenue raising bills must originate in the House of Representatives and Obamacare originated in the Senate. Calling it a tax, the Supreme Court exposed this glaring constitutional violation.

Not to fear, the next step is bringing that to the Supreme Court and there are already cases moving through the courts to do just that, but it takes time. The Supreme Court has recently accepted another case, which argues that in states with no state health care exchanges, the federal subsidies for those who sign up for Obamacare are against the law. The Obamacare law specifically states that federal subsidies can only be paid to states with state exchanges. Most states haven't, but their residents are receiving the subsidy. Basically, the U.S. government is handing out subsidies to the poor in all 50 states to make it affordable enough for them to sign up, but the law specifically says this can only be done in states with state exchanges

If the Supreme Court finds that the Obamacare law is being broken, which it very clearly is, then roughly half of the Obamacare enrollees will have to drop their coverage, an enormous blow to the so called Affordable Care Act.

You have no right to good health or to health care. Your health care is your own responsibility. If you rely on others who don't even know you exist to manage your health care, you are in for a rude awakening one of these days. If health care is important to you, prioritize your own spending and put good health insurance over having the latest and greatest phone or flat screen TV. People who run around in $300.00 Nike Air Jordans carrying an iPhone 6 have no business asking anyone else to pay for their health care.

Possibly the most devastating fake right is the fake right to vote. You do not have a constitutional right to vote. We are conditioned from early childhood to think that we do have a right to vote, but we don't. I repeat, you do not have a constitutional right to vote. Even people on the right start throwing a fit when this is pointed out, because the false premise that we have a right to vote has been so successfully ingrained in everyone's beliefs. Keep in mind; the United States is a Constitutional Republic and not a Democracy.

To make this easier to understand, remember that all legal resident immigrants who are not citizens, enjoy all of the same constitutional rights as the rest of us. Non-citizen residents have the right to bear arms, they don't have to incriminate themselves, they cannot be unreasonably searched, etc. Constitutional rights cover everyone who is legally in our country and since non-citizen residents can't vote, it is perfectly clear that voting is not a constitutional right.

It is often brought up in discussions that only male land owners could vote when our country was founded. Well, this isn't entirely accurate and in and of itself, sets up a false premise that voting rules are made at a national level, which they are not.

States decide who can and cannot vote. New Jersey allowed women to vote in our nation's infancy. Each state had its own rules as they do now, although the rules are very similar from state to state. There are some differences. Some states allow felons to vote, although most don't. Virginia allows absentee voting for federal, but not state elections.

The Federal Government has no constitutional authority to make any decisions on who can or cannot vote. Four amendments to the Constitution involve voting rights. The colloquial term "voting rights" should not be misconstrued to presume that voting is a constitutional right. Even when voting rights are mentioned in the Constitution, they are not referred to as absolute or universal or they would just say so. They are merely recognition that rights may exist at state levels. The four amendments regarding voting rights were ratified by the states, not by Congress. Congress cannot amend the Constitution.

The first amendment to address voting rights is the 15th. Many people claim that the 15th Amendment[27] grants voting rights for all. Well, if that were the case, there would be no need for the 19th[28], 24th[29], or 26th Amendments[30]. Their content would be moot if everyone had the right to vote. The 15th Amendment says, "Section 1. The right of citizens of the United States to vote shall not be denied or abridged by the United States or by any State on account of race, color, or previous condition of servitude-. Section 2. The Congress shall have the power to enforce this article by appropriate legislation."

What does that mean? Exactly what it says. States can't use race, color or previous enslavement against you when granting voting rights. At the point that the 15th Amendment was ratified, states could still deny women from voting. Thus, the 15th Amendment did not grant any voting rights whatsoever, especially to all. It merely stopped states from denying voting privileges from people based on race.

The 19th Amendment came 50 years later and addressed women. It says, "The right of citizens of the United States to vote shall not be denied or abridged by the United States or by any State on account of

---

[27] See page 254

[28] See page 256

[29] See page 260

[30] See page 262

sex. Congress shall have power to enforce this article by appropriate legislation." Now the rest of the states would catch up with New Jersey. Now everyone has the right to vote, right? No. Now states can't hold race or sex against potential voters. They can still use anything else to approve or deny a right to vote in their state. To this day, if states wanted to limit voting to property owners, they could.

Curiously, states could allow non-citizens to vote, should they choose to. There actually are several cities in the United States that allow non-citizens to vote in local elections. Support will probably never be there for this to occur at a state level, but it is not forbidden. As a matter of fact, states could allow non-citizens to vote and then restrict their voting privileges in the ways the Constitution won't allow them to restrict citizen voters.

If a state chose to, they could allow non-citizens to vote only if they are over the age of 30, even though the 26th Amendment forbids states from revoking voting rights based on age over 18, because the 26th Amendment only applies to citizens. The same applies to all four Amendments that address voting rights. The states can't disenfranchise citizens based on certain criteria, but can disenfranchise non-citizens, should non-citizens ever obtain the privilege to vote.

It seems very complicated. It is a subject that causes many headaches for people contemplating it until it all clicks and then it's hard to believe it wasn't always so obvious. In a nutshell, you have no right to vote, but states can't hold certain criteria against you when granting voting rights, unless you aren't a citizen, in which case, if they allow you to vote, they can hold those criteria against you.

The 24th and 26th Amendments stop states from using any age over 18 or a poll tax against citizens who are potential voters. These two amendments are among several that should probably never have been ratified, because they have done far more harm than good. Now we allow uneducated, inexperienced 18 year old kids and people with no skin in the game to vote. States gave up too much power by agreeing to allow high school seniors to vote.

As for the poll tax, the mere hint of supporting such a thing can bring on serious wrath from liberals and even right wingers who don't know any better. They have all fallen prey to the false premise that it is just greedy and mean to deny people the right to vote for not paying a poll tax. Well, the truth is, taxpayers all pay a poll tax for welfare deadbeats to vote. We pay taxes so that democrats can use welfare to bribe their constituency to vote democrat. If that isn't a poll tax, on us, the taxpayers, I don't know what is. It grows tiresome paying a poll tax for votes to be cast against my interests: even more so considering that all federal entitlement programs are unconstitutional.

So, the Constitution provides 4 things states can't use against their residents when determining voting rights: Race, sex, age over 18, and poll tax. Not one of them mentions being an entitlement recipient. I am possibly the first to think of this, but I advocate the complete revocation of all voting rights from federal entitlement recipients. States are completely within their rights to do so and it would result in an amazing reversal of the damage done to our country. Fewer of us are pulling the cart while more are along for a free ride in the cart and giving us directions on where to pull it.

While states can revoke voting rights from welfare deadbeats, it would be more effective as a constitutional amendment. It would be worded something like this, "Voting in federal elections is prohibited for all recipients of federal entitlements for a period of 7 years after receipt of the final entitlement payment." Seven years ensures that people can't go off and on the programs just to vote and would have to sit out an entire senate election cycle if they chose to prioritize taking handouts from tax payers over having a voice in our government. The choice would be everyone's to make. Be a taker or be a decision maker.

Some may claim that it's not fair to revoke voting rights from people and that everyone should have a say. We are not a democracy and we are becoming a country where two wolves and a sheep are voting on what to have for dinner. Allowing people to continue voting to steal from others has got to come to a stop. The only problem with amending the Constitution to revoke voting privileges from entitlement recipients is that it would give the appearance of legitimizing those federal entitlements, which are unconstitutional to begin with. However, the prospect of ending those entitlements becomes much more realistic when those who receive them can't vote.

The Bill of Rights[31] were amendments which primarily outline actual rights. Further amendments are assumed by many to do the same, give the people more rights. This is not entirely true and often just the opposite is the case. There are several amendments which we would be better off without and I personally think should be repealed.

The 14th Amendment[32] should be repealed, because it is badly misinterpreted. It was ratified in 1868, but it wasn't until later that it begun to be misinterpreted to automatically allow citizenship to anyone born on U.S. soil. For some reason, the words "subject to the jurisdiction thereof" seem to be written in invisible ink, because an anchor baby to illegal immigrants is not subject to U.S. jurisdiction, but rather to the country the parents are from which legally holds a claim of allegiance on the child.

The 14th Amendment is also misinterpreted as saying that states must abide by all of the same restrictions imposed on the Federal Government in the Constitution, thereby negating the 10th Amendment.[33] This is patently absurd, but believed by many. It does say, "No state shall make or enforce any law which shall abridge the privileges or immunities of citizens of the United States; nor shall any State deprive any person of life, liberty, or property, without due process of law; nor deny to any person within its jurisdiction the equal protection of the laws."

Some contend for instance, that this means that states are limited by the 1st Amendment[34] just as Congress is, because they can't make or enforce laws which abridge these 1st Amendment privileges. This is not true. This falsely assumes that the 1st Amendment grants privileges, but it doesn't, it merely restricts Congress. If you want to have a peaceable assembly, you are still very likely going to be required to get a permit from your state or local government.

---

[31] See pages 249-251

[32] See page 253

[33] See page 251

[34] See page 249

Most of the 1st Amendment freedoms are also covered in State Constitutions as well, making all of this moot. In short, the 14th Amendment is too confusing and too easy to misinterpret and causes a lot of damage, so it should be repealed.

The 16th Amendment[35] should be repealed simply because we don't need it. The Federal Government wastes more money on unconstitutional spending than it brings in from income tax, so it's time to repeal this monstrosity and stop the ongoing legalized theft. While replacing income tax with another form of tax, such as the Fair Tax or Flat Tax would be an improvement, they are also just diversions. Rather than arguing whether we should pay a tax at all, we are merely arguing over how to pay it. It's a shell game and there is a ball under every shell.

The Founders were smart to allow the people to elect our House of Representatives and the State Legislatures to select the Senators. The people and the states are represented in this way. The 17th Amendment[36] took this representation away from the States and gave the election of Senators to the people. Now the States have no power or representation in the Federal Government.

We have drifted further from a republican form of government and closer to a democratic form with mob rule at the helm. This amendment should be repealed as quickly as possible. The people already have their representation in the House of Representatives and they elect their own State legislatures as well, which is as much influence over the selection of Senators as they need. The 17th Amendment transferred power directly from the States to the Federal Government, so it belies logic that the States ever ratified it in the first place.

The 24th and 26th Amendments[37] keep States from revoking voting rights from uninformed youths and keep States from requiring a poll tax. Voters should be contributors, not leeches on society and

---

[35] See page 255

[36] See page 255

[37] See pages 260-262

should have some idea of what it is they are voting on, so repealing both of these amendments has the potential to bring sanity back to the electoral process.

Finally, the 27th Amendment[38] should also be repealed. It was proposed in 1789 and finally ratified in 1992. Why did it take 203 years after proposal to be ratified if it was such a great idea? It took that long to dumb down the people enough to misunderstand it. The way it is written seems to make it out to be a good thing by limiting how often Congress can give themselves raises, but in reality it actually guarantees that Congress will give itself a raise every two years.

There are some good ideas for amending the Constitution, but repealing many amendments should be considered first, especially, the 14th, 16th, and 17th[39].

---

[38] See page 262

[39] See pages 253-255

Chapter 5   The Supreme Court

SUPREME USURPATION OF POWER

- Judicial Review is not in the Constitution.
- Precedent and Case Law are legislation from the bench.
- The Constitution enumerates no power to the Supreme Court to interpret the Constitution.
- Read the Constitution. It belongs to you. Read it.

The Supreme Court is absolutely lawless. Almost everything the Supreme Court Of the United States (SCOTUS) does anymore is unconstitutional.

Everybody knows that it's the job of the Supreme Court to interpret the Constitution and decide whether something is constitutional or not, except for the fact that everybody is wrong. SCOTUS has been performing this task known as Judicial Review for a very long time and it has become more and more their primary function even though it is unconstitutional.

Article 3[40] of the Constitution enumerates all of the power and authority of the judicial branch making no distinction between the Supreme Court or lower courts as to their roles other than the fact that the Supreme Court is higher than the lower courts. Article 3 is very short, because there is really not much for the courts to do other than decide which side wins any particular case, based on the law. Article 3 does not grant Judicial Review authority to any court let alone the Supreme Court.

States are well within their rights to grant judicial review authority to their courts regarding their state laws, but federal courts have no such power granted by the Constitution. The Supreme Court cannot interpret or invalidate laws or any part of the Constitution, yet that is basically all they do. The Constitution was written in plain English purposefully, so that any person could read and understand it with ease without the aid of an attorney. No interpretation is required, except to serve an unconstitutional agenda.

How does SCOTUS get away with wielding power they have no authority to wield? Quite simply because the masses are ignorant and SCOTUS has been doing it for so long that the practice is institutionalized and never questioned by even our brightest scholars. There is too much to be gained by those who are able to take advantage of judicial review for anyone in power to upset this powerful apple cart.

Some people defend the power of Judicial Review by pointing out that the practice predates the U.S. Constitution. Well, yes it does, as does British Common Law, but we don't fall under British Common Law. We fought and won the Revolutionary war, severing any allegiance to the British government or its laws. Judicial Review was not included as a power for American courts in the Constitution.

Judicial Review began in the United States with the case of Marbury vs Madison in 1803. If you ask anyone what the case was about, they are unlikely to know. The actual case was inconsequential compared to the ramifications it had on our country as a side effect. It was basically William Marbury petitioning the Supreme Court to order James Madison to deliver some documents. The Supreme

---

[40] See page 242

Court decided that the documents were withheld illegally, but that the SCOTUS didn't have the authority to order their delivery. Many questions arose as to what the remedy would be if Congress passed laws that conflicted with the Constitution and Chief Justice Marshall argued that the Courts have to side with the Constitution, which is basically what became Judicial Review.

From that point on, SCOTUS has evolved from a court that decides cases on a case-by-case basis, to a legislative body that writes case law by making decisions on the constitutionality of each case brought before it. This of course requires the justices to interpret the Constitution. The Constitution says what it says very plainly, yet we often see 5 to 4 decisions in the Supreme Court, which is clear evidence that interpretation can result in getting it 180 degrees wrong.

Everyone loves when a Supreme Court decision falls in their favor and effectively legislates new law from the bench. Winning feels good, even if it's unconstitutional. In an effort to vaccinate myself from any accusation that I am biased, I will explain using an example of a Supreme Court case that was solidly in my favor and explain why it is still unconstitutional for the Supreme Court to interpret the Constitution.

In 2003 a lawsuit was filed against the District of Columbia challenging the D.C. Firearms Control Regulations Act of 1975. As a side note, this is proof that even older, institutionalized laws should be challenged if they are unconstitutional. Most federal laws are unconstitutional, so challenge them all. Those who are strong proponents of the 2nd Amendment[41] applauded the Heller vs D.C. decision, which basically upheld that the 2nd Amendment is a right for the people, not a right for the militia to keep and bear arms. There is a little more to it and how it applies to federal enclaves, but that is the gist of it. Since that is exactly what the 2nd Amendment says, who needs SCOTUS to substantiate that? To question it is lunacy, since the words are clear. "The right of *the people* to keep and bear arms, shall not be infringed." The SCOTUS decision was great and yes, it even made me happy, because had the decision gone the other way it would have been disastrous.

---

[41] See page 250

The way the Supreme Court practices an unconstitutional role is why the case had to be filed the way it was in the first place, which was a challenge to an unconstitutional law. If the Supreme Court kept its role within constitutional confines, the unconstitutional law would have been rendered inert years ago if those who fell victim to it simply appealed their cases and were found not guilty and sued DC for damages. This sounds ridiculous on the face of it, considering what our courts have become.

Mass ignorance of the Constitution keeps us "in our place." Imagine that the populace was educated and after D.C. passed the unconstitutional Firearms Control Regulations Act of 1975, all of the people who were arrested for bearing arms actually knew their own rights. The district would have had to press charges and take them to court. The cases would have met with jury nullifications and not guilty verdicts and the victims of the bad law would have a class action lawsuit to sue D.C. for damages and the D.C. officials could face criminal charges for violating their rights. Inevitably D.C. government officials would actually be the ones doing time behind bars. But, because we now rely on courts and SCOTUS to interpret the Constitution and the fact that people only bring cases against the unconstitutionality of laws rather than against the culprits who pass them, we continue to see one unconstitutional law after another passing at every level of government. Rather than fighting to have a law thrown out, we should be fighting to have lawmakers thrown into jail. We'd see far less rights violation in law making if lawmakers were held accountable.

I have no choice but to agree with the decision of Heller vs D.C., because it was constitutionally accurate to say that the people have the right to keep and bear arms, but the fact that they made a decision at all is unconstitutional. People may think that is crazy, because people like what they are used to. It's hard to admit that you have been hoodwinked all your life and difficult to accept change even when the reality is that stripping SCOTUS of their judicial review power would be bringing us back in line with the Constitution. The Constitution doesn't enumerate this power to The Supreme Court; it was usurped by the Supreme Court in 1803, during our country's infancy. It would take an enormous level of education, a populace who cared, and a Congress with more interest in keeping their oaths, than lining their pockets to censure and possibly impeach the Supreme Court Justices to rein them back in.

Judicial Review remains one of my biggest concerns in the realm of unconstitutional abuse of power, but I have little hope that anything will ever be done about it. Many people argue that "someone" has to have the job of interpreting the Constitution. This is a lazy and uninformed argument. It is also defeatist. This excuse is admission of willful ignorance or at least a personal belief in one's own incapability to read the Constitution on their own. Anyone who thinks that someone has to interpret the Constitution for them must prefer having a ruler over taking responsibility for their own lives. They need a babysitter.

The fact is that our founding fathers meant for we the people to be able to read the Constitution for ourselves. If they thought that someone should be empowered to interpret the Constitution, they would have enumerated this authority within the Constitution. It's not there. Having the ability to interpret the Constitution and then pass judgment on the people based on that interpretation is tantamount to tyranny.

The Constitution is meaningless if its meaning is entirely up to a single person in a black robe who casts the swing vote, when 4 black robe wearers believe it means one thing and 4 others believe it means the exact opposite. Words mean things. If two people are able to interpret the exact opposite meaning from any given clause in the Constitution, then one of them is clearly a liar.

Everyone should read the Constitution for themselves. Do not rely on anyone else to tell you what it means. People go to school for years to learn law, yet most law school graduates don't know the first thing about what the Constitution really says. Much of what they are taught is case law. Case laws are laws, which aren't really laws, because they are derived from the judiciary. This is referred to as legislation from the bench. The very first sentence of the Constitution after the Preamble outlaws case law as a form of legislation. Article 1 Section 1[42] is the end of any argument on the validity of case law. "All legislative Powers herein granted shall be

---

[42] See page 233

vested in a Congress of the United States, which shall consist of a Senate and House of Representatives."

Read The Constitution[43] yourself. Read a paragraph per day. It's a very short document, so you'll be finished before you know it. Read it word for word. Understand it for yourself. It's not difficult at all. If you have any questions, ask them! But ask them of yourself. Read it again. Everything I know about the Constitution I learned from reading the Constitution. Always keep the 10th Amendment[44] clear in your mind when you read any of it. You'll find that by doing this you can debunk the constitutionality of just about every domestic federal law on the books. You'll clearly see the unconstitutionality of any federal regulatory agency.

If the Constitution doesn't specifically say the Federal Government can do something, they can't. But they do anyway. Our ignorance allows them to get away with it. Don't be one of the ignorant. Arm yourself with the truth. The Constitution includes a staggering amount of wisdom for a document that is so short. It is the most brilliant document ever written. It empowers you, the individual, with more liberty than anyone else in the world, yet millions in government, media, and education are always diligently at work ensuring that you don't know what it says. Read The Constitution!

---

[43] See pages 232-248

[44] See page 251

Chapter 6
Flat Out Unconstitutional
The Blog

BLOG POSTS FROM JULY, 2015 – JUNE, 2016

After the release of Flat Out Unconstitutional in e-book format, Flat Out Unconstitutional The Blog was born, because there is always more to say. The first year of blog posts are now included in the book, many of which compliment what is already covered while others cover different topics altogether based on current events of the time.

My blog posts included many web links, which have been converted to footnotes with the text of the web addresses for the printed version of this book.

Since this is not a book for young children or liberals, pictures from blog posts are not included.

GUN CONTROL: IT'S ALL UNCONSTITUTIONAL

POSTED JULY 25, 2015

The left wing and its media will never let a crisis go to waste! The easiest way for those who want power to gain it is to scare you into giving it to them willfully. There is no reason to use force to control you if you volunteer to be enslaved. With the bully pulpit of the entire main stream media at their finger tips, the left depicts an America where we have to live in constant fear. They bully dissenting voices into towing their party line. Political correctness keeps the dissenters in line for fear of being called names like right wing radicals. We've come to a point where the Constitution of the United States is considered right wing radicalism. Freedom is radical. Liberty is insanity! We are called names by the very people who fit those names, yet those of us on the right are always cowered into never calling out the hypocrisy. Intolerant of anything traditional or having morals and family values, the left calls us intolerant if we dislike abhorrent behavior. If we want people to behave, we're called racists. If we read the Bible, we're homophobes. In this way, they keep everyone afraid to speak their minds. If we're silent, it's easier to control us, because we all feel alone.

Once we're silent and those we elect in landslide elections are also kept silent, the fear mongering is employed. While every type of gun related crime is sharply down as gun ownership has steeply climbed over the past several years, it doesn't stop the media from making it look like the exact opposite is occurring. Gun crimes are down, but media hysteria is way up! Every statistic has shown that as gun ownership increases, crime drops, even in places like Chicago. The left constantly repeats the number 30,000 as in the number of gun deaths every year, which still doesn't reach the number of vehicle related deaths. They will never break that number down, so that we know that 18,000 of those deaths are suicides. Robin Williams didn't need a gun. They want it to sound as if there are 30,000 murders every year and that they could only occur if guns are involved. Truthfully, there are closer to 12,000 murders in America each year and dropping, a country of 320,000,000 and 8,400 with guns. This number has come down tremendously during the Obama Administration, but the left wing media doesn't want you to know that. You would think that should be something positive they could attribute to Obama, but not really. It has to do with the fact that gun manufacturers have had to triple production to keep up with the demand for new gun purchases during Obama's administration. More guns equal less murders.

Another figure they don't want broken down out of that 30,000 is how many gun related deaths are justifiable. With an average of 2.5 million uses of guns in self defense every year, the vast majority of them never having to come to a point where a gun is fired, a few actually do end up in the deaths of a mugger, a rapist, a burglar, a robber, or an attempted murderer. Good riddance. Some gun deaths are good gun deaths. When you lump all gun deaths into one number and scream it across every media platform as a fear mongering tactic, then you're not only being dishonest, but you're going so far off the deep end that you're no longer credible. This is the point the left has missed and why the gun control groups like Moms Demand Action for Gun Sense in America have failed so miserably. They jumped the shark on the gun control debate and revealed themselves for who they truly are: control freaks.

What about all the mass shootings? Well, there aren't that many to be honest and the rate of their occurrences is down too. The media coverage of each one is off the charts, though! With every mass shooting, comes a claim that it's some crazy conservative shooting up a place, yet once the story gets fleshed out a little more we find out that almost every one is a lunatic liberal or jihadi muslim. We also find out that it happened in a gun free zone, where no one could shoot back.

Let's take a look at the South Carolina church shooting by Dylann Roof for instance. The media and the left still keep trying to call him a radical right winger, because in one picture he held a Northern Virginia Battle Flag (commonly misconstrued as The Confederate Flag). Well, the tell tale sign that he was a lefty starts off with another picture showing him burning the American Flag. If there is one thing that no conservative does, it's burn the American Flag. As a matter of fact, the pastor of the church and South Carolina State Senator who Roof shot and killed, Clementa Pinckney, voted to keep the Dixie Flag on capitol grounds and also voted to disarm the flocks of every church in the state without permission of the pastor of each church to carry a gun for self defense. Pastor and Senator Pinckney, God rest his soul, did not give such permission in his church, so he laid the groundwork for his own and his flock's inability to shoot back when fired upon by a raving lunatic. No flag was to blame for the deaths of 9 people in this South Carolina church. Dylann Roof is of course the most at fault, followed in second place by Pastor/Senator Climenta Pinckney, God rest his soul. That's right, I said it. If you disarm yourself and others against those who would do you harm, harm may befall you. It may not sound pretty, but there you have it.

Being politically correct won't allow the cold hard truths to be told without people attacking you with comments such as "how dare you say such a thing?" Truth is still there though for anyone with eyes opened to it. Too many people are afraid to speak the truth, because of the ridicule from the left that it invites, which makes it so much easier for the left to get away with spreading their lies.

There are so many gun control laws and so many ways that they have gotten people hurt, killed, or unconstitutionally jailed. They are all unconstitutional. The 2nd Amendment[45] doesn't say, "The right of the people to keep and bear arms, shall not be infringed, unless…" There is no reason to infringe. Every time our rights are infringed, people get hurt. Nothing good comes of it.

It's been discovered that Dylann Roof should have failed a background check before buying a gun. Why? A person who is intent on shooting up a church will get a gun whether a background check passes or fails. Bad guys do bad things. The background check itself is the problem. What are they checking for? If the 2nd Amendment is clear that your right shall not be infringed, then nothing they check for can be used to infringe. Why check? Well, because they do infringe. They violate the Constitution. Background checks violate the 4th and 5th Amendments[46] as well. Your background is being searched without a warrant and you are forced

---

[45] See page 250

[46] See page 250

to incriminate yourself on the forms you fill out or face years in prison. No right to remain silent. You're guilty until you prove your innocence.

The Unconstitutional Gun Control Act of 1968 doesn't allow felons to own guns. By creating this unconstitutional 2nd class citizen without rights, they have created the incentive to come up with more ways to put people into that class. Its almost impossible to get through life without becoming a felon anymore. If someone is so evil and violent, there are no guns in jail and that's where they should be. Don't let them out, because if they truly intend to do harm, banning felons from owning firearms never stops them. We only stop those who don't intend to do harm, but who might want to get their life together again and have a desire to protect their family. Only those felons who have decided to become law abiding citizens end up remaining disarmed. Most of these felons have broken unconstitutional federal laws to earn that title in the first place, which is another discussion in and of itself. Our country did just fine for two centuries before we decided to create a 2nd class citizen called felons.

Take my advice. Arm yourself and your family. Stand up and fight unconstitutional gun control laws. If you don't know which ones are the unconstitutional ones, they all are. If you're proud of your concealed weapons permit, you've already been brainwashed. You should need no permit to exercise a right. Many states are starting to move toward Constitutional Carry, where permits are no longer required. Sometimes only in baby steps. Missouri and Maine are two of the latest. Texas finally allows open carry of modern pistols, but only with a permit. Next step: repeal the law requiring a permit. Keep up the good work, because truthfully, we have been having a 2nd Amendment awakening and have made a lot of positive progress. It's not time to start hitting the brakes though, it's time to push harder on the gas.

DON'T LET REPUBLICAN PRIMARIES DIVIDE US!

POSTED JULY 27, 2015

If there is anything that liberals are better at than conservatives it's uniting. They are community organizers after all. Liberals are group thinkers, whereas conservatives are individual thinkers. Liberals are used to taking marching orders and doing as they're told without even taking the time to wonder why. The reason doesn't necessarily matter to them, as long as they can be part of the group. Belonging is very important to liberals.

Democrats have 5 candidates running in their 2016 presidential primary, but really only have two who stand out, criminal Hillary Clinton who can't even name a single one of her own accomplishments when asked, and admitted socialist Bernie Sanders. Both candidates are obvious hazards to our nation, yet liberals will rally behind whichever one wins the Democratic nomination without a second thought about their previous allegiance to the other candidate during the primary. It helps that many of them are bribed with unconstitutional welfare and food stamps and are bused from poll to poll to vote more than once. This is why they are so dead set against voter ID of any kind.

Forcing ethical standards in elections is detrimental to all liberal causes, because the majority simply does not agree with them and dead voters can't show their IDs.

Republicans have 16 candidates in the race at last count, but who can keep up. Republican candidates range from the most constitutionally grounded with Conservative Review[47] Freedom Scores of (96%-A) for Ted Cruz and (93%-A) for Rand Paul, to the bottom of the pile, Chris Christie, Lindsey Graham, and Jeb Bush [48]whose scores aren't given, probably because they are such low Fs.

---

[47] https://www.conservativereview.com/

[48] https://www.conservativereview.com/2016-Presidential-Candidates

We also have Donald Trump, who has a lot of flaws, has supported gun control and other liberal ideas and has contributed to democrats. Unlike the rest of the pack though, Trump is saying all the right things right now, telling it like we've all wanted to hear it for a long time. When the media tries its regular tactics to silence Trump or force him to apologize for something he said, he doubles down and his poll numbers go up. This would work for every candidate if they just had the spine Trump has.

For various reasons, us right wingers support different candidates in the Republican Primary, whether it is because we want the most constitutionally conservative candidate or the one who has the spine to ignore political correctness and speak his mind, exposing the truth on immigration issues. Some people choose a candidate because they are from their home state. I have personally not chosen to back a particular candidate at this time, because I want to see all of them fully vetted, so that my decision can be better informed. Certainly there are some I like much better than others and some I'd like to see drop out of the race right now, but I'll wait a little longer before I make my final decision on who to support publicly and financially.

What I have been noticing a lot among right wingers in social media is that many have already made the decision on which candidate they are supporting in the primaries and they have done so to almost a rabid degree. It is a blind, uncompromising level of sycophancy I normally only see from liberals for Obama or Hillary Clinton. Right wingers and conservatives who otherwise agree with one another on almost every issue are arguing in social media over primary candidates and blocking one another out of rage. I have seen none of this happening among liberals. Hillary and Bernie supporters get along great with one another and they will all join forces seamlessly to back whichever one of their candidates gets the nomination.

We have got to stop the squabbling. We are going to need to unite for the general election. We can't sit out the election and allow another 4 or 8 years of this destruction to go on at the hands of Hillary or Bernie. Even if it means, God forbid, holding our nose and voting for a liberal light like Bush or Christie, we are going to have to do it. Let's just pray that it doesn't come to that and work as hard as we can to nominate a conservative. We can't allow the media to control the nomination process.

If the media tells us that one candidate or another isn't "electable" it's because they are leftists and they are afraid of that candidate. Remember, we nominated McCain and Romney, because the media told us they were electable. We can see where that got us. By all means, continue to debate with one another. Discuss the candidates, both their strengths and their flaws. They all have flaws. Do not be a sycophant. Your candidate of choice does have flaws. There isn't a single candidate in the race who is perfect. Discussing them in a positive way with one another is a good thing. We all stand to learn something new every day. Just don't allow the discussions to become hateful and drive us apart. Don't be easily offended by other conservatives when they say something negative about the candidate you favor. If you're getting angry, table the conversation for a later time. Cooler heads can prevail.

While I am not fond of this cliché, this is a time where agreeing to disagree is a better option than blocking friends over something so temporary as a presidential primary. There are many issues and many more elections to come, where we will do better if we are united than if we divide over a single issue or election. Those of us on the right all agree in the general direction we want to take this country and that it's far to the right of where we have been taken by Obama. We all agree that we need to move to the right, even if we disagree on how far right. We can disagree on the details without allowing it to divide us. Remain friends and let's keep our eye on the bigger ball, the general election.

SAY "YES" TO A $15.00 MINIMUM WAGE!

POSTED JULY 29, 2015

The minimum wage in 1963 was over $15.00 per hour, so why not return to those rates? Let's give liberals what they want and raise the minimum wage to $15.00 per hour and even more! So, how do we do this? Should Congress just vote to raise the federal minimum wage and let Obama sign it into law? Of course not, a federal minimum wage is flat out unconstitutional. There is absolutely no enumerated power in Article 1, Section 8[49] of the Constitution which allows Congress to legislate mandatory wages for employees.

Now that I appear to have gone completely bonkers, it's time to explain. The minimum wage in 1963, setting aside its unconstitutionality, was actually $1.25. Adjusted for inflation, that is $9.49 in 2015 dollars. The current $7.25 minimum wage is equal to 92 cents in 1963 dollars. Inflation has gone out of control, because any time the federal government wants, it can just print more money. Doing so automatically devalues all of the rest of the money in circulation. Your wealth is quite literally stolen from you when more money is printed. You still have the same number of dollars, but their purchasing power drops.

Take a look at this chart of historic gold prices. Gold: 1792 – 2014[50]

While the United States was on the gold standard, you can see that the price of gold barely changed from 1792 to 1932, never budging from the 19-20 dollar range. Gold holds its value fairly solidly over the course of centuries. In 1933, Franklin Delano Roosevelt took the United States off of the gold standard, so paper currency was no longer backed by anything of tangible value. The federal government unconstitutionally outlawed the ownership of most gold coins and bullion, demanding that everyone turn it in to the Federal Reserve for the current price of $20.67 per ounce. Once

---

[49] See page 237

[50] http://onlygold.com/Info/Historical-Gold-Prices.asp

the government had a virtual monopoly on gold after rounding it all up out of private hands, they arbitrarily set a new price of $35.00 per ounce for gold. It was magic! Suddenly all of the government's gold almost doubled in value!

Beginning in 1964 the United States began removing silver from our coins. All of our coins dated 1964 and prior, with a face value of 10 cents or more, were 90% silver. The half dollar coins continued to contain 40% silver though 1970. The last of the silver was removed from U.S. coins in 1971. The last driblet of actual value was stripped from the currency. Sure, the federal government still set a value of $35.00 for an ounce of gold, but they had all of the gold and the people couldn't buy it. It was still against the law to own it. At least having the set value stifled inflation.

1971 got worse! Without a drop of silver left for the people, Richard Nixon put the final nail in the coffin of the gold standard. After all, the government can't inflate money by printing more if they have a fixed price for gold. Even though people couldn't buy the gold, printed money had an artificial value that didn't waver, because of its pretend gold backing. Nixon removed the government fixed price on gold, completely severing any real value from printed money once and for all.

If you refer back to the chart of gold prices from 1792 – 2014 you can see the sudden skyrocketing price of gold beginning in 1972. At first glance it looks fantastic, but other than some gold certificates that started being legal to buy in 1964, no one had any gold to sell as the price rose. The price didn't rise because people valued gold more. It rose, because the Federal Reserve was printing more and more money. The value of gold versus any other general commodities remained the same, but the number of dollars needed to purchase those commodities rose.

Amazingly, in 1975 when the price of gold hit $139.00, seven times what the Federal Government bought it all for, it became legal to own gold again. Now gold was for sale, but there was only one major seller: Uncle Sam. This makes me wonder if there is anything left in Fort Knox. That's a question no one can honestly answer and a conspiracy not worth delving into right now.

What does any of this have to do with a $15.00 minimum wage? The five quarters that made up the $1.25 minimum wage in 1963 were 90% silver with a 2015 melt value of over $15.00! Reversing all of the damage the federal government has done to our currency since 1933 would put a real value back on our money rather than the artificial value the Federal Reserve places on it. Dropping the minimum wage back to $1.25 per hour and minting our coins from silver again would immediately put more wealth in the hands of burger flippers than the current $7.25 in Monopoly money they currently earn.

It is always easier to do damage than it is to repair it. Reversing the direction the government has taken with our currency and going back onto the gold standard could have some growing pains if deflation were allowed to happen. It would have to be done relatively slowly and in managed stages. Deflation can be worse than inflation. As money becomes more valuable, debts become more of a burden, because wages go down.

We are a nation of people who love our debts. Debt isn't necessarily a bad thing. It's because of our ability to go into debt that we can afford to put mortgages on houses and cars and pay for them over time. If you have a debt such as a mortgage, inflation makes it easier for you to pay over time, because money is less valuable and you have more of it, and your debt doesn't inflate with the money. Debts couldn't remain static when facing a large deflation or everyone would lose their properties even as their monetary wealth remains the same. This is why the deflation would have to be managed to decrease debt at the same percentage that increased value in money decreases our incomes.

Going back onto the gold standard and managing the deflation that would come along with it, especially with the return of silver coins, is one solution, but quite frankly it is an unconstitutional one. It wouldn't be advisable to repair damage that was done unconstitutionally, by doing something else unconstitutional. The federal government has no enumerated power to decrease the debts people owe one another just because of deflation. There is another solution, which passes constitutional muster and would take far less time. It could even be painless.

Congress is empowered to coin money. They can also regulate the value of money. These powers are expressly enumerated in the Constitution. There are several reasons we can't change the name of our money, but we could replace it.

If we were to go back onto the gold standard, Congress could print Dollars 2.0! The gold price could be immediately set to $20.00 per ounce and all U.S. dollar wealth and debts in existence adjusted accordingly. It would be perfectly fair, across the board. Liberals love fair, right? They would also love the fact that there would be no more billionaires. Even people who hoard gold and other commodities would remain unaffected. Their wealth would remain intact. The value of everything would remain the same and it would stay that way. Any value could be set in stone for an ounce of gold with Dollars 2.0, I just like $20.00. This rate would drop the current $7.25 minimum wage down to about 4 cents per hour, but it's all relative. I think 4 cents per hour is the perfect minimum wage!

Thank you to http://onlygold.com/ for their wonderful chart of historical gold prices!

PARTS IS PARTS!

POSTED JULY 31, 2015

The left wing has jumped the shark now. There is no longer any excuse they can come up with to justify their evil. They have been pushing immorality for as long as there has been a left wing. Evil is their core. They have always gone through great lengths to disguise their evil intentions as good ones and using sinister tactics to ridicule those with high moral values if they speak out against them.

Everything liberals support or advocate is evil. They get away with it by trying to erase history or by appealing to the moral high ground of the right wing with false premises that their goals are liberty and freedom oriented. They accuse the right of atrocities that belong solely to the left. We're taught in public schools that the left/right paradigm is a circle and that if you go far enough right or left, you come out the other side, basically that the left and right meet in the middle at an extreme position. This is patently false. The scale of left to right is a straight line where totalitarian tyranny can be found on the far left and complete freedom and anarchy are the furthest to the right. The Constitution is very far to the right, but not so far as to lead to anarchy, which could never be sustained. There is always some leftist who will seek power. Anarchy would erupt into gangs run by warlords.

Hitler was as far left as a leader can get. He was a socialist, fascist and dictator who ruled with an iron fist. Freedom was not a NAZI virtue. Leftist history professors and public school teachers all want us to believe that fascism is right wing. Total government control is somehow a result of too much desire for freedom. No, it doesn't matter how free a people are, even if they are a complete anarchy, the move from freedom to totalitarian control doesn't move from right to left by going around a circle. It moves from right to left by being conquered by a leftist tyrant. The left wing owns NAZI Germany and Hitler, lock, stock and barrel. There was nothing right wing about them at all. If you point this out to liberals their next step is to argue that NAZIs were Nationalists and that Nationalism is right wing. That is a false premise that can be negated with any dictionary. Nationalism has no left/right paradigm, it is simply a strong patriotism, regardless of the type of government the people are loyal to. Hitler was a Nationalist. He was also a socialist, fascist, leftist tyrant. Obama is an Anti-Nationalist, socialist, fascist, leftist tyrant. The only differences between Hitler and Obama in their ideology is that Hitler actually loved his country.

Liberals, who have completely taken over the Democrat party now, have always found it difficult to get what they want through legitimate means. They have pushed unconstitutional legislation through Congress such as welfare entitlements, the 1968 Gun Control Act, and the Civil Rights Act. The Constitution enumerates no authority under Article 1, Section 8[51] for Congress to legislate in these areas. If any of these things truly had merit, getting the states to ratify constitutional amendments should not have been difficult.

Far more often than not, liberals are unable to convince legislators to pass their evil bills into law, so they rely on courts and activist judges to thwart the will of the people, as they recently did with gay marriage. Marriage is not a constitutional purview of the Federal Government at all. Time and time again, the will of the people by popular vote, state government legislation, or state constitutional amendments have outlawed gay marriage. Liberals claim to have 60% support for gay marriage, yet the issue never wins when voted on. In every case, judges abuse power they are not authorized to wield in order to unlegislate by throwing out laws. Article 3[52] of the Constitution grants no authority for courts to legislate or unlegislate. Interpreting the Constitution and other laws are usurped powers. The role of the judiciary is meant to determine if a law is broken, not if the law should exist.

Since the Supreme Court decision on Roe vs Wade, which legalized abortion by unconstitutional legislation from the bench, the left has been claiming that abortion is virtuous, because it's all about the health of the woman. We're supposed to believe that almost 60 million women would have died if they didn't have that dangerous and pesky tumor called a fetus removed! God designed women to get pregnant and have children. With the help of modern medicine,

---

[51] See page 237

[52] See page 242

actual risk to a woman's life due to pregnancy is so rare as to be almost nonexistent.

Liberals have done themselves in this time and exposed their evil for what it is. There is no recovering from the latest transgression on the right to life after it has been revealed that Planned Parenthood has been selling baby parts. Their decades old claim that a fetus isn't a baby can no longer hold water if the fetus is made up of baby parts that can be sold on the black market.

The Center for Medical Progress obliterated any hope that Planned Parenthood could ever have of keeping up the appearance of being good, by releasing videos that show that Planned Parenthood is in the baby parts selling business. The videos just keep coming and the White House and other leftists keep jumping to their defense, but only serving to make themselves look stupid in the process. This is indefensible and the more they try to defend it, the more their evil is exposed for what it truly is.

The left wing media is always ready to cover up the truth, but they can't spin this one, so the only trick they have left is to make you watch the left hand, so you can't see what the right hand is doing. By diverting our attention with other stories, especially if they tug on our heart strings, they can hopefully calm down the story on baby parts, before any major damage is done to their beloved tax payer funded, baby killing organization, Planned Parenthood.

Dixie flags and lions are the latest media distractions. Dixie flags distracted us from talking about the hazards we face when gun control statists disarm us. The story about a dentist killing a lion is just what the media needed in their left hand to get our attention off the baby parts in their right hand. Don't fall for these media tactics. Keep your eyes on the ball. I'm not suggesting that we can't be engaged with multiple stories at the same time, only pointing out the technique being used to try to pry our attention away from the ones that truly matter.

Personally, I am no huge fan of trophy hunting, but I am a huge supporter of hunting in general for sustenance whether you need it or not. Let's face it, you can't buy a venison tenderloin at Kroger and I love venison tenderloin. My opinion on trophy hunting though, isn't the point. I have neither condemned nor defended the dentist or anyone involved with killing the lion. I am condemning the notion that he be extradited to Zimbabwe over the incident and firmly against any presidential or federal involvement in the matter. It is not only a smoke screen over more important issues, but an unconstitutional one if the federal government gets involved.

Our focus right now with regard to these issues should be firmly on the complete and utter destruction of Planned Parenthood. All federal funding should be cut off to them immediately and not only because it's unconstitutional for the federal government to provide subsidies to any companies or people, but because as a Christian, my money should not be stolen from me by government to pay for atrocities. Planned Parenthood is evil. Evil must be shut down. Don't you think? How much do you enjoy having the money you earn spent on murder, which then turns even more profit when they auction off the aftermath to the highest bidder?

WELFARE DEADBEATS SHOULD NOT VOTE!

POSTED AUGUST 2, 2015

There is no constitutional right to vote. Argue all you want, but it's a simple fact. To understand this, we need to set aside everything we were taught in public schools using a curriculum that is put in place by the unconstitutional Department of Education. It's not in the government's best interest to teach you how to limit the government, so very little is taught about the Constitution any longer. There are two types of rights and we can't get them confused. There are natural rights, those that are God given, many of which the Founding Fathers enumerated in the Constitution and Bill of Rights[53], such as the right to bear arms. Then there are legal rights, which are those granted by government, so they really aren't rights at all, since the government can take them away just as easily as they granted them.

The right to vote is a legal right and one that is granted by states, not the federal government. When our country was founded most states required voters to be land owners, because it's a good idea for those who have a say in government to also have a stake in it. Most states didn't allow women to vote, but New Jersey did. There is no single set of rules for the entire United States with regard to voting.

In 1870 the states ratified the 15th Amendment[54] to the U.S. Constitution. Contrary to popular belief, this did not give blacks or other minorities a *right to vote*. What it did was take race out of the infinite number of reasons a state could use to revoke voting rights. The 15th Amendment has the word *right* in it, but doesn't grant a right. It merely recognizes that the *legal* right may exist in the states. Now a state could not base a person's eligibility to vote on their race. If the 15th Amendment actually granted all minorities a right to vote,

---

[53] See pages 232-251

[54] See page 254

then it would have included black women as well, but it didn't. States could still bar women from voting.

Fifty years later, in 1920, the states ratified the 19th Amendment[55]. By doing this they relinquished the ability to use gender as criteria in determining who could vote. Like the other amendments dealing with voting, this one doesn't grant women a right to vote. It says that their right to vote "shall not be denied or abridged by the United States or by any State on account of sex." So, they can't deny you the *legal* right to vote on account of sex, but they sure could for any other reason except for race. Legal rights to vote could still be denied based on age or a trillion other reasons.

In 1964, the 24th Amendment[56] was ratified eliminating the ability for states to charge a poll tax to vote. After all, how can a deadbeat's vote be bought with welfare checks if they couldn't afford to pay a poll tax to vote? This amendment ensured that the decline into socialism in the United States would speed up dramatically. This finished setting the stage which was set by the New Deal to ensure that people could vote for more and more handouts. When people vote for their own government dependencies, it's easier for the government to maintain that dependence. A dependent citizen is a compliant citizen. Scratch that... A dependent citizen is a slave.

The myth that we have a constitutional right to vote makes people feel good, because it sounds fair, so it makes a poll tax seem unfair and a way for the rich to control things. Well right now the rich do control things, because so many of the poor depend on government for handouts. Another way of looking at it is that the deadbeats control things as they steal from us and vote to steal more.

Giving deadbeats the ability to vote by eliminating the poll tax wasn't good enough. The government wanted more deadbeats voting and the more ignorant, the better. Along came the 26th Amendment[57]. It was decided that it would be wise to allow

---

[55] See page 256

[56] See page 260

[57] See page 262

uneducated, inexperienced, clueless children to vote. States no longer have the ability to determine who can vote based on age, over 18. The way it is written they can not abridge the legal right to vote for anyone over 18 on account of age, but they still can abridge that legal right for anyone under 18. Or not! A state could decide not to abridge the legal right to vote for 12 year olds if they wanted to. Then anyone 12 and up could vote! Again, like the previous three amendments, the 26th Amendment doesn't grant a right to vote, it merely subtracts a reason from the unlimited number of reasons that states can use to revoke the ability to vote.

The 15th, 19th, 24th, and 26th Amendments never mention a word about welfare or other entitlements. They are free game. Every federal entitlement is unconstitutional with the exception of pensions. For instance, military retirees have earned the benefits that were part of their contract when they signed on for service. It would be perfectly legal and tremendously beneficial for states to revoke the legal right to vote from all recipients of unconstitutional entitlements. I may go so far as to grant an exception for Social Security, due to the fact that we have no choice to opt out. That is a an entirely different conversation.

I would like to see voting rights revoked from all recipients of programs like Welfare, HUD, Food Stamps (EBT), WIC, and Planned Parenthood, federally funded abortions. The revocation should last 7 years beyond the final receipt of any of these benefits to ensure they are forced to sit out one full election cycle, including senate races. I would reduce it to 5 years if the 17th Amendment[58] is repealed and senate elections go back to state legislatures where they belong.

Legal residents of the United States who are not citizens enjoy all the rights that the Constitution protects. They even have the right to bear arms. I know legal residents who buy guns. The fact that no state allows legal residents to vote in federal elections is all you need to know to realize that voting is not a constitutional right.

It's time to ban deadbeats from the voting booth! People can set their own destiny. They can choose to be a contributing member of

[58] See page 255

society in every way including voting, or they can choose to be a leech, in which case they can no longer choose what they leech. Which would you choose?

YES WE CAN…DEPORT ALL ILLEGAL ALIENS!

POSTED AUGUST 4, 2015

The left has done a wonderful job of making it taboo to talk about deporting illegal aliens. How many years now have people been screaming, "Build the fence first?" We have been subconsciously convinced that the only way to make progress on stopping illegal immigration is to make a stand for securing the border first to stop the influx invaders before we address the ones who are already here. I don't want a fence built. I want a great wall built with a No-Mans Land filled with land mines, gun turrets every 400 yards, and in ground motion detectors. I want it built right now, but it doesn't have to be *first*. We can tackle the rest of the immigration problem at the same time.

We spend billions and billions (Carl Sagan voice) on illegal immigrants every year. In 2013 alone, the city of Los Angeles spent 1.6 billion on various entitlement programs for illegal aliens as well as, schooling, medical care and increased law enforcement. What does America get out of it? Crime, poverty, low unemployment due to cheap labor, and a loss of our American identity.

If we diverted all of the money that we spend on illegal immigrants into stopping illegal immigrants the problem would be quickly and easily solved. Masons would be laying bricks for the great wall tomorrow. Every illegal child should immediately be kicked out of every American school. Hospitals should refuse any treatment that any illegal doesn't pay for up front, out of pocket. Every illegal that is arrested for any minor crimes should be deported immediately. If they are arrested for high crimes or violent crimes, they should be imprisoned, serve out their entire sentence and then be deported. Once we deport an illegal alien they should be disqualified for having an entry visa into the United States for life.

Much of the tax payer money that is currently being spent to give illegal invaders a comfortable American lifestyle, should be diverted to bounties. Bounty hunters have to operate under strict guidelines, so the excuses that bounty hunters would go rogue and start shooting everyone are without merit. Bounty hunters have been a major contributor to law enforcement for our entire history and they currently serve a valuable purpose and do so with honor.

We should take a page from Obama's handbook. Obama targeted children. He bused in 10's of thousands of illegal, measle ridden children and spread them all over the country. Of course this laid the groundwork for bringing the parents into the country next. We blamed the measles on Disney Land. Now Obama could look humanitarian by bringing the parents to America and reuniting the families. We're supposed to forget that he's the one who split them up in the first place. I think it would only be consistent with this new found tradition of transporting children first if we doubled the price of bounties on children. Create an incentive to deport them first. If we kicked them out of our schools it would be important for them to return home quickly anyway, so they could get back into a class room! Many of the parents would immediately self deport to go after their children.

I'm sure it will be said that sending so many kids to their home countries all at once will cause massive logistical and financial problems for the governments of those countries. So what? Who cares? No one seemed to care when the problems were dumped on us. It isn't our problem. Get rid of it. The parents will follow. If they don't, the bounty hunters will eventually get them. It will all work itself out. They would be going right back where they came from.

Hiring an illegal alien should carry with it the penalty of jail time. No fines, just jail time. Renting a home to illegal aliens should also result in jail time. Admitting illegal aliens into any college or private school should result in jail time. Once a few CEOs and college deans end up behind bars, the message will be clear that we mean business.

As if illegal aliens coming crossing the Rio Grand weren't bad enough, now the Obama administration is importing muslim refugees by the 100s of thousands and placing them all over the country. The U.S. Department of State is paying dozens of *volunteer* organizations billion and billions of dollars to manage the refugee relocation programs. The cities and towns they end up in aren't getting paid anything, but are bearing the sudden burden on their resources. Most of the places these jihadis are being sent to are small towns that don't have massive public housing projects to put them into. They don't have the utility infrastructures to accommodate the sudden increase in population and they don't have schools equipped to take in thousands of non-English speaking, 3rd world kids. Their hospitals and clinics certainly aren't equipped or trained to handle the exotic diseases they carry.

It goes without saying that these muslim refugees have started demanding sharia law all over the country, but that is another topic altogether.

The left isn't simply allowing our beautiful country to be destroyed by an invasion of illegal aliens and muslim refugees, they are causing it. Congress could put a stop to all of this if they cared. They don't. Democrats want more voters and crony capitalist RINO Republicans want cheap labor. Obama wants more muslim jihadis. Congress has been allowing Obama to get away with illegally granting amnesty by executive order. The words *executive order* do not appear in the Constitution and is not an executive power. An executive order is legally nothing more than an order a president can give within his own chain of command. Executive orders can not legally order anyone who is not in the executive branch of federal government to do anything. The president is not a king.

By all means, let's build a massive wall, especially on our southern border. Let's start building it as soon as possible. Don't allow liberals to continue fooling us with the false premise that we can't multitask. We can deport, deport, deport. States can take it upon themselves to do it too. They don't need the federal government. In fact, Article 1, Section 10[59] of the Constitution allows states to go to war against invasion when the federal government does nothing about it. There are a lot of easy solutions to this problem. All we need are backbones.

---

[59] See page 239

ISLAM: THE RELIGION OF PEACE

POSTED AUGUST 6, 2015

Islam is an evil cult. Islam was founded by a slave trading, mass murdering, pedophile, rapist named Muhammad. Muslims claim to worship the same God as Abraham, but call God Allah, after a pagan, Sumerian moon god. The Bible and the Koran make several similar references which leaves a logical person to conclude that Allah is Satan. Muslims will tell you that Allah means God, because Allah says so. Okay, then by that logic Rachel Dolezal really is black.

The Bible often refers to Satan as a deceiver. Revelations 12:9 "And the great dragon was cast out, that old serpent, called the Devil, and Satan, which deceiveth the whole world: he was cast out into the earth, and his angels were cast out with him." Islam credits Allah with being the greatest of deceivers. Koran 3:54 – And they (the unbelievers) planned to deceive, and Allah planned to deceive (the unbelievers), and Allah is the best of deceivers. Koran 8:30 – And (remember) when the unbelievers plotted deception against you (O Muhammad), to imprison you, or kill you, or expel you. They plotted deception, but Allah also plotted deception; and Allah is the best of deceivers.

Conclusion: Allah is Satan. Credit belongs to Answering Muslims[60] for the Koran verse numbers. I don't make a habit of memorizing the Koran.

The Book of Galatians in the Bible tells us that Islam is accursed. Muslims claim to have descended from Abraham, worship the same God as the Jewish and Christian God, but that Islam is the latest and greatest in the word of God. Galatians puts an end to that argument by telling us that any future gospel will be accursed! Galatians 1:8 – But though we, or an angel from heaven, preach any other gospel unto you than that which we have preached unto you, let him be accursed. Galatians 1:9 – As we said before, so say I now again, If

---

[60] http://www.answeringmuslims.com/2014/03/is-allah-best-of-deceivers.html

any man preach any other gospel unto you than that ye have received, let him be accursed.

Islam says that the angel Gabriel brought revelations to Muhammad to bring forth the birth of Islam. Obviously, the angel Gabriel lied to Muhammad or never spoke to him in the first place. Either way, Islam is accursed.

Islam has been at war with the rest of the world since it began 1400 years ago. It has been at war with the United States since 1801 when Thomas Jefferson was president and refused to pay tribute to the Barbary States of North Africa. American merchant ships were captured and the people held as hostages. Muslims love taking hostages. It's how they roll. The Marine Corps Hymn pays a tribute to this day, to the Battle of Tripoli. "From the Halls of Montezuma To the Shores of Tripoli; We fight our country's battles. In the air, on land and sea." After two sea battles and a land battle the muslims were forced to sign a treaty.

While the United States may not have an officially declared war against Islam, Islam certainly has declared war on us and it's well past time for people to realize it. Islam constantly terrorizes the western world and yet everyone keeps trying to appease it rather than defeat it. Muslims migrate to countries all over the world and rather than assimilate into the local culture, then plant seeds of Islam and Sharia law and spread like a virus. The left continually covers for them. When muslims commit atrocities the media tries to hide the fact that the issues are related to Islam. At best they will blame muslim extremists and will keep beating the drum that Islam is the religion of peace. If it is so peaceful, shouldn't the muslim extremists be extremely peaceful?

When muslims chopped off Colleen Hufford's head in Oklahoma, Obama and the sycophantic media call it work place violence. Larger muslim terrorists attacks are referred to as man caused disasters. Muslims make no secret of their intentions. The left is in complete and utter denial. As crowds on the streets of Iran chant "death to America" for all the world to see, Obama unconstitutionally signs a treaty with Iran to allow them to build nuclear weapons while giving them 11.9 Billion dollars of U.S. taxpayer money! This is insanity and Congress ignores it even though they have the power to stop it immediately. Congress doesn't have to come up with a 60 vote majority to override Obama's veto on the Iran deal. According to Article 2, Section 2[61] of the U.S. Constitution, Obama needs 67 votes in the Senate to sign the deal in the first place.

Obama is shipping hundreds of thousands of muslims into the U.S. as refugees. None of them are vetted, which would be moot anyway, because the Koran teaches muslims to lie. More on the refugees can be found here: Yes We Can Deport All Illegal Aliens[62].

None of them can be trusted. Every time another muslim goes on a terrorist killing spree, his oblivious friends and coworkers say, "we never expected he could do anything like that!" They sure should have expected it! The only radical muslim is a peaceful muslim. The Koran teaches muslims to deceive and kill all infidels. It is impossible to be a devout follower of the Koran without at least supporting the savagery of these evil doers. Where are all of the so called peaceful muslims speaking out or fighting to stop the extremists?

It's time to start getting angry and stop being politically correct over these heathens. Wherever they gather they are trouble, whether it's Rotherham, England where they systematically raped 1200 children for years, or ISIS ordering the murder of American soldiers on U.S. soil followed by the attacks on the recruiting centers killing five. Obama couldn't lower the flag to half staff fast enough when drug addict Whitney Houston died, but took almost a week under enormous political and public pressure, to lower it for our five fallen heroes who were left disarmed while at their posts.

Importation of more Islam has to stop. Deportations have to begin. The only reason needed is that they are from Islamic states and we aren't taking any more chances with them in our own backyards. As responsible citizens we must take our 2nd Amendment[63] rights seriously and consider it more than a right, but a

---

[61] See page 241

[62] See page 66 - Yes We Can... Deport All Illegal Aliens!

[63] See page 250

responsibility. When these savages have been stopped in the middle of their terrorist attacks, such as in the Oklahoma beheading or the Garland, Texas Muhammad Cartoon Contest, it has been by an armed cop or civilian. Armed civilians are almost always quicker, so don't leave yourself or your family unprotected. The war is on our soil whether our government and media admit it or not.

DO #BLACKLIVESMATTER?

POSTED AUGUST 10, 2015

The most deadly predator of black people is black women. If not for the genocidal rampage that black women have been on for the last four decades, the black population in the United States would be around 18% of the total population rather than 12.6%. Black women have caught up with Hitler in a holocaust of their own. Hitler killed 6 million Jews with the might of a massive army behind him. Without a single tank, canon, gun, or plane, American black women have successfully rid the planet of 6 million black people since 1973. Black women must really hate black people.

How do black women kill so many? Abortion. 1,876 black babies have their lives snuffed out each day in the U.S. At only 12.6% of the population, blacks are responsible for 34% of the total abortions. Per capita, blacks are by far the leading race when it comes to murdering babies. Margarette Sanger, founder of Planned Parenthood, hated all babies. She said that she believed no more babies should be born. She was particularly hateful of blacks and in a letter about regarding her "Negro Project" she wrote, "We don't want the word to go out that we want to exterminate the Negro population, and the minister is the man who can straighten out that idea if it ever occurs to any of their more rebellious members." She felt that blacks were stupid and superstitious and that the best way to talk them into aborting their babies was to get black doctors and ministers on her side to do the convincing. It worked. To this day, black women abort their babies at alarming rates.

Second only to black women when it comes to murdering black people, are black men. They are in a distant second place, because it's not easy to catch up when first place is 6 million. According to FBI Murder Statistics[64], 2,491 blacks were murdered in 2013. This is

---

[64] https://www.fbi.gov/about-us/cjis/ucr/crime-in-the-u.s/2013/crime-in-the-u.s.-2013/offenses-known-to-law-enforcement/expanded-homicide/expanded_homicide_data_table_6_murder_race_and_sex_of_vic itm_by_race_and_sex_of_offender_2013.xls

without counting the 684,740 aborted black babies. Of the 2,491 blacks who were murdered, 2,245 were at the hands of blacks. Roughly 2000 of the murderers were black men. Whites, who are constantly being accused of being racist against blacks and who vastly outnumber them, killed a whopping 189.

The #BlackLivesMatter crowd isn't concerned with black on black crime. They seem to be perfectly okay with that. They only become alarmed in the ultra rare instances when someone who is not black kills a black person. What really gets them upset is if a police officer is somehow involved with the death of a black person. The reason is never of any interest to them. It also doesn't matter that twice as many whites are killed by cops as blacks.

The #BlackLivesMatter movement started when George Zimmerman, during a neighborhood watch shift, shot and killed Trayvon Martin. Zimmerman was on neighborhood watch duty when he caught sight of Martin in his neighborhood. Thinking that he appeared suspicious, Zimmerman called 911. Martin noticed Zimmerman following him and didn't like that very much, so his first reaction was to attack Zimmerman and start pounding his head into the pavement. Luckily Zimmerman was able to reach his concealed pistol and put a stop to Martin's attack with a single shot. Curiously the burglaries in the neighborhood ceased with the death of Trayvon Martin. Some stolen goods were allegedly found in his book bag. The #BlackLivesMatter movement was born, because facts don't matter to racists like Al Sharpton, Eric Holder, and Barack Hussein Obama, who pounced on the chance to create a racial divide. It's always easiest to blame white people, so the media quickly labeled George Zimmerman as a White Hispanic.

In Ferguson, Missouri, Gentle Giant Mike Brown exited the liquor store where he just completed a successful strong arm robbery. He wanted some cigars really bad, so he grabbed the owner and shook him until he got the message. Loot in hand, Brown figured it would be wise to jaywalk in front of a police car. He was a brilliant scholar after all, headed to college soon! When Officer Wilson directed him to move out of the street, Brown rushed him him a fit of rage and started pounding the pulp out of Officer Wilson. It was all Wilson could do to grab his gun as Brown tried taking it from him. The guy with his finger on the trigger wins, so Brown came crashing down with six fresh holes in him.

Now the #BlackLivesMatter crowd were growing, so they wasted no time in burning down their town and looting everything but work boots from the stores. Eric Holder and the Obama Administration again wasted no time in stoking that fire. A slogan appeared and spread like wildfire, even though it was based on a lie. Hands up, don't shoot! Millions of dollars were made in t-shirt sales! The only problem was that Mike Brown never put his hands up and never said, "don't shoot."

The next black man to die at the hands of a cop and garner national attention was Eric Garner, in New York. He was selling loosies, single cigarettes. The owner of the store property he was standing on was getting tired of him running his shady business there, so he called the cops. Garner had a lengthy police record, but all were mostly minor crimes. Selling loosies probably wouldn't have been such a problem if he would have stayed off of the property he was on. Generally, no one thinks that Eric Garner was really that bad of a guy. When the police did arrive though, he allegedly resisted arrest, at least enough to require physical restraint. During this restraint Garner was suffocated. It was most certainly not intentional to kill him and his death has been attributed to either a preexisting medical condition or misapplied restraint techniques. It could have been both. It didn't matter to the #BlackLivesMatter crowd. To them it was cold blooded murder, so the #ICantBreathe hashtag was born. They love their slogans. Anything that doesn't take a lot of wit to remember and can be chanted in groups is acceptable for the creation of slogans for leftist and racist groups.

Finally, when Freddie Gray, yet another repeat offender, was arrested in Baltimore, Maryland, he was thrown in the back of the paddy wagon. People have been thrown in the back of motorized paddy wagons for a hundred years. This time was different though. This time the passenger wouldn't live to tell the tale. A week after his ride, while still in custody, he died from spinal injury allegedly sustained during transportation in the paddy wagon. A fellow passenger who was separated from Gray by a partition, claimed he could hear Gray pounding his head into the door. He later recanted when the #BlackLivesMatter crowd made it clear that his life didn't matter if he didn't shut up. The autopsy confirmed that Gray had sustained injuries consistent with banging his head into the door handle. Now 6 police, some black themselves, are charged with the murder of Freddy Gray, because thug #BlackLivesMatter more than the truth matters.

With the blessing of Baltimore Mayor Stephanie Rawlings-Blake, the blacks in Baltimore burned down their neighborhood and looted all of the stores of everything but work boots. Baltimore has had 185 murders in 2015, 42 in the month of May following the Freddy Gray incident and 45 in July. None of those #BlackLivesMatter, apparently.

So, do #BlackLivesMatter? Well, I think they do. I think all lives matter. Saying that really makes the #BlackLivesMatter crowd angry though. To them #OnlyBlackLivesMatter, but not all black lives. Only the very few black lives that are taken by non-blacks or cops matter. If they really believed that #BlackLivesMatter, they would be address the issues that cause the most deaths of blacks. They won't. Bill Cosby did, but the media silenced him for good. For these racists, #BlackLivesDontMatter. #RaceBaitingMatters.

FERGUSON RIOTS 2.0!

POSTED AUGUST 12, 2015

We can no longer play games with savages. It's time to start retaliating. There are several ways to retaliate that are perfectly legal and effective in stopping this kind of insanity. Simply allowing the riots to go on in Ferguson, as Baltimore Mayor Stephanie Rawlings-Blake did, can no longer be tolerated. Both police officers and regular law abiding citizens have it within their power and rights to make an effective stand against the looting, arson, vandalism, and physical attacks being perpetrated by the animals of Ferguson and other similar locations.

Officer Darren Wilson was acquitted by grand jury of any criminal charges in the death of Mike Brown. It's been proven that the claim that Mike Brown had his hands up and said, "don't shoot," is a complete fabrication. Brown's several autopsy reports have repeatedly shown that he was the aggressor and was shot dead while attacking Wilson. It's time for the heathens of Ferguson to get over it. They hurt their racist Black Lives Matter crusade by protesting the death of a thug by becoming thugs themselves. At this point, anything negative that happens to these raving lunatics is brought upon themselves.

In this 2015 reenactment of the violent Ferguson, Missouri protests, they are chanting, "This is what democracy looks like" and "Black Lives Matter." What they fail to realize is that they are only showing examples of anarchy and crime and what they are doing just helps convince the country not to care much about black lives. Stereotypes are never free, they are earned and the Ferguson crowd is bending over backwards to ensure a perpetual negative stereotyping of blacks. The many black across our country who have done no wrong and who live productive and positive lives are incapable of countering the bolstering of negative stereotypes from these unlawful throngs of hoodlums. Negative traits always outshine the positive ones in peoples' perceptions.

The time for political correctness and trying to grant respect to these people has come and gone. The law needs to make examples out of each and every one of them. There are several types of non-lethal force that police can use to subdue most of them, so that they can be arrested and removed from the equation, saving lives and property. In some cases lethal force may need to be used, such as in the case of Tyrone Harris Junior who pulled out a gun and started firing at police officers. The officers fired back hitting Harris and now he is lying in critical condition in the hospital. Too bad, so sad. He is no martyr. He's a thug and his fate is entirely his own fault. He doesn't deserve a single tear shed for him. This isn't a case of people utilizing their 2nd Amendment rights[65] to protect themselves from tyranny. These are animals who are violating the rights of others. Stopping people like this is why we have law enforcement. So far 57 of these so called protestors have been arrested. We can only hope that they face the maximum jail time for each of their crimes. Among the prominent instigators who were arrested were Cornel West, Johnetta Elzie, and DeRay McKesson.

The media is full of stories now about four Oath Keepers who are walking the streets of Ferguson bearing arms. They're making it very clear that they are white men. They are being called inflammatory and extremely anti-government. In fact, they are not anti-government, they are only against tyranny and lawless government that violates the Constitution. They have all sworn an oath to protect and defend the Constitution against all enemies foreign and domestic and it is the government itself which swore them to this oath. They are exercising their 2nd Amendment rights and carrying arms, just as Missouri confirmed they could last year. They are not throwing Molotov Cocktails through windows or shooting cops. They are not trying to force themselves against police barricades into the federal courthouse like barbarians. They may be the four most peaceful people in Ferguson right now and if there were more of them, perhaps the town wouldn't be overrun with thugs. The key thing to note about these Oath Keepers is that they have not been arrested. They have done nothing wrong. For the media to be attacking them in the midst of the horrors that actually are going on, is disingenuous and a dereliction of their profession.

---

[65] See page 250

Anyone who owns shops and businesses in Ferguson that are targets of vandalism, arson, and looting should be standing their ground on their properties, in unison and well armed. This hooliganism, does not have to be tolerated. No one is required to allow their property to be destroyed and their lives threatened without being able to fight back. The best way to avoid the need to fight back in the first place is to make a strong presence visible for all to see. Even savage animals will refrain from attacking when the odds are clearly against them. It is high time we stop tolerating these degenerates. Protesting is one thing, but doing it violently or disruptively is unacceptable. These professional protestors who run around stirring up the hatred and violence, usually through race baiting, should go away for a long time.

ARREST HILLARY CLINTON NOW!

POSTED AUGUST 14, 2015

If the media did their job Hillary Clinton would have been in jail years ago. Let's face it, if the media did their job there would hardly be a left wing in America. They constantly cover up for and even glamorize the corruption, racism, murder, and filth that the left is involved in and peddles. With the pressure of political correctness, normal people are afraid to speak out. We are forced to tolerate and even openly endorse a growing evil in our midst. With the help of corrupt politicians who are on the take and unconstitutional federal agencies, such as the Department of Education, our children are being dumbed down and indoctrinated to confuse sinful behavior with something to be proud of.

The left has convinced us that it is a constitutional right to commit 57,000,000 abortion murders. The Constitution says nothing of the sort. At best it is a state issue, at worst it is a violation of 57,000,000 peoples' right to life. We have been indoctrinated to believe that the Supreme Court has the power to legislate and throw out laws. These powers do not exist for the judiciary in the Constitution. We have come to blindly accept the power of the courts to rule over us. When the people speak out in vast majorities, as they have done time and time again against gay marriage, the court steps in and throws it all out, claiming to legalize gay marriage. Really? How is it legalized if dozens of state laws forbid it and no legislation at any level makes it legal? This reverence we have for the courts to rule over us is a sickness that must end.

We're all constantly called racists and bigots unless we're black or gay, then it's impossible to be either. If someone commits a crime there is an immediate clamor from the left to label it a federal hate crime, because it must have bigoted motivation. Never mind the fact that a federal hate crime law is unconstitutional. No power to legislate or enforce a hate crime law is enumerated in the Constitution. It makes the race baiting leftists happy to have another way to convict people when their agenda outweighs the truth. It is an end run on the 5th Amendment[66], because it is double jeopardy. All heinous crimes are motivated by hate. Throw the book at criminals for the crime, not the motivation. There is no need to throw two books. It is none of the federal government's business in any case. The Black Panthers can block polling booths to keep whites from voting, put bounties on the head of George Zimmerman, and rally outside a Texas Sheriff's office screaming, "Off the pigs!" That's all okay with the left wing and they see nothing hateful about it.

The media is fully on board with protecting the left's rabid and relentless attack on America and our values. Few have been more corrupt and wrapped up in crime after crime that the media dutifully covers up than Hillary Clinton. If she were to drown a bag full of kittens the media would spin it by playing it backwards and claim she rescued them.

The Whitewater scandal was enough to put Bill and Hillary behind bars, but when they got to appoint their own investigators, like Janet Reno and Robert Fiske, they could get away with anything. Just ask Vince Foster. Oh wait, he was found dead shortly after Bill Clinton became president. Of course it was ruled a suicide. Then and only then did the White House agree to turn over Whitewater documents to the Justice Department, including documents from Foster's office. The Clintons could ensure the documents were properly cherry picked if Foster wasn't around.

Hillary became an expert at covering things up when she did so for Bill and his alleged rape of Juanita Broaddrick, as well as his other escapades with various women such as Kathleen Wiley, Gennifer Flowers and Paula Jones. Let's not forget Monica Lewinski. Hillary's cover ups weren't good enough to keep Bill from being impeached, but she has gotten much better at it now that she is looking out for herself and not her cheating husband. Let's face it, the media laughed it off when Hillary was caught illegally obtaining FBI files in Filegate. Hillary laughed it off too as she made her way out of the Whitehouse with the silverware.

While running for president herself in 2007, Hillary made a big deal out of being the one who could answer the 3:00 A.M. phone call.

---

[66] See page 250

Well, she not only missed the 3:00 A.M. phone call from Benghazi, she ignored it. Hillary Clinton is directly responsible for the deaths of U.S. Ambassador Christopher Stevens, Sean Smith, Tyrone Woods, and Glen Doherty. They called for help. Help was available, but was refused by Hillary and Obama. They could have easily been rescued. Stevens was the first U.S. Ambassador killed in the line of Duty since Adolph Dubs in Kabul during the Carter Administration. She was in the perfect position to prove that she could keep a campaign promise, yet she failed miserably. Why would anyone believe a word that comes out of her mouth during her current campaign?

Time after time, Hillary Clinton has been embroiled in controversy and the media continues to whitewash it and bail her out. The list goes on and on, but her latest scandal is becoming harder and harder for the media to cover up. Journalists still try though. Now her private e-mail server has been confiscated by the FBI. It has been proven that Hillary feloniously sent and received top secret information through that private server. Journalists such as John R. Schindler of The Daily Beast are trying their best to play down Clinton's involvement, as if it had nothing to do with her. In his article[67], Schindler says, "Hillary Clinton has decided to turn over her private email server to the Department of Justice." He also says, "it now appears increasingly likely that someone on her staff violated federal laws regarding handling of classified materials." No Mr. Schindler, no one else on her staff used her e-mail server. No one else is to blame for Hillary's e-mails. The e-mails are in her name. They are also Top Secret, which is far worse than simply calling them classified. In all fairness to Mr. Schindler, he does do a better job of explaining the situation if you scroll down further in his article than the average liberal ever scrolls. You can almost always find snippets of the truth if you scroll far enough down, even in left wing journalism. In this case, it's becoming very hard for the media to hide the facts.

Hillary Clinton has never answered a single question regarding her accomplishments. New York Times columnist Thomas

---

[67] http://www.thedailybeast.com/articles/2015/08/12/the-spy-satellite-secrets-in-hillary-s-emails.html

Friedman asked her, " When you look at your time as Secretary of State, what are you most proud of, and what do you feel was unfinished, maybe love to have another crack at someday?" Hillary replied, "Look, I really see my role as secretary, and in fact, leadership in general in a democracy, as a relay race. I mean, you run the best race you can run, you hand off the baton. Some of what hasn't been finished may go on to be finished." In other words, *bupkis*.

Hillary did have two major accomplishments. She accomplished getting four Americans killed in Benghazi and she accomplished being the highest ranking federal official to ever compromise Top Secret information on a daily basis for years at a time. As Secretary of State, Hillary ordered the illegal e-mail server to be set up. When asked why, she told us that she was incapable of using two e-mail addresses or two devices to separate her private and official communications. It only took a few minutes before that lie was exposed with footage of her using two devices.

Hillary is running around campaigning with Huma Abedin, whose entire family including her mother is part of the Muslim Brotherhood. We now that Hillary has zero regard for national security. Are we supposed to believe that with all of the Top Secret information she was sending and receiving through an unsecured, private e-mail server that she never CC'd her Muslim Brotherhood "companion" Huma? Hillary can't blame simple negligence when she is sleeping with the enemy.

Not one of the republican candidates has the blood on their hands that Hillary has. We need to weed out the RINOs in the Republican Primary and nominate a conservative who will respect the Constitution and do everything in their power to roll back the damage of the Obama administration. Failing that, in a worst case scenario, if we were stuck with a liberal like George Pataki as our nominee, it would be a far better choice than Hillary Clinton. Under no circumstances can we allow her back into the White House. Not even for a cocktail. Hillary Clinton has betrayed the United States of America and not just once. She has made a career out of betrayal us. The media should be universally ashamed of itself for not doing its job and reporting on her honestly. It is time to press charges, put the cuffs on and arrest Hillary Clinton. She has every right to a speedy and public trial. The 6th Amendment[68] of the Constitution grants her that right and I say the more public, the better.

UPDATED AUGUST 23, 2015

With all of the attention given to the 14th Amendment[69], it should be noted that it does NOT grant birthright citizenship to babies of illegals, but it does actually prevent Hillary Clinton from running for President of the United States or even voting.

14th Amendment, Section 3:

No person shall be a Senator or Representative in Congress, or **elector of President** and Vice President, or **hold any office, civil or military, under the United States**, or under any state, **who, having previously taken an oath, as a member of Congress,** or as an officer of the United States, or as a member of any state legislature, or as an executive or judicial officer of any state, to support the Constitution of the United States, **shall have** engaged in insurrection or rebellion against the same, or **given aid or comfort to the enemies** thereof. *But Congress may by a vote of two-thirds of each House, remove such disability.*

---

[68] See page 250

[69] See page 253

HOMOGAYDOM IS A JUDICIAL BLITZKRIEG ON CHRISTIANITY!

POSTED AUGUST 16, 2015

Few are more rabidly intolerant than the homosexuals. They are already vile sinners, so being disingenuous by demanding tolerance from everyone else while tolerating no opposing views themselves, is no surprise. Why should anyone be shocked that people who practice evil would also be dishonest? They are not happy practicing their sinful ways in private. Homosexuals seek the approval of everyone else for their sick activities. Perhaps they know their actions are sinful, so they are trying to obtain justification or vindication from others.

It is not mere acceptance of their lifestyle that they want from the rest of us. Obtaining tolerance isn't enough. They want full endorsement, participation and a total cultural immersion into their debauchery. You can hardly find a television show anymore that doesn't push the homosexual agenda in our faces. Even shows that should be completely politically neutral, such as The Walking Dead, have forced us to watch gays in action. It's sickening and the people are growing weary of it.

Homosexuality is a sin, which by it's very nature, should not affect anyone else outside of the bedroom. Almost no one would care what gays did if they kept it to themselves. That isn't good enough for them. Gays want others, especially Christians, to be forced to participate and be effected by their homosexual sins. Whether it be forcing a Christian baker to bake a cake for a gay wedding or pushing the legality of that wedding on us and forcing us to subsidize it with our taxes in various ways. Our religious rights do not exist if we are forced to abandon our beliefs with a government boot on our throat.

When it comes to gay marriage, it should be noted that if the federal government had not unconstitutionally involved itself with marriage in the first place, the entire argument would be moot. No one would care what gays do, because it wouldn't affect anyone else. It isn't marriage that gays are truly after, it's the entitlements, tax breaks, and other benefits that come along with marriage, thanks to the unconstitutional meddling of government in marriage that created these things.

Marriage is primarily a religious institution for the creation of a nuclear family unit. A large majority of homosexuals are atheist, so it belies credibility that they want to take part in a religious ceremony, because the faith is so important to them. If the faith were really that important, they would cease their sinful ways and repent. Marriage has a definition. Homosexuals have never been barred from marriage. Like everyone else, they have always had the right to marry someone of the opposite sex. Again, it isn't marriage that they really want. They want to destroy religious institutions and traditions and do so at the expense of the tax payer.

All levels of government already have their tentacles wrapped in the institution of marriage. Ideally we'd remove government from the equation altogether, but that isn't very likely. In the mean time, it falls within the jurisdiction of the states to decide how to handle marriage and gay marriage. No federally enumerated power exists to legislate on the matter, so it is a 10th Amendment[70] issue.

All across the United States, the people have put gay marriage to a vote. The people have spoken loudly and clearly to be firmly against the legalization of gay marriage. Even in the fervently liberal State of California, the people voted in Proposition 8, to outlaw gay marriage. Every step of the way, homosexuals have taken it to courts to have the laws and state constitutional amendments which ban gay marriage, thrown out. Never mind the fact that courts have no authority to legislate or throw out law. We have been dumbed down so thoroughly that the vast majority of people don't know the limits of courts, so we allow them to get away with it. All it takes now is a single, biased and activist judge to throw out a majority vote. There is no shortage of liberal activist judges, so eventually every case will find its way in front of one. Our government is not designed to be thwarted just by finding a judge who has a bias.

The homosexual community, including the White House, celebrated when the Supreme Court legalized gay marriage. There is

---

[70] See page 250

only one problem. Gay marriage wasn't legalized! Few Americans are constitutionally educated enough to understand this. The Supreme Court can't legislate. Article 3[71] of the Constitution does not allow them to unlegislate, either. No authority is granted to any court to legalize anything or prohibit any laws. All they can do is determine if a law is broken, not whether or not the law is legitimate. There is no constitutionally grounded argument that can refute this. The power that the Supreme Court wields on a daily basis, is done so without constitutional authority. It has been usurped.

The Supreme Court decision is both illegitimate and illegal. States can and should nullify it by simply ignoring it. Colorado has shown us how easily it is to nullify unconstitutional federal drug laws. The Supreme Court has no power to enforce their decision on others. Americans have a serious and urgent need to educate ourselves on the Constitution. We have been lead astray by those in power, so that they may remain in power. Our ignorance is vital for that power to me retained. The power that rightfully belongs to the people and the states, must be revoked from those in the federal government who have usurped it.

Illegally using the courts is the only way that homosexuals, who make up 2.5% of the U.S. population can impel their will on the rest of us. There is no law that says any business has to provide a service or product that they do not offer. If a baker does not have gay wedding cakes on the menu, they can not be forced to bake one. That is, unless the homosexuals can find a judge to make an illegal decision. Gays also like to cite the Civil Rights Act, which is both unconstitutional and doesn't mention anything about sexual deviancy being a protected class. That's right, Congress had no enumerated authority to pass the Civil Rights Act. If it were really so fantastic, a constitutional amendment would have been the legitimate way to make it law. That is beside the point though, because The Civil Rights Act does nothing to protect homosexuals from bakers who refuse to violate their Christian faith by taking part in a gay wedding.

If a baker can be forced to bake a cake for a gay wedding, can a photographer also be forced to film a gay porn film? Can a Jewish

---

[71] See page 242

tailor be forced to sew NAZI uniforms? Can black carpenters be forced to build crosses for the KKK to burn? Can a Walmart be forced to bake a Dixie Flag cake? Apparently not, because Walmart will no longer bake a cake with a Dixie Flag on it and there are far more southerners and Sons of Confederates who hold their southern heritage dear than there are homosexuals. Southerners don't force others to fly their flags or take part in their celebrations. Only gays want to force everyone else to embrace their beliefs at the expense of their own.

NORTH AMERICAN ARMS AND SAFETY!

POSTED AUGUST 19, 2015

I have been around guns my entire life. So that makes me a know it all, right? Nope. Every time I buy a new gun or have the opportunity to use a gun I haven't used before, I approach it as if I am entirely inexperienced. I personally don't want to take chances by being cocky. I always ask the owner or seller to explain the intricacies of the gun that I am new to and more often than not, I end up learning something.

Not long ago, I purchased a North American Arms (NAA) .22 Magnum, 5 shot revolver. I haven't shot very many small pistols, Derringers, or Saturday Night Specials. I wanted to have a little pocket revolver as a backup. I opted for a .22 Magnum due to its incredible power for its size. The quality of the NAA revolvers is very good. The first thing I did when I purchased this little guy was ask the seller to show me how to operate it. I knew it was a single action, but I wanted to know if there were any oddities to consider when loading it and I was especially curious about his preferred method for keeping it safe. Everyone I knew who had a similar single action revolver either kept one chamber unloaded, so the hammer wouldn't rest on a cartridge, or they kept their guns at half cock. I don't really relish either method, but was prepared to keep only four rounds loaded in a 5 shot revolver to stay on the safe side.

I am really glad I asked the seller these questions, because he showed me that the NAA revolvers actually do have a built in safety and a very good one! I can't honestly say that I would have ever figured this out on my own. After purchasing mine, I started running into more and more people who had NAA revolvers and none of them realized that they had a safety built in. They were always thrilled when I show them how the safety works.

The safety feature on these revolvers almost seems to be a secret, so I felt like it would be a good idea to put this out there for anyone else who may be interested. You can find similar instructions in other places, but you have to know to look for them. Guns are dangerous, so don't blame me if things go wrong. Follow these instructions at your own risk. If you plan on trying to sue me over helping you to be safe, because you harm yourself, just quit reading and go find a crying pillow.

Putting the revolver on safe is tricky. Once you get the hang of it, it's fairly easy, but it takes getting used to, because you need a little muscle memory to be really good at it. On the back of the cylinder you will notice a notch between each chamber. The key to putting the revolver on safe is dropping the hammer into one of those notches, so that it is firmly locked into place between two rounds and the cylinder cannot turn. The reason this is tricky is that the cylinder doesn't spin freely unless you draw the hammer back slightly beyond half cock.

Make sure your revolver is unloaded and practice doing this over and over until you feel comfortable doing it. Then practice it some more.

Pull the hammer back, while holding it firmly, so you don't accidentally let the hammer drop. If you are right handed you'll want to pull the hammer back with your right thumb. Once you pass the half cock point, the cylinder is released and can rotate freely. With your left hand, rotate the cylinder to align one of the slots between the chambers with the very top, so that when the hammer comes back to rest, it will fall into the slot. This is where it gets precarious and why you want to practice a lot before doing it with a loaded revolver. Now, with the hammer held past half cock, once you have the slot on the back of the cylinder aligned at the top, pull the trigger. Don't let go of the hammer! With the trigger pulled, you can now ease the hammer back down to rest and gently guide it into the slot between chambers.

Once the hammer is resting in the slot, it is very safe. The hammer is locked between rounds, therefore can't strike the rim of a round. The cylinder can't turn, because the hammer is locking it in place. It's single action, so the trigger can't cause the hammer to draw back. It's as safe as it can be. But remember, a gun is never safe. Treat it as if it is always unsafe and loaded.

Now that you have gotten that down pat you are finally ready to do it again at least 200 more times before you attempt it while loaded! It's well worth it, so don't let a little practice discourage you!

NAA revolvers haven't always had this feature, so if you have one that is older and don't have the safety notches, you can call North American Arms at 800-821-5783 to find out how to update your gun.

One more important thing that all NAA Revolver owners must know. Never, ever, ever, ever use PMC brand .22LR or .22 Magnum ammunition. North American Arms has extended this advisory to include any ammunition made under subcontract to PMC, such as ARMSCOR and FIOCCHI. Basically, they are saying to steer clear of Filipino ammo. There have been occurrences of double-discharge. As you can imagine, two rounds going off in a revolver that only has one round in battery (aligned with the barrel) is something that you probably never want to experience.

THE 14TH AMENDMENT DOESN'T GRANT CITIZENSHIP TO BABIES OF ILLEGAL ALIENS!

POSTED AUGUST 21, 2015

The 14th Amendment[72] does not grant birthright citizenship to everyone born in the United States. In order to assume that it does, a person has to actually ignore what it says. The Supreme Court set the precedent of birthright citizenship by misinterpreting the 14th Amendment. Poor education about our history and government ensures that We the People never get uppity over this unconstitutional misinterpretation. The purpose of the 14th Amendment was to give citizenship to former slaves who were in the United States through no fault of their own.

The 14th Amendment was ratified in 1868. If it granted citizenship for no reason other than being born on U.S. soil, you would think that the U.S. would have started granting birthright citizenship in 1868, right? Wrong. They didn't, because that isn't what the 14th Amendment says. The 14th Amendment says, "All persons born or naturalized in the United States, **AND** *subject to the jurisdiction thereof*, are citizens of the United States…" Two years prior to its ratification, Senator Jacob Howard explained the actual intent of the 14th Amendment. He said, "Every person born within the limits of the United States, and subject to their jurisdiction, is by virtue of natural law and national law a citizen of the United States. This will not, of course, include persons born in the United States who are foreigners, aliens, who belong to the families of ambassadors or foreign ministers accredited to the Government of the United States, but will include every other class of persons. It settles the great question of citizenship and removes all doubt as to what persons are or are not citizens of the United States. This has long been a great desideratum in the jurisprudence and legislation of this country."

---

[72] See page 253

The key to inheriting birthright citizenship is being subject to the jurisdiction of the United States. Foreigners are subject to the jurisdiction of the countries they are citizens of. We deport illegal aliens back to the countries that they are subject to the jurisdiction of. If they were subject to the jurisdiction of the United States, then they would have all privileges and rights that go with that jurisdiction including voting, enlisting in our armed forces, and running for public office. Not being part of our jurisdiction, they are ineligible. They can do so in their home countries. The Supreme Court held to this in the 1884 Elk vs Wilkins case. They decided that the children of foreign ministers were not granted birthright citizenship based on the fact that they weren't subject to the jurisdiction of the United States. An American Indian was not granted citizenship, because his parents weren't completely subject to U.S. jurisdiction, being also subject to an Indian nation. If an American Indian was not granted American Citizenship by birthright after the 14th Amendment was ratified, then we can certainly conclude that birthright citizenship isn't granted to foreigners by the 14th Amendment. Congress didn't grant citizenship to American Indians until 1924!

It wasn't until 1898, 30 years after the ratification of the 14th Amendment, that a case came in front of the Supreme Court that changed things. Keep in mind that the 5th Clause of the 14th Amendment specifically gives congress the power to enforce the 14th Amendment, not the Supreme Court.

Wong Kim Ark was a Chinese man who was born in the United States to Chinese citizens. They returned to China and took little Wong with them. Eventually Wong wanted to come back, but he wasn't allowed due to the Chinese Exclusion Act of 1862 that prohibited all immigration of Chinese laborers to the United States. Wong sued and his case went all the way to the Supreme Court and they pulled a rabbit out of their hat and said that the 14th Amendment granted him birthright citizenship, which it clearly doesn't. The Supreme Court often misinterprets the Constitution, which is why the founding fathers did not give them the power to interpret the Constitution to begin with. They purposefully left judicial review out of the list of enumerated powers that the Constitution authorizes the courts. The Supreme Court usurped this power in Marbury vs Madison and it hasn't yet been properly challenged. I have my hopes.

Now that Won Kim Ark was granted citizenship based on a misinterpretation of the Constitution, the other unconstitutional power of the Supreme Court kicked in, which is to set precedent, effectively legislating a new law. Now it applied to all babies born on U.S. soil. This went on until 1965 when it was no longer good enough to liberals to merely give birthright citizenship to the children who were born in the U.S. No, liberals wanted this birthright to extend to the family of the baby.

Congress passed the unconstitutional 1965 Immigration Act. This gave birth to the term "anchor baby." Listen carefully to those on the left like Jeb Bush who keep saying, "If you're born in this country, you're a citizen!" They are deflecting the issue. The term "anchor baby" has nothing to do with the citizenship of the baby. It's far worse now. The baby is granted birthright citizenship straight out of *illegal* alien womb and instantly *legalizes* the alien who birthed it. The baby anchors the mother to the U.S. with a green card. It keeps getting worse, because the chain on this anchor has gotten longer and now applies to a growing list of extended family members. When an illegal alien squeezes out a kid out on American soil now, the kid is holding a bag of green cards for the whole family waiting on the other side of the border.

Even if you are stupid enough to believe that the 14th Amendment grants citizenship to any baby born on American soil, it's asinine to assume this extends to the entire family. Granting birthright citizenship to the baby of an illegal alien is unconstitutional enough, but the 1965 Immigration Act is borderline treasonous.

Always question the constitutionality of any law that Congress passes. Most are unconstitutional. If they pass a law called an Act, you can safely bet your house that it's unconstitutional. The Gun Control Act and The Civil Rights Act are just two more of many unconstitutional and dangerous laws that Congress has passed. They always do it under the guise of being caring and yet they always infringe our liberties and/or sovereignty.

There is no need to ratify another amendment to get rid of birthright citizenship, because it doesn't exist. We merely have to stop applying unconstitutional Supreme Court decrees to the populous. They can't legislate. All we need to do is read the 14th Amendment and follow what it actually says. This is not to say that I wouldn't love to see the 14th Amendment repealed anyway. There are other reasons that I want it repealed, which I cover in more detail in Chapter 4 of this book and Chapter 6, "The 14th Amendment – Equal Protection Explained."

HOW TOLERANT IS A GAY, BLACK LIVES MATTER RACIST?

POSTED AUGUST 27, 2015

Juan Williams blamed gun loopholes. Criminal Hillary Clinton and White House Press Secretary Josh Earnest quickly jumped on the bandwagon to blame guns. The left blatantly disregards the fact that gun sales have been through the roof in Virginia for the past decade and gun crimes are way down.

The one person that Juan, Hillary, Josh or any of the left will not blame is liberal whack job, Vester Lee Flanagan, AKA Bryce Williams after he shot and killed two reporters, Alison Parker and Adam Ward who were giving a live television broadcast. He also severely wounded Vicki Gardner, the woman being interviewed, by shooting her in the back. He filmed the whole thing and posted it on Twitter and Facebook. He was upset, because he claimed that Alison made a racist comment. Hours later, Vester did the world a favor by shooting himself while being pursued by police. He died after they got him to the hospital.

In his rambling and racist manifesto he wrote that he did it because he was discriminated against for being gay and black. Speaking about the Charleston Church shooting, which was perpetrated by another liberal nut job, Dylann Roof, he said, "The church shooting was the tipping point...but my anger has been building steadily...I've been a human powder keg for a while...just waiting to go BOOM!!!!"

More quotes from his manifesto:

"What sent me over the top was the church shooting. And my hollow point bullets have the victims' initials on them."

"As for Dylann Roof? You (deleted)! You want a race war (deleted)? BRING IT THEN YOU WHITE ...(deleted)!!!"

Referencing the Columbine and Virginia Tech shooters he said, "Also, I was influenced by Seung–Hui Cho. That's my boy right there. He got NEARLY double the amount that Eric Harris and Dylann Klebold got…just sayin.'"

He says he has suffered racial discrimination, sexual harassment and bullying at work.

He says he has been attacked by black men and white females.

He talks about how he was attacked for being a gay, black man.

Shouldn't we be blaming and banning a flag or two now?

Vester was a product of the racist Black Lives Matter movement and the Force Homosexuality Down Our Throats movement all wrapped in one. He was indeed a human powder keg, but one that was designed and created by the race baiting, homosexual pushing, divisive Obama Administration. Obviously, he was a very evil, gay, black man who could not tolerate the fact that others didn't see eye to eye with his chosen lifestyle. Vester figured that he could take advantage of the racial divide that has been created by the left and particularly the Obama Administration to give him a violent outlet for his anger. The Gays and the Black Lives Matter movements have a lot in common. They are both groups that are supported very strongly by the left wing for their ability to divide Americans. They are both filled with angry, bitter, and vile followers. They both resist the word of God. Their major difference is in how they pursue their goals. Gays use illegal, activist court decisions to throw out the will of the people and the Black Lives Matter savages use violence. When you wrap both up in one package and put a bow on it, you get Vester Lee Flanagan.

The immediate reaction from the top levels of the left wing are to address Vester's murders by attacking our 2nd Amendment[73] rights. The left thrives on this sort of thing. They cannot let a crisis go to waste! A crisis gives them an opportunity to sway the populous who is in temporary shock, to give up our rights in the interest of safety. That safety never comes. It can't be provided by those who promise it. You don't see Obama standing on the soap box decrying the murders for what they are, evil and reprehensible actions of a Gay, Black Lives Matter, Racist. You don't see Obama giving his

---

[73] See page 250

condolences to the families of the victims, like he did for the families of thugs like Trayvon Martin and Mike Brown when they were put down. Vester is a hero to the left. He provides the kind of opportunity they salivate for. The crisis he enables is used as a fear tactic to scare We the People into submission.

We must immediately put up our intellectual guards against the propaganda onslaught from the left that will ensue after this outrageous, cold blooded murder perpetrated by one of their own gay, racists. Vester is an example of why everyone should buy more guns, more self defense training, and more ammunition. While these types of violent attacks are actually extremely rare, in a nation of 320 million people they are still bound to happen occasionally. Left wing media hype about these events is on a sharp rise, because they want to beat the drum that we live in a violent society and that guns are to blame. Gun ownership across the country has been climbing fast over the last decade, especially among women and gun crime has been plummeting. Don't be fooled by the tricksters in media who try to spin every bad story to garner support for more government tyranny. If you heed anything Hillary Clinton says, you have other problems that probably can't be helped. The fact of the matter is, had Alison Parker, Adam Ward, or Vicki Gardner been armed, there would have been a better chance to stop the carnage at least a little sooner. You can't avoid being ambushed, but you can stop an attack sooner and keep casualties lower if innocent, law abiding civilians are able to shoot back.

Buy more guns. Follow your state and local laws, even if they are unconstitutional. Fight the battles to repeal unconstitutional gun control laws in your state legislatures and courts. In the mean time, abide by the laws you may be constricted by and get permits if you have to. Keep yourself armed at all times. Even if you have used guns for your entire life, it never hurts to get more defensive and safety training. It's not expensive and it's fun. You may never need your gun or your training. Chances are you never will, but it's better to be safe than sorry. The Boy Scouts of America sum it up in two glorious words. Be Prepared!

OPEN LETTER TO ANDY PARKER, FATHER OF ALISON PARKER

POSTED AUGUST 29, 2015

Mr. Parker,

I sympathize with you and your family's tragic loss, as I do for the family of Adam Ward. Vicki Gardner is also in my prayers and I hope that she recovers quickly and well.

That said, I would kindly like to ask you to get off of my back! Your new found crusade to attack me, other Virginians, and Americans who had nothing to do with the evil actions of Vester Flanagan, is uncalled for and driven by unchecked emotion and ignorance. I am sick and tired of you leftists who hate liberty using every tragedy as a soap box to stand on to attack the freedoms that our founding fathers have secured for us and that our men and women in uniform have protected for over two centuries. You liberals always want to take advantage of every shocking event to catch the public off guard in a moment of despair, so that we will willingly relinquish more of our freedom in the false hope that it will be replaced with more security.

I challenge you sir: how do you expect me to be safer if we pass any new gun control law? Name one gun control law that will leave the liberty of all free Americans intact while somehow disarming the people who are willing to ignore law to commit murder? If you can't answer this question, then you have no business harassing Virginians or other Americans with your impotent agitation. I have the RIGHT to keep and bear arms and that right shall not be infringed, by you or anyone else.

Why do you think that violating *my* 2nd, 4th, and 5th Amendment[74] Rights will do anything to prevent a single crime? We are already forced to undergo unconstitutional background checks. Vester Flanagan passed one of your statist checks. Obviously they don't work. They force us to incriminate ourselves against our 5th

---

[74] See page 250

Amendment rights. They allow an unwarranted search of our past, violating our 4th Amendment rights. The 2nd Amendment doesn't say, "Shall not be infringed UNLESS..." There is absolutely *nothing* that can be searched for, which can be used to infringe on our right to keep and bear arms, so why do the check in the first place? If there is something so horrible in our past that should prevent us from owning a gun, then it should also prevent us from getting out of prison in the first place. You cannot convict me or anyone else for a crime we did not yet commit. If you can't keep a truly violent person behind bars *after* they have committed a crime, then there is a problem with the system. Address *that problem* if you like, because it is a real issue. Leave free Americans alone.

I don't know what kind of new gun control laws you seek, but it doesn't matter. You statists will always take every step you can on your never ending march to push us to the left, but this time you won't get to take that step. You have been all over the media, primarily MSNBC, cackling about how it's time for *reasonable* gun control. Using adjectives like *reasonable* to advance a false premise no longer works. We the People are sick and tired of *reasonable* violations of our rights and principles as Americans. The talking heads on MSNBC are wringing their hands, giddy with excitement and glee over the fuel you are providing them to put freedom under a torch. It's a sick thing to see in America, especially in Virginia. I am a Virginian, sir. Virginia is where the Revolutionary War was won! We are *not* going to bow down to your proposed boot of tyranny on our throats.

Virginia has a fantastic history of throwing gun control bills out while still in committee before they are even brought to a vote by the full Senate or House of Delegates. Thankfully, your admittedly tragic situation will lose all of its shock value by the time the Virginia General Assembly begins the 2016 session. You aren't going to be able to ride a wave of emotion over the better judgement of the Virginian people to ambush our rights with a sneak attack. Cooler heads by that time will prevail over your hot headed ranting.

Your daughter's situation was absolutely horrible and there is little she could have done to protect herself under a surprise attack by a crazy person. However, had Adam or Vicki been armed, they could have possibly done something before Vester's attention turned to them. It is indisputable that they would have had a better chance to mitigate at least some of the damage had they been armed. We have now witnessed on live TV how easy it is for a bad guy with a gun to go unchallenged when firing upon a group of unarmed innocent people. Nothing that you propose would stop the bad guy from having a gun. You only make it harder for the good guys to defend themselves.

Year after year the FBI continues reporting increased gun sales and decreased crime, especially gun related crime. In the U.S. in 2013 around 20 million guns were sold and murder fell by 6%. Burglary fell by 14%. Assault fell by 1.6%. Over the course of a decade we've seen fantastic numbers like this reported by the FBI, yet you people on the left continue your drum beat against guns! All statistics show the same results and even more so in Virginia. If you, Mr. Parker, want to do something to actually bring about a positive change, then why don't you direct your energy toward something that will actually do some good? Why don't you fight to make punishments fit the crime? Instead of letting the most violent criminals out of prison early, why don't you fight to have them kept there. There will be plenty of room for them in prison if we stop filling our prisons with people who commit victimless crimes. Lock up the truly violent among us and throw away the key. Those who are free, even the felons, would be able to enjoy all of the rights that the Constitution protects and the truly evil among us will be behind bars where they can do no more harm.

Unfortunately, locking up the truly violent criminals for good doesn't fit your liberal agenda. You on the left *need* those violent criminals out, so that they can commit more crimes that can be used as emotional catalysts to attack our freedoms again and again. As the left likes to say, "never let a crisis go to waste."

I completely understand that you are suffering a heartbreaking misfortune right now. I know that it has your emotions running high. However, your feelings do not and will never trump my God given, constitutional rights! Stop blaming innocent people and inanimate objects for the evil actions of an extremely finite number of monsters. Stop looking to government to violate the constitution in order to appease your misplaced desires. You are spitting in the face of those of us who would have been most willing to reach out and comfort you. Instead, you are joining the chorus of a bunch of leftists who couldn't care less about you or your daughter, but merely exploit you as another convenient tool in their effort to take down freedom. Vester Flanagan is the intended result of the rabid vitriol of the leftists you are siding with. You need to step back and examine the facts without an emotional bias and get off *my* back!

BLACK LIVES ARE EXPENDABLE TO BLACK LEADERS

POSTED SEPTEMBER 1, 2015

Buy guns and ammo. Always be prepared, because Black Lives Matter savages will start creeping up on you! At least that is the message the Racist New Black Panthers have for police. They stood outside a Houston jail and screamed and hollered at the police saying they "will start creeping up on you in the darkness." It seems as if they have already been doing quite a bit of creeping up. They are a bunch of violent, racist, race baiters who have already begun their murder spree. The best advice to everyone is to arm up and watch out for black people creeping up on you under the cover of darkness. If they creep up on you, defend yourself.

Threatening the police that they would creep up on them wasn't the extent of their ebonic rant. Using the word *off* as a verb, like only a ghetto thug can, they chanted in unison, "The revolution is on! Off the pigs! Oink! Oink! Bang! Bang!" We're not describing a bunch of honor students here, we're talking about blacks who have been purposefully dumbed down by liberals to enslave as voters. Keeping a group of people stupid and dependent on government also makes them sheepish and prone to group think. The black community has become a large group of brainwashed people who are easily swayed by the power of suggestion to do whatever the loudest one among them says. They have been brainwashed of any ability to think independently. Culturally, the left has turned the black community into a race of puppets. They empower a few puppet masters to pull all of the strings.

The puppet masters are being upgraded. Al Sharpton and Jesse Jackson aren't getting the air time they are used to having. The people of Ferguson, Missouri actually sent Sharpton packing. These race baiters aren't violent enough to foment the true hate that the Obama Administration wants. The division has to be deep enough to cause a race war. Sharpton's and Jackson's days of merely demanding a piece of the pie are over. Violence is the goal now and they need new leadership to bring that about. New puppet masters.

People like Deray McKesson, whose only claim to fame is quitting his job to become a full time hater and agitator. You won't see Deray actually committing the violence he advocates. He likes to let others do the really dirty work while he sits back in the clear. He's a coward. Much like a muslim who sends children into a crowd with a suicide bomb vest. Deray is garbage. A laughing stock. But he's just the kind of leadership the Black Lives Matter crowd needs. Loud, racist, and hateful. On his own he can't do jack. He needs a group of ignorant miscreants to do his bidding.

Deray was an inspiration to the recent murderer, Vester Lee Flanagan who shot and killed two journalists, Alison Parker and Adam Ward and then also wounded Vicki Gardner, the innocent woman being interviewed at the time. Some were saying that Deray and Vester followed one another on Twitter, but that's hard to confirm now that Vester's account is suspended. Right after the shooting, Deray, the chicken that he is, tried to distance himself and the Black Lives Matter organization from the evil murders that his group inspired by claiming that Vester was white. He tweeted, "Some say 'disgruntled employee,' others say 'terrorist.' Whiteness will explain away nearly anything." He later deleted his tweet when his lie proved to be too blatant to cover up. No one said "terrorist" and no one said "disgruntled employee." Everyone said, black, racist, homosexual, just as Vester's manifesto described himself. Vester also claimed to be starting a race war. This is what Deray wants. He's just unwilling to be the patsy when there are plenty of willing pawns to do his bidding for him.

Another, slightly more silent puppet master is Baltimore Mayor, Stephanie Rawlings-Blake who ordered cops to stand down and allow the savages to loot and burn the city. A responsible mayor would stopped the riots before they got out of control. Mayor Rawlings-Blake's influence doesn't reach that far beyond Baltimore though, except for causing a little more unrest among blacks with her rhetoric. Her overt inaction was her way of tugging on the puppet strings. Her puppets danced just as she dreamed they would.

A good example of a new age, black puppet master is former New Black Panther Party Chairman, Malik Zulu Shabazz. He recently told a group of fellow Black Lives Matter savages that they "need to finish the mission of killing slave masters and their G**

D*** families." Again, like the other Black Lives Matter leaders who are willing to talk the talk, he is too afraid to walk the walk. His intention is to pull the puppet strings of the blacks whose lives don't matter, inspiring them to commit violence.

Over and over again the black leadership inspires their minions to go out and kill in the name of Black Lives Matter. The first actual killing under the Black Lives Matter banner was done by Ismaaiyl Brinsley. He shot his ex-girlfriend dead in Baltimore, then drove to New York where he killed Wenjian Liu and Rafael Ramos, two New York City police officers. This put a lot of smiles on the faces of a lot of bigots in the leadership of Black Lives Matter.

The latest black life that the puppet masters pulled the strings on is allegedly Shannon Miles, the man arrested for the heinous murder of Harris County, Texas Sheriff's Deputy, Darren Goforth. Whether it is proven to have been Shannon Miles or not, one thing is certain: a Black Lives Matter representative followed the New Black Panthers missive to creep up on a police officer under the cover of darkness to murder him. Deputy Goforth was minding his own business filling his car with gas. His murderer crept up from behind, in the darkness, and did the unthinkable. Unthinkable until Black Lives Matter became a movement. Now it's becoming all too common.

This is sick and it's intentional. The left wingers in power, such as the Obama Administration, cultivate this evil. They bestow a certain level of power to the leadership of the divisive, racist, Black Lives Matter and New Black Panthers movements. These leaders are then more than happy to pull the puppet strings to beguile their dimwitted pawns to commit acts of violence. The pawns get to feel like they are part of something big, when in fact they are nothing but dutiful rubes who get to take the fall. The Derays and Maliks are willing to sacrifice a lot of pawns. They could care less about black lives. Their goal and the goal of those in power who sanction them, is to create a division among the American people. Liberals divide and conquer according to the Alinski model. It's how they hold onto power.

For at least a generation, racism was all but dead and buried in the United States. Now Black Lives Matter is doing everything it can to stoke the racist fire and give people good reasons to become racists. When people of one race publicly demand a race war while killing innocent civilians, police, and journalists, it's harder and harder for anyone to ignore the stereotype they are creating for themselves. Their leadership doesn't care at all about black lives and to them, the less value that others place on black lives, the better. This week at the Minnesota State Fair, they chanted "Pigs in a blanket! Fry 'em like bacon!" Their chant writers aren't really cut from the same cloth as Mark Twain or William Shakespeare.

Remember when the Tea Party was accused by the entire media and the left for being a racist organization? Although there are black Tea Party members and no evidence whatsoever of racism, they were vilified. A black Tea Party member selling t-shirts at a Tea Party gathering was beaten to a pulp by the tolerant left wingers who saw him there. The IRS illegally audited Tea Party organizations and shut them down, so that they couldn't participate in the election process like left wing organizations and unions could. We don't hear a peep from the media today about the racism being spewed by Black Lives Matter, even though they have blood on their hands and admit that it's *race war blood*.

Yes, it is time to arm up, folks. Purchase firearms and ammunition. Learn to use them. Take some defensive weapons training, even if it is a refresher. If you are a certified trainer, offer discounts or even free courses for the elderly. Two Black Lives Matter savages just played the Knock Out Game on an old white woman inside a church. Conceal or open carry wherever you go. Always be on the lookout for a Black Lives Matter thug creeping up on you in the darkness, especially if he's gay!

IRAN NUKE DEAL IS ILLEGAL

POSTED SEPTEMBER 3, 2015

How have we gone this mad? I keep seeing headlines everywhere, such as the Washington Times saying, "Obama Secures Votes to Preserve Iran Nuclear Deal Despite Majority Opposition."[75] This is *asinine*! This isn't how it works! Where is Mitch McConnell calling the President and the media out on this? This is illegal. This is Flat Out Unconstitutional![76] Mitch McConnell could end this with one press conference by simply laughing and saying, "Obama thinks he's God or something, because he clearly has no such power. This deal is not happening. Enjoy the rest of your day folks."

Article 2[77] of the Constitution enumerates the powers of the President. Every power he has must be listed. According to the 10th Amendment[78], he has no power that is not specifically *delegated* to him by the Constitution. Article 2, Section 2, Clause 2[79] says, "He shall have the power, by and with the Advice and Consent of the Senate, to make Treaties, provided ***two thirds of the Senators present concur.***" Two thirds of the Senate is 67, the last time I counted. So how on God's green earth is 34 his magic number? It's not! It's a lie. The entire federal government is in on it. The media is gleefully backing this backwards abuse of power by not reporting the truth. Everyone, and I mean everyone in the media is either completely ignorant or guilty of complicity. No one is reporting this.

The media has continuously been reporting about the 34 votes in the Senate that Obama needs to provide a veto proof Congress, so he

---

[75] http://www.washingtontimes.com/news/2015/sep/2/obama-secures-votes-to-preserve-iran-nuclear-deal-/

[76] https://flatoutunconstitutional.com/

[77] See page 239

[78] See page 251

[79] See Page 241

can get away with his deal to arm Iran with nukes. Veto? What veto? He doesn't have 2/3 consent, therefore there is no treaty. There is nothing to veto. Congress doesn't have to pass a law to block a president from forming a treaty. The Senate has to consent to it with a super majority of two thirds! The House of Representatives has absolutely nothing to do with the process. It is impossible for a treaty or lack thereof to be vetoed! Congress doesn't vote down treaties and then need a big enough majority to block a veto. My God, people! Wake the heck up!

Semantics is also playing apart in this crime. Obama knows that We the People are too stupid these days to understand something so simple as renaming a rose. Yup, now a rose by another name is a turnip. All he has to do is call a treaty a deal and wha-lah! He also knows that no one in the media or the Congress will call him out on his word games. It doesn't matter what you call it. When one country strikes a deal with another country, it's a treaty. This isn't a complicated or misinterpreted word in our dictionary.

treaty | ˈtrētē |
noun (pl. treaties)
a formally concluded and ratified agreement between countries.

This Iran nuke deal is impeachable. Everyone involved is impeachable. This is treason. It is providing aid and comfort to our enemy. Iran is an ardent enemy of the United States of America. Iran has a holiday each year called Quds Day, which centers around rallying cries of "Death to America" and "Death to Israel." They burn our flags and images of our leaders in effigy. They make no bones about their role as our enemy or their hatred for us. Obama has no business making treaties with this evil regime, but even if he did, he must do it legally and constitutionally, with 2/3 consent of the Senate. Make no mistake, this is *treason*! Every member of the senate who doesn't speak out against this emphatically and call it what it is, *treason*, is also committing treason. They should all be impeached. The Senators who are complicit need to be impeached, removed from office and replaced before Obama can be removed from office. We need actual patriots who cherish the Constitution as Senators to remove Obama from office after the House impeaches him.

Honestly, I want Mitch McConnell to be the first one impeached. He is a traitor.

This could never have happened 20 years ago. I want the republican presidential candidates to immediately and convincingly start calling this what it is. **Treason**. I want them to vow that they will undo this on day one, should they be elected. I demand it! I cannot believe how far we have fallen and how stupid we have become. This is sheer lunacy and I hope to God I wake up and find out this is all a dream. America, for the love of God, please tell me what went so wrong?

KIM DAVIS BROKE NO LAW!

POSTED SEPTEMBER 7, 2015

For days people have been arguing about Kim Davis's refusal to hand out gay marriage licenses in Kentucky on social media. This issue isn't even about gay marriage. The Supreme Court unconstitutionally threw out the laws and constitutional amendments of all states which banned gay marriage. This was a large majority of the states. These laws were legislated by legislative branches of government or voted on by the people and passed legitimately. The Supreme Court has no constitutionally enumerated authority to rule on the Constitutionality of a law or to throw out a law. None. You will not find these powers listed in Article 3[80] of the U.S. Constitution, as the 10th Amendment[81] requires.

Federal Judge David Bunning found Kim Davis to be in contempt of court when she refused to break Kentucky state law and hand out marriage licenses to homosexual partners. She based her decision on religious grounds. Her religious beliefs are protected from the federal government. The 1st Amendment[82] says, "***Congress*** shall make no law respecting an establishment of religion, or prohibiting the free exercise thereof." This makes it impossible for there to be a federal law that Kim Davis broke.

In 2003, Judge Bunning ordered Boyd County High School to allow a gay club against the will of the school and the parents. Part of his order was that the school implement a mandatory reeducation program for the school staff and students to learn about diversity and be forced to accept homosexuality. None of his order was constitutional or legal. Ordering civilians around is not a constitutionally enumerated judicial power. Neither is force feeding sinful propaganda to people in violation of their religious core beliefs.

---

[80] See page 242

[81] See page 251

[82] See page 249

No power is enumerated to the federal government or judiciary to mandate what schools teach or what clubs they allow. This judge is a verified gay activist, rogue. He should immediately be impeached.

Liberals and dime store conservatives (a term I am coining right now, to mean people who claim to be or may want to be conservative, but whose knowledge of the Constitution isn't worth 10 cents), have been jumping on the talking point bandwagon that Kim Davis broke the law. Not one person has been able to cite the law she is accused of breaking. There is no law which says that she must hand out gay marriage permits. The Kentucky State Constitution says the exact opposite and outlaws gay marriage. There is no federal law, which legalizes gay marriage. The federal government has no jurisdiction over marriage. Kim Davis has been falsely arrested.

Liberals and dime store conservatives are also saying that being in contempt of court is why she was arrested. Really? What court gave her an order? What court case had her on the docket? Are we seriously being told that the Supreme Court has the power to give a blanket order to all Americans at large now? Can someone please provide the Constitutional Amendment, which grants this power to the Supreme Court? The Constitution allows courts to decide a case based on the law, not change the law and apply it to the nation. I would like to see the court order from the Supreme Court directed to Kim Davis, which she violated. As far as I know, no such order exists. You can't be held in contempt of court if you were never party to the trial and courts can't legislate or give orders to the public. It's terrifying that we actually have a populace who is so dumbed down, that they are gleefully surrendering their liberty in favor of judicial tyranny.

Liberals and dime store conservatives are trying to justify the Supreme Court's decision on gay marriage with the 14th Amendment[83]. Let's set aside the fact that the Constitution does not allow the Supreme Court to interpret the constitution or to determine the constitutionality of laws. This isn't even the real topic at hand, but just to get this out of the way, the 14th Amendment does not

---

[83] See page 253

protect gay marriage. If it did, gay marriage would have been around since 1868 when the 14th Amendment was ratified. It's amazing how much this election cycle is riding on arguments over an amendment, which was never even legally ratified in the first place. That is a topic for a different time.

Equal protection of the laws does not mean equal privileges. Marriage has always been defined as being between opposite genders. Everyone, straight or gay have always had the same, equal opportunities to get married if they wanted to. What homos want is a change in the definition of a word. They don't want equality, they want extra privileges. They want same sex partners to be able to marry one another, but only if they are homos. I asked someone on Twitter, "Why cant a woman marry her mother based on the same fallacy that the 14th Amendment's equal protection clause allows it?" He replied, "Because that's incest!" He didn't even see his own hypocrisy. So what if it's incest. Homosexuality is gay! Who is he to decide that gayness is better than incest? If he wants free and open marriage to be defined by the equal protection clause, then he is not allowed to draw any lines in the sand.

Where the left gets really confused is when they think the issue over gay marriage is about equal rights. There is no constitutional right to get married. The federal government has no authority over marriage. This issue is not even about marriage, especially for a constitutional conservative. This is about usurpation of power by the judiciary and a populous who is too stupid to understand it. This is about federal encroachment in state issues. This is about 5 people in black robes, abusing power they don't legally have, to thwart the will of the vast majority of 320,000,000 people.

I have just shown how easy it is to get off course and start talking about gay marriage, when that isn't the real issue regarding Kim Davis. The action of Federal Judge David Bunning is what we should be discussing. It doesn't matter what the issue is, Judge Bunning had no authority to make his ruling and the fact that the Kentucky law enforcement are blindly going along with it is a sad day for Kentucky. Shame on you Kentucky for capitulating to unlawful orders. Read your own constitution, Kentucky!

A message to all of you liberals and dime store conservatives out there. If you jump in on this debate and all you have for your side of the argument is a claim that Kim Davis broke a law, was held in contempt of court, or that the 14th Amendment protects homosexual marriage, then you have already lost the debate. Kim Davis broke no law. Courts can't hold you in contempt for disobeying the ruling of a court case you weren't involved in. Whether the 14th Amendment protects homo marriage is not part of this issue and it's a diversion. The 14th Amendment grants equal protection of the laws, not equal legislation of the laws or equal privileges. We can argue about marriage until the cows come home, but this isn't about gay marriage, it's about judicial tyranny. The subject of the 14th Amendment is moot. If you are so eager to allow the Supreme Court to usurp power they don't have in order to give dictatorial decrees to America, then God help you when your turn comes to have the hammer brought down on something you cherish. You shouldn't be so hasty to give up your liberties to 9 rogue justices in black robes.

One last nugget to chew on. If Kim Davis can be held in contempt of court for not obeying the Supreme Court decision over a case she took no part in, doesn't that mean that every school in Federal Judge David Bunning's jurisdiction is in *contempt of court* if they don't also have a mandated gay propaganda class and a school sanctioned gay club? This is why people not involved in a case can not be held in contempt. Where would it end? Judicial tyranny has to stop. The only way we have a chance to stop it is to wake America up. Educate your friends and family. Don't let them be victims of federally influenced public education.

THE 14TH AMENDMENT – EQUAL PROTECTION EXPLAINED

POSTED SEPTEMBER 23, 2015

I am so sick and tired of people who just can't grasp the 14th Amendment[84], but think they are experts, because they heard something on a liberal rag like Huffington Post. Let's see if I can help clear things up a bit regarding the most controversial parts of the 14th Amendment. First, I would like to make it clear that the 14th Amendment was never even legally ratified. There is plenty of information already out there on this, so it's not necessary for me to go into it. Start here: There is No 14th Amendment![85]

What must be understood with crystal clarity about the 14th Amendment, Section 1 is that NONE of it prohibits Congress from violating equal protection. It applies solely to the states. The 14th Amendment is designed to rip power from the states and give it to the federal government. This is why the states would not vote to ratify it and didn't. It takes states to ratify an amendment to the Constitution: 75% of the States... unless Congress illegally stops them from voting.

Now, for the purpose of the rest of this post, I will work with the assumption that the 14th Amendment is valid, since I'm not going to be able to convince anyone in state governments otherwise. So, let's say that I would love to see the 14th Amendment repealed. It is a mess. People of rudimentary intelligence can't understand it and are easily duped into believe it says things it doesn't. There is nothing beneficial about it and every court ruling based on it ends up being destructive to our nation.

Let's start with the claim that liberals and even dime store conservatives make, which is that the 14th Amendment repeals the

---

[84] See page 253

[85] http://www.constitution.org/14ll/no14th.htm

10th Amendment[86].   This claim is made because the 14th Amendment says, "No State shall make or enforce any law which shall abridge the privileges or immunities of citizens of the United States." You have to really try hard to warp this into meaning what liberals think it means. They think states can't make any laws that the federal government can't make, based on this. For instance, the 1st Amendment protects certain freedoms from Congress, but what they don't teach us in schools is that it doesn't protect those freedoms from states. As a matter of fact, the 1st Amendment[87] acted to protect state religions from Congress. So, liberals think that if a state passes a law to abridge the privileges in the 1st Amendment, they violate the 14th Amendment now. Except that the 1st Amendment grants no privileges, it only limits Congress. It's purpose isn't to grant anything. It's purpose is to protect us from Congress. States aren't violating the directive (Congress shall make no laws) of the 1st Amendment in any way by requiring a permit to peaceably assemble.

Congress is limited by the 10th Amendment and all powers that are not specified to Congress in the Constitution are left to the people or the States. If liberals were right and the 14th Amendment repealed the 10th, then how could any state pass any law, ever? It was my privilege to smoke in bars. But we have liberal smoking bans everywhere now. But wait! I thought the 14th said, "No State shall make or enforce any law which shall abridge the privileges or immunities of citizens of the United States?" They are making and enforcing laws against my privileges every day. You don't hear a peep out of liberals when states pass 22,000 unconstitutional gun control laws. Gun control laws abridge my privileges and RIGHTS more than any other laws. The 2nd Amendment[88] even says that my right to keep and bear arms *shall not be infringed*!

I have already covered the false claim that the 14th Amendment gives us anchor babies here: The 14th Amendment Doesn't Grant

---

[86] See page 251

[87] See page 249

[88] See page 250

Citizenship to the Children of Illegal Aliens.[89] I have also shown how The 14th Amendment, requires Hillary Clinton to have a 2/3s approval of Congress to even be allowed to run for President here: Arrest Hillary Clinton Now! [90] That's a fun topic that you don't hear liberals bringing up the 14th Amendment about. I don't need to go into those subjects in detail again, because I just gave you the links!

Moving on to the latest abuse of the 14th Amendment in order for the Supreme Court to throw out the laws of states. Liberals are hanging their hats on the Equal Protection Clause in the gay marriage issue. The equal protection clause is in the same sentence they think repeals the 10th Amendment, so here is the entire sentence. "No State shall make or enforce any law which shall abridge the privileges or immunities of citizens of the United States; nor shall any state deprive any person of life, liberty, or property, without due process of law; nor deny to any person within its jurisdiction the equal protection of the laws." Keep in mind that liberals do not want to discuss the depriving of liberty part with regard to Kim Davis, or her equal protection under the law, which is a legitimate point, since she actually followed the law that was legislated.

Equal protection of the law… what is it? Well, it's not equal rights. It's not equal protection of rights. It's not equal anything at a federal level, as it states, "no State shall…" Equal protection of the law is not a directive on how to write laws. It is a directive of how to apply laws. Laws just are what they are. We all have to follow them even if they seem unfair. Even Cornell University, the "go to" source for bad information on the Constitution, gets it partially right. They say, "The equal protection clause is not intended to provide 'equality' among individuals or classes but only 'equal application' of the laws." Well, what does this mean? It means that if a state law says that marriage is between a man and a woman, then we all live under that same law equally. We all obey it equally. We can all marry someone of the opposite sex equally. The only thing stopping us is finding someone who can put up with us!

---

[89] See page 92 - The 14th Amendment Doesn't Grant Citizenship to Babies of Illegal Aliens

[90] See page 80 - Arrest Hillary Clinton Now

What equal protection of the law is really supposed to ensure is that if someone commits a crime, they aren't treated differently based on their station in life. A Wall Street banker and a janitor should face the same justice. That goes for Senators and Presidents too!

Marriage isn't a right. Redefining marriage isn't an equal protection of the law. The Supreme Court decision to throw out marriage laws in the majority of our states was unconstitutional. Nowhere does the Constitution say that if courts think a law is unfair or doesn't apply to everyone equally, they can throw them out. It doesn't say it in Article 3[91], which enumerates every single power the courts have and it doesn't say it in the 14th Amendment. States should nullify this Supreme Court decision by ignoring it. But they won't, so there is something everyone needs to understand about this Supreme Court decision. They determined that equal protection of the law means that you can marry whoever you love. If you love both your dad and your brother, let the wedding bells ring! They drew no line in the sand and neither do liberals. Liberals will promise not to cross some lines we draw if we compromise and allow them to cross others. Once across, they immediately go to work crossing the line they promised not to. It always happens. The media is now trying to "normalize" pedophilia. This isn't going to end well.

By the way, the 14th Amendment doesn't count American Indians as people if they aren't taxed! Wait, what? They aren't counted? They get no representation in Congress? What about equal protection of the law? Wait, why don't they have to pay taxes? I don't want to pay taxes either! Where is my equal protection of the law on that? Same amendment, folks.

I just read a news article that provides a great way to illustrate how wrong liberals are about equal protection of the law. It all sounds well and good, when the only subjects are gay homos who just want to love each other and live happily ever after. Now, let's take a look at Islam. Angry Muslims Taunt New Jersey School Officials! "We'll be the majority soon![92]

---

[91] See page 242

[92] http://www.thegatewaypundit.com/2015/09/video-muslims-taunt-nj-school-officials-were-going-to-be-the-majority-soon/

The muslims of New Jersey have now grown sufficiently in population to stop yelling, "We're the religion of peace!" and start yelling, "You will bend to the will of Allah!" By the liberal definition of equal protection of the law, these muslims can use the 14th Amendment to force the New Jersey School System to implement muslim holidays. Mark my words. This 14th Amendment baloney is just getting started. Equal protection of the law doesn't mean that if we celebrate Christmas in America, we have to celebrate every religious holiday on earth or it's a 14th Amendment violation. Does this example make it any clearer to anyone that Equal protection of the laws is not equal privileges based on different beliefs, feelings, wants, desires, or deviant impulses? Happy Ramadan!

DID GOD PROTECT GEORGE WASHINGTON?

POSTED SEPTEMBER 28, 2015

After watching a couple of debates with Dinesh D'Souza making mince meat out of atheist Christopher Hitchens and liberal terrorist Bill Ayers, I figured I would watch his documentary, "America, Imagine the World Without Her." I don't know why I waited so long to watch it. It's an extraordinary movie, especially having been made by an immigrant who has learned more about our country than most people who are born and raised American.

The first scene in the movie shows a few very small events, which could have gone another way and easily lead to a future with no United States of America. First among them was George Washington getting shot and killed in battle. This immediately brought to mind something I hadn't thought about in a long time. It was something I remembered reading in an encyclopedia as a kid, before you could Google anything and after real history stopped being taught in schools. So I wondered if many people even knew about it any longer. So while this topic isn't a current event, it seems like a great idea to bring it up and let people know. I'm sure plenty is written about it with more detail than I will go into, but it takes knowing about it to search for it. I encourage everyone to do so.

George Washington was more than just a great general. Some people claim he wasn't all that great, especially at first. Yet George Washington took a ragtag bunch of men who were not prepared for war, had never trained for war, were short on supplies, not outfitted for sustained campaigns, and were suffering from starvation, disease, and bitter weather and beat the most powerful army in the world. It was George Washington who Cornwallis surrendered to in Yorktown. There was more to George Washington though. He appeared to be singled out and protected by God Himself. By all rights, George Washington should have been dead several times over and it's incredible he was even alive to be a general during the Revolutionary War.

Long before the Revolutionary War was the French and Indian War, from 1754-1763. The British and French both claimed trade routes with Indians going into the Ohio country. Don't think of the modern state maps. This began in the area of modern day Pittsburgh, Pennsylvania. Two rivers, the Allegheny and Monongahela join in Pittsburgh and become the Ohio River. In 1753, 21 year old Major George Washington was sent by the Virginia governor, Dinwiddie to deliver a demand from the British to the French that they stop building forts in the area. Dinwiddie then ordered William Trent to go and build a British fort in the area. The French refused the British demand. When Washington returned to Virginia with the refusal, Dinwiddie responded by promoting Washington to Lt. Colonel and ordered him to put together forces and to return and assist William Trent in building the fort.

Before reaching the location for the planned new fort, Washington ran into a small French contingent. Washington ambushed them and had an easy victory, but realized he couldn't go further at this point and would have to fall back and quickly build another fort out of necessity. One of the Frenchmen escaped the battle and Washington knew a retaliation would soon come. He named the fort Necessity. It was built quickly and out of not much else than a 7 foot tall ring of sticks. Sure enough, 1200 French soldiers under the command of General De Villiers attacked Fort Necessity and Washington's 400 men. Washington and his men fell under an enormous barrage of musket fire. The assault lasted for a solid 9 hours and only 30 of Washington's men were killed. In the end, the French offered Washington a chance to leave if he surrendered and Washington accepted. The lack of British casualties was remarkable considering they sat in the middle of a circular barrage of musket balls for 9 hours.

By 1755, the conflict with the French had become such that interest was taken higher up in the chain of command than the governor of Virginia. Major General Braddock was sent from England to take over from this point and engage the French. He took Washington with him as an unpaid aid. This is because of a complicated quirk of the way the British Army ran things back then. Basically, a military officer wasn't necessarily always on active duty, as we think of it today. When Washington returned after his surrender at Ft. Necessity, Governor Dinwiddie disbanded Washington's regiment and only kept people on active duty who were ranked Captain and below. For Washington to remain on active duty he would have had to take a demotion. Instead, he just went off of active duty. When Braddock showed up and wanted Washington to join him, Washington was able to refuse and he did so based on the other little quirk the British Army operated under. Regulars were British Army, through and through. Provincial Army were more or less, colonists in the Army. You could think of it like today's regular army and the reserves. Not quite the same, but similar enough. The Officers of the regular army always outranked all officers of the provincial army who were below Colonel. So, as a Lt. Colonel, Washington would be outranked by Regulars who were Lieutenants. Washington wasn't having any of that and preferred going with Braddock as an unpaid aid without having *butter bars* outranking him.

They set off, along with Lt. Colonel Thomas Gage with roughly 1400 soldiers (100 of which were Washington's) toward Fort Duquesne along the Monongahela river near modern day Pittsburgh. Washington warned Braddock that the French and Indians were using guerrilla tactics, hiding behind trees and rocks, but Braddock didn't give Washington's advice any merit, due to his much lower rank. So when they ran into a French and Indian army they weren't prepared for what came. Both sides were surprised, but the French and Indians quickly hid behind trees and rocks while Braddock ordered columns. Only Washington's men followed suit with the French and Indians and took cover, but this infuriated Braddock, because like most British officers of the time, he considered this cowardly. He ordered them to line up in formation as well. They got destroyed. All the while, Washington was in the front of battle enforcing Braddock's orders, going back and forth. He had two horses shot out from under him. General Braddock was killed. Washington organized a retreat, which in the light of the situation got him reinstated in the provincial army and promoted to Colonel.

Many were surprised that Washington could have possibly survived the battle. One British soldier is quoted as saying, "I expected every moment to see him fall. Nothing but the superintendent care of providence could have saved him." Washington's coat had four musket ball holes in it, yet he was unscathed. The Indians claimed that there was a shield around Washington that protected him.

15 years later, this battle led to what many know as the Indian Prophesy of George Washington in 1770. Washington was approached by a group of Indians, the chief among them took part in the battle and brought Washington this message. *"I am a chief, and the ruler over many tribes. My influence extends to the waters of the great lakes, and to the far blue mountains. I have traveled a long and weary path, that I might see the young warrior of the great battle. It was on the day, when the white man's blood, mixed with the streams of our forest, that I first beheld this chief: I called to my young men and said, 'Mark yon tall and daring warrior? He is not of the red-coat tribe- he hath an Indian's wisdom, and his warriors fight as we do- himself is alone exposed. Quick, let your aim be certain, and he dies.' Our rifles were leveled, rifles which, but for him, knew not how to miss- 'twas all in vain, a power mightier far than we, shielded him from harm. He cannot die in battle. I am old, and soon shall be gathered to the great council-fire of my fathers, in the land of shades, but ere I go, there is something, bids me speak, in the voice of prophecy. Listen! The Great Spirit protects that man, and guides his destinies- he will become the chief of nations, and a people yet unborn, will hail him as the founder of a mighty empire!"*

This all occurred before the Declaration of Independence. Now, on to the Revolutionary War. Washington, unlike many generals, actually lead the armies from the front. This is a habit that you would think only a bulletproof general would adopt. In battle after battle, Washington came out unscathed where he should have been riddled with bullets. Just focusing on the most miraculous escapes from death, let's jump 2 years into the Revolutionary war into 1777.

In January of 1777, Washington was focused on Cornwallis, but his attention became diverted when an American militia under the command of Brigadier General Hugh Mercer, not far away in Princeton, New Jersey was being defeated by two British regiments commanded by Lt. Colonel Charles Mawhood. One day after defeating a British attack in Trenton, Washington rode in with his army to save the day against Mawhood forcing British surrender! It doesn't sound amazing that reinforcements arrive and save the day. What is amazing is how it happened. Washington arrived while the militia were in full retreat and getting mowed down. He hollered out, "Parade with us, my brave fellows! There is but a handful of the enemy, and we will have them directly." The militia complied and immediately rallied. Washington ordered them not to fire until his command. He led them, riding on a horse in front, to within 30 yards of the enemy before ordering his men to fire. So many shots were fired that it was reported that the smoke in the air was too thick to be able to see a thing. Washington was in the middle of both sides firing away! It was sheer insanity! When the smoke cleared, Washington was again unscathed.

Later in the same year of 1777, Washington had yet another brush with death, but which can be said to have be averted by God in a different way, by influencing the heart of a man. The British army, like other armies were known for lining their armies up in a chivalrous battle formation. But don't be fooled into thinking this is the only way they fought. And for those out there who think the 2nd Amendment[93] only protects muskets, because the Revolutionary War was only fought with muskets, think again. The British had snipers. Their targets were officers. We've been taught that the officers were sort of off limits to aim at in Revolutionary times, but this isn't the case at all. British snipers had one main purpose. Take out the commanders, at all costs!

Washington, while riding alone with another cavalry officer inadvertently ran into the edge of a fresh 12,500 member, British army. He ran directly into a sniper team lead by Captain Patrick Ferguson who were waiting for just such an encounter with orders to shoot and kill any American officers they laid eyes on. Ferguson and his men were armed with breech loading, fast repeating rifles that Ferguson designed himself. Assault rifles! Not Muskets! Ferguson hollered out to Washington, who gave a casual glance, then nonchalantly turned and slowly left, along with his companion. It was Ferguson's job to shoot to kill, but he later said, "I could have lodged half a dozen balls in or about him, before he was out of my reach, but it was not pleasant to fire at the back of an unoffending individual, who was acquitting himself very coolly of his duty—so I let him alone." Ferguson did his job every other day, why not this day?

There are many more examples of Washington escaping death where he shouldn't have. He was always in the thick of battle and stood out like a sore thumb by the way he dressed. He was tall and

---

[93] See page 250

rode tall horses. He was instantly recognized by the enemy anywhere he met them. He was the biggest target the British army wanted taken out and he always offered himself up to be targeted as easily as possible. It was almost as if he knew he was bulletproof and could waste enemy fire by taking it himself and drawing it off of his men. I know of no other general that is comparable in all of history, especially who has seen so many battles.

All I've pointed out regarding possible divine intervention is Washington's impervious nature when it comes to being shot at, but so many other things were also incredibly fortunate that the sheer numbers of events belie statistical credulity if only luck were involved. I could go on for days about those events, but just one example is when Washington sent Henry Knox to Fort Ticonderoga for supplies. To make a long story short, this was a wasted effort under the time constraints they were under, because it couldn't be successful. It required that it be warm enough for a river and lake to be traversable for precisely long enough to float tons of canons & supplies to one point and then for it to snow like crazy and everything to freeze so they could continue on from that point with dozens of sleds. It worked like clockwork as if Washington could predict the weather.

It is my belief that divine intervention was a daily part of George Washington's life, because God wanted The United States of America to be founded. Anyone is free to believe what they like, but they can't prove me wrong.

Sources, mainly to ensure correct dates, ranks, names, and details I didn't trust to memory[94].

---

[94] Wikipedia; http://www.tworiverscc.org;
http://www.retraceoursteps.com; http://www.historynet.com

UMPQUA COMMUNITY COLLEGE ENABLED CHRIS HARPER MERCER'S MASSACRE!

POSTED OCTOBER 4, 2015

Our 2nd Amendment[95] rights are not up for debate. Reality continues to confirm this each time the left starts dancing on the graves of victims of a violent shooter. We the People have grown weary of the constant clamor to curtail our rights, so the grave dancing continues to backfire on the left. Mass shootings are incredibly rare when measured on a per capita basis against a U.S. population of 320 million, but with that many people they are inevitable. With each mass shooting the left's grave dancing starts sooner, long before any actual information about the event comes out. Social media quickly spreads news of the occurrence of a shooting, but doesn't speed up the time it takes for law enforcement to decide to release the details.

With absolutely nothing to go on but his disdain for the Constitution, Obama immediately attacked the 2nd Amendment in the wake of the Umpqua Community College shooting in Oregon. Obama showed no true concern for the victims or for the American People as a whole. In fact, he showed hatred for the American people by making it very clear that he blamed the NRA and he would go after the 99.999999% of Americans who did not shoot anyone at Umpqua Community College and make it political, his agenda being against our natural right to bear arms. The kind of rhetoric he used is precisely why gun sales keep going up and the anti-gun movement continues its pattern of failure.

The shooter, who we later found out was Chris Harper Mercer, was the only person who wasn't stopped from carrying guns by the "No Guns Allowed" sign. Everyone else in the school valued the sign more than their own lives. Mercer was certainly the bad guy, but he didn't make his crime possible. Umpqua Community College

---

[95] See page 250

made the shooting easy for Mercer by denying a core American right from the students and faculty of the school. The families of the victims should immediate ban together to sue the school for its role in the massacre. This would send a clear message to other schools, businesses and institutions, that if you deny the people their God given right to defend themselves, then you are 100% responsible for guaranteeing their safety and held culpable and responsible if you fail.

The first bit of detail that most of us saw regarding Mercer's shooting was that he asked people if they were Christian. Then he shot the Christians in their heads, killing them and shot everyone else in the legs. Everything else being talked about was pure speculation.

Information about Chris Harper Mercer seems to trickle in slowly. At first, many liberals were quick to jump on the fact that Mercer's MySpace page claimed that he was a Conservative Republican. Absolutely nothing about his social media fingerprint even suggested he knew want conservatism in America is. Liberals must think that it's impossible for a mass murderer to lie on MySpace. The same page said he kills zombies and eats brains. His profile also said that he was non-religious, but spiritual. For those of us who think logically, targeting Christians doesn't seem to correlate with a non-religious spiritual person. It's not as if there is a jihad against Christianity among growing sects of budding, young Agnostic Buddhists. As a matter of fact, further information came to light that he had sympathies for the Irish IRA terrorist organization and his MySpace friend Mahmoud Ali Ehsani appeared to be an islamic terrorist sympathizer.

Even days later, we still don't know all of the details. There are surprisingly few facts that we have to go on with regard to Chris Harper Mercer. We've seen claims that he was part of Black Lives Matter and there have been doctored photos of him to make his skin look whiter, to emphasize the media narrative that he is white. It has been claimed that he is not white, or that he is black or mulatto. There is at least one report[96] that he is on the Russian terrorist watch list and that Russia has passed on this information to the U.S., but

---

[96] http://www.eutimes.net/2015/10/oregon-mass-shooter-on-terror-list-obama-refused-to-take-from-russia/

that the Obama Administration has ignored it. ISIS actually claims that his actions were under their direction. Now it is said that Mercer is British born.

With as little as we know about Chris Harper Mercer, some conclusions are obvious. He was anything but a Conservative Republican. It was Mercer, not the NRA, and not any other law abiding, gun owning American who shot the victims in the school. We know that Mercer's dad was shocked and surprised that this could have happened, as is the case with all similar shootings when it comes to the friends and family of the shooter. We know that every one of his victims wished they had a gun. We know that a gun free zone isn't a very safe place to be.

There is little choice for rational people, but to wait until more facts come in before jumping to crazy conclusions such as this being a false flag shooting that was pulled off by actors just to push the anti-gun agenda. Whether an incident is real or fake, the reaction of the left is always the same: attack the 2nd Amendment. They salivate while waiting months on end for another ultra rare mass shooting to occur, so they can immediately hit the air waves and social media with the same, tired, old talking points, which blame you and I. They want more and more gun control, but can never name a single new law, which could have prevented any shooting.

The left's incapability to justify new laws doesn't stop them from wanting them, because public safety isn't the reason the left wants gun control. The left loves mass shootings. They aren't concerned about the victims; they can't wait for the next group of victims. In fact, it's conservatives who give more to charities of the victims. Gun control is not sought to stop people from shooting one another. The real goal is government control. The corrupt and lawless government we have today does not like the idea of an armed populous any more than Hitler, Stalin, or Mao did. Disarming the people is an absolute prerequisite to full government control. Sure, some of the brainwashed rubes, who the left uses to spread their lies and talking points, might think they have good intentions, but they are *pawns*. They mindlessly push forward on their march. The people who know the real reason that gun control is sought are the ones in power who want to control us. The *rooks, knights, bishops, kings, and queens* are all in government or in some position to benefit from a tyrannical government.

There are two undeniable truths about gun control in the last 7 years. *First,* gun control activists have come out in record numbers and pushed harder than they ever have to infringe on our 2nd Amendment rights. They have spent more to combat the 2nd Amendment than ever before. Moms Demand Action for Gun Sense blew through 50 million dollars in an anti-gun campaign that resulted in nothing but complete and utter failure. *Second,* patriotic Americans who value our rights, especially the 2nd Amendment have been winning at record rates. New gun control bills have been defeated and existing laws have been repealed. Several states including Texas and Missouri have legalized open carry and some states including Missouri have restored the right to bear arms to teachers. Washington D.C., California, and even Illinois have been forced to recognize the right to bear arms by repealing laws outlawing it or issuing concealed carry permits. The zealotry with which the left has attacked the 2nd Amendment has cost them dearly. They exposed how venomous they are. They weren't careful enough to brainwash all of their rubes with the right talking points and many let the cat out of the bag in social media that their end game is to disarm everyone. We the People could clearly see that if we gave an inch, we'd lose a mile.

Our rights are no longer up for a debate. When the rabid gun grabbers start dancing on another grave and throwing fits, just point at them and chuckle. A shooting is tragic and should be talked about, yet when a shooting happens, the left's topic of conversation turns from the shooting to their hatred of America and our rights. Had the victims in Umpqua Community College not been stripped of their rights, the results could have been far less tragic. Mass shootings are stopped by armed civilians all the time. We don't hear about these, because they don't become mass shootings if they're stopped by a bystander and these stories counter the leftist agenda. You have the **right** to bear arms. You have the right to protect yourself. Don't let a sign on a door stop you from exercising your rights! No one in a gun free zone will protect you. You are always responsible for your own protection. Is your life worth complying with a *Gun Free Zone* sign?

I want to repeat one point and be very clear about it. I want to see the families of Mercer's victims sue the living daylights out of Umpqua Community College. The NRA should be leading and funding this lawsuit. This is what we pay dues to the NRA for. If a college revokes your rights, they must pay the price for it. Demand it!

ALERT! U.N. MILITARY INVADING AMERICA WITH OBAMA'S BLESSING!

POSTED OCTOBER 6, 2015

Every American should be infuriated! Thanks to Pamela Geller at D.C. Clothesline, as well as other sources, we learned that the Obama administration is allowing the Sharia Law compliant United Nations to start establishing a presence in American cities with a Global Police Force, ostensibly to fight extremism, called the *Strong Cities Network.*[97]

First of all, our cites already have police forces. Also, the American people are very well armed. American civilians have more arms than the rest of the world combined. There is nothing that the U.N. has to offer us that we don't already do better. The level of unconstitutionality this reaches is beyond belief. The Constitution does not enumerate any authority to the federal government to police Americans, let alone bring in foreign militaries to do it. It doesn't matter what false premise the Obama Administration uses to justify it. There is no justification that passes Constitutional muster.

Even if policing were not the plan for the U.N. Global **Police** Force, allowing any foreign military presence to base itself on American soil would require a treaty. The U.N. does not hold any authority over the United States of America on our soil. According to Article 6[98], The Constitution and any treaties made *under the authority of the United States* are the highest law in the land. The only way this could pass a constitutional smell test would be for a treaty to be made with other nations, agreeing to this police force. But we know there is no such treaty, because Obama doesn't make treaties, he makes unconstitutional DEALS, aka Executive Agreements, as he did with the Iran Nuke Deal. Making a treaty requires 2/3 of the

---

[97] http://www.breitbart.com/big-government/2015/10/02/obama-administration-and-un-announce-global-police-force-to-fight-extremism-in-u-s/

[98] See page 245

Senate to Consent. Article 2, Section 2, Clause 2[99] of the U.S. Constitution, while describing the powers enumerated to the President says, "He shall have Power, by and with the Advice and Consent of the Senate, to make Treaties, provided two thirds of the Senators present concur." When did 2/3 of the Senate concur with quartering foreign soldiers on American soil?

This is treason. This president has gone so far rogue that any other man in his position would have been impeached long ago. Everyone in Congress is either afraid to do anything about it, quite simply because they don't want to be part of taking down the first black president, or they are complicit and traitors themselves.

I urge everyone to contact your congressmen, both your representatives in the House and your two Senators and demand this be stopped! This cannot happen! We can't just roll over and allow our country to be invaded by a foreign army while our treasonous President Obama and Attorney General Loretta Lynch, laugh about it. Nothing that this administration has done so far, no matter how vile, evil, treacherous, or treasonous should scare you more than this. The Iran Nuke Deal was chump change compared to this, but it set the unconstitutional precedent for Executive Agreements to take the place of treaties, so that this could happen. Call your Congressmen! Write to your Congressmen. Do the same with your governors, state legislators, mayors, sheriffs and police chiefs. Contact everyone. Make them all aware and put a stop to this. This isn't a matter of drawing a line in the sand. There can be no line in the sand, because these foreign warriors can't be allowed to even step foot on our sand. The line has to be drawn in the ocean.

Giving credit where it is very much due and very much appreciated, I am posting the text for the Department of Justice Release below, copied from the D.C. Clothesline link from Pamela Gellar. We owe Ms. Gellar a deep debt of gratitude for staying on top of these things! Please visit her site for more details on the story itself. My post is less about the details, which are already available, and more for the purpose of explaining its unconstitutionality and garner a call to action! Spread this and share it EVERYWHERE!

---

[99] See page 241

Also, remember that it is your responsibility to protect yourself. Police are never there when you need them. Some police it seems will be here even though we DON'T need them. Embrace your right as an American to keep and bear arms. If you do not own a gun, buy one. If you do own a gun, buy another. Join classes for various types of gun training, such as safety and self defense. It's fun for the whole family!

UPDATED NOVEMBER 7, 2015:

A few deniers have called this a conspiracy theory and doubt there is anything nefarious about this. They have their heads in the sand, especially considering the Obama Administration's track record. This isn't just about sharing information. That can be done with an e-mail address from Geneva. If you are in doubt, look no further than their own web site[100]. Click "About Us" and then "What is the Strong Cities Network." Pay attention to the key words. "**Pool Resources?**" Pool means they have some *resources* to share too. Share for what? They tell you. To "**Mobilize Local Action**." Ask yourself, what kind of resources could the U.N. provide that are capable of mobilizing local action? It's time to wake up America!

Official DOJ Release:

FOR IMMEDIATE RELEASE: The Department Of Justice, September 28, 2015 (Thanks To Debra)

Cities are vital partners in international efforts to build social cohesion and resilience to violent extremism. Local communities and authorities are the most credible and persuasive voices to challenge violent extremism in all of its forms and manifestations in their local contexts. While many cities and local authorities are developing innovative responses to address this challenge, no systematic efforts are in place to share experiences, pool resources and build a community of cities to inspire local action on a global scale.

"The Strong Cities Network will serve as a vital tool to strengthen capacity-building and improve collaboration," said Attorney General Loretta E. Lynch. "As we continue to counter a

---

[100] http://strongcitiesnetwork.org/

range of domestic and global terror threats, this innovative platform will enable cities to learn from one another, to develop best practices and to build social cohesion and community resilience here at home and around the world."

The Strong Cities Network (SCN) – which launches September 29th at the United Nations – will empower municipal bodies to fill this gap while working with civil society and safeguarding the rights of local citizens and communities.

The SCN will strengthen strategic planning and practices to address violent extremism in all its forms by fostering collaboration among cities, municipalities and other sub-national authorities.

"To counter violent extremism we need determined action at all levels of governance," said Governing Mayor Stian Berger Røsland of Oslo while commenting on their participation in the SCN. "To succeed, we must coordinate our efforts and cooperate across borders. The Strong Cities Network will enable cities across the globe pool our resources, knowledge and best practices together and thus leave us standing stronger in the fight against one of the greatest threats to modern society."

The SCN will connect cities, city-level practitioners and the communities they represent through a series of workshops, trainings and sustained city partnerships. Network participants will also contribute to and benefit from an online repository of municipal-level good practices and web-based training modules and will be eligible for grants supporting innovative, local initiatives and strategies that will contribute to building social cohesion and resilience to violent extremism.

The SCN will include an International Steering Committee of approximately 25 cities and other sub-national entities from different regions that will provide the SCN with its strategic direction. The SCN will also convene an International Advisory Board, which includes representatives from relevant city-focused networks, to help ensure SCN builds upon their work. It will be run by the Institute for Strategic Dialogue (ISD), a leading international "think-and-do" tank with a long-standing track record of working to prevent violent extremism:

"The SCN provides a unique new opportunity to apply our collective lessons in preventing violent extremism in support of local communities and authorities around the world", said CEO Sasha Havlicek of ISD. "We look forward to developing this international platform for joint innovation to impact this pressing challenge."

"It is with great conviction that Montréal has agreed to join the Strong Cities Network founders," said the Honorable Mayor Denis Coderre of Montreal. "This global network is designed to build on community-based approaches to address violent extremism, promote openness and vigilance and expand upon local initiatives like Montréal's Mayors' International Observatory on Living Together. I am delighted that through the Strong Cities Network, the City of Montréal will more actively share information and best practices with a global network of leaders on critical issues facing our communities."

The Strong Cities Network will launch on Sept. 29· from 4:00 p.m. to 5:30 p.m. EDT, following the *Leaders' Summit on Countering ISIL and Violent Extremism*. Welcoming remarks will be offered by the United Nations High Commissioner for Human Rights, Prince Zeid Ra'ad Al Hussein and Mayor Bill de Blasio of New York City, who will also introduce a Keynote address by U.S. Attorney General Lynch. Following this event, the Strong Cities International Steering Committee, consisting of approximately 25 mayors and other leaders from cities and other sub-national entities from around the globe, will hold its inaugural meeting on Sept. 30, 2015, from 9:00 a.m. to 4:00 p.m. EDT.

Courtesy of Pamela Gellar from her story here: http://pamelageller.com/2015/10/obama-administration-and-un-announce-global-police-force-to-fight-extremism.html/

Original DOJ source: https://www.justice.gov/opa/pr/launch-strong-cities-network-strengthen-community-resilience-against-violent-extremism

I DON'T HAVE ENOUGH FAITH TO BE AN ATHEIST!

POSTED OCTOBER 12, 2015

Atheism is a religion. Atheists act like Dracula confronting a cross when faced with the fact that their beliefs rely solely on faith. They hate the word faith, even though it's all they've got. They try to make the claim that their religion is based on science, although actual science doesn't support their claims any more than science can prove the existence of God. When they are called out for having faith, they'll say something like, "An absence of belief isn't faith," yet their claim of an absence of a belief is a lie.

Atheists most definitely have beliefs, such as life starting somehow out of no life. Basically there were rocks, then all of a sudden a single cell organism came to life out of nowhere. This is called abiogenesis. A spontaneous generation of life where there was none. They use fancy words, like "primordial soup," yet have no scientific evidence that any such soup ever existed and have no idea what it would be composed of if it did. They try to steer the conversation away from abiogenesis, to evolution. They can't stand the fact that their belief in abiogenesis is rooted entirely in faith. There isn't the tiniest shred of evidence that abiogenesis ever occurred and even if it had, there could be no scientific way to prove that God wasn't behind it. Some atheists, such as Richard Dawkins have made the foolhardy mistake of trying to avoid the topic of abiogenesis by making the claim that perhaps aliens seeded life on Earth. Fantastic! So how did abiogenesis create the aliens? It must be noted that a single cell is millions of times more complex than anything we have ever created as mankind. It would be far more likely for a Buick to appear on Mars than for a living cell to have suddenly been constructed out of primordial soup.

Afraid to even debate abiogenesis, atheists often try to steer a discussion into evolution, because many scientists agree that evolution has existed. The fossil record tends to show a progression of species, however the sciences of paleontology and geology are far from perfect. There are two types of evolution, micro and macro.

135

Micro evolution can be seen. We breed different types of dogs. They're still dogs, though. Macro evolution, would give us something other than a dog when breeding dogs, maybe a bear. Macro evolution has no proven evidence thus far. The fossil record fails to show any true evolution from one kind of animal to another. This isn't to say that it couldn't have happened. Christianity in particular wouldn't be threatened if macro evolution were a proven fact. It's a moot point. Christians would not mind seeing the evidence. Atheists on the other hand have firmly held beliefs in macro evolution with very poor evidence to go on. That's called faith.

One other problem with the fossil record is that it is based on a geological assumption made by Nicolas Steno in 1669, which is that sedimentary layers must be older the further down you go. It's a logical assumption to make, but an assumption all the same and it wasn't until the past few decades that actual experimentation has been performed to study how layers are deposited. Oddly enough, in flood situations all of the layers are laid simultaneously. You can see this explained very well here, but be prepared for a somewhat dry video. Flood Geology and Stratification Experiments.[101] Geology is still taught in colleges based on Steno's assumptions.

Regardless of what is ever proven scientifically in the fossil record about evolution, it remains moot. A God who is powerful enough to create an entire universe and a planet teaming with life could have easily developed evolution as well. Evolution could never prove or disprove the existence of God. Atheists turn to this topic merely to try to claim that they have science on their side.

One thing that science has always shown to be true is that there can never be an effect without a cause. Atheists have a lot of faith in the Big Bang occurring without a cause. Scientists and mathematicians have worked long and hard to determine the nature of the universe before the Big Bang and the consensus is that there was nothing. It's hard to imaging nothing. Nothing means no mass, no energy, no space and no time. We are expected to believe, as atheists do with much faith, that in total nothingness, without any

---

[101] https://www.youtube.com/watch?v=5PVnBaqqQw8

time, that all of a sudden nothing exploded into a Big Bang and produced everything, including time. It's very important to grasp the absence of time before the Big Bang. Without time, there could be no before or after. There were no ticks or tocks. It would be impossible for there to be an "*all of a sudden.*" Without a tick and a tock there can be no advancement from nothing to Bang! The lack of time would prevent any change whatsoever. This means that without question, the Big Bang was an effect without a cause. Or was it? If a Creator is eternal and lives without the limitations of space and time that we are accustomed to, perhaps He was the cause.

One simplistic way to think of it is to compare the Big Bang, Creation, and even Evolution to a video game like The Sims. If the game was far more advanced and the characters actually had consciousness, you as the player at the computer could pause the game. Then you could resume the game. The characters in the game would never notice the pause. Time for them is determined by when the player decides to allow the game to run. The characters in the game would find it very hard to contemplate your ability as the player to simply stop time in their world while you get up to grab a beer. It would probably never occur to them that you could also boot up the game on a different computer at the same time and instantly create an entirely new Sims universe that has a beginning, that you caused by booting it up, but the cause of which would not be discernible by characters in that game. There are actual scientific theories that propose that our universe is nothing more than a very advanced computer simulation and that we aren't very far from having the technology to do something similar ourselves if we had almost unlimited resources such as RAM, and hard drive space. The amount of those which would be required are astronomical.

So, what we know about atheists is that they claim that science is on their side, which it is not and that their beliefs in the origins of the Universe and Life are completely based on faith. They will never admit this faith though, but it's obvious, so their denials are laughable. Those of us with religious convictions, such as Christians admit our faith. We don't try to claim that we can prove what we can't. At least we aren't disingenuous about having faith. Atheists are liars, because they deny the faith which makes up their core beliefs. At least agnostics aren't liars. They admit they don't know anything. Remember all of this next time a rabid atheist tries to evangelize. They evangelize a lot!

Note: a follow up to this blog post[102] was written on August 18, 2016, which isn't included in this book. It includes many full color pictures, which are an integral part of the article. It is called "Evolution for Dummies." The entire theory of evolution gets completely debunked.

---

[102] https://FlatOutUnconstitutional.com/2016/08/18/evolution-for-dummies/

THE 2ND AMENDMENT: SHALL NOT BE INFRINGED!

POSTED OCTOBER 20, 2015

A well regulated Militia, being necessary to the security of a free State, the right of the people to keep and bear Arms, shall not be infringed.

I have the right to keep and bear arms. So do you if you are an American citizen, legal resident or even a visitor. People ask if illegal aliens also have this right and the answer is yes, sure, but they have no right to be in the U.S. in the first place, so they should be granted their rights under the 5th Amendment[103] to have a speedy and public trial and be deported back where they came from. Remember, the rights in the Bill of Rights[104] are considered to be natural rights or God given rights. The Bill of Rights doesn't grant us our rights, it protects them from government. As natural rights, everyone in the world has them, but the United States is the only place that recognized that these rights must be protected from government infringement. The Bill of Rights isn't necessary to grant us rights. It's important, because it reminds us that we have rights and who is out to take them from us at all times: government.

Notice that The 2nd Amendment[105] doesn't say anything such as, "The people are hereby granted the right to keep and bear arms." It assumes the right already exists. It says, "The right of the people to keep and bear Arms, shall not be infringed." In other words, the right is there already. It isn't in question. The only expressed mandate the 2nd Amendment puts forth is that it forbids anyone from infringing on this right. It doesn't say, "shall not be infringed by Congress," in the same way that the 1st Amendment[106] only

---

[103] See page 250

[104] See pages 249-251

[105] See page 250

[106] See page 249

restricts congress. It doesn't say, "Shall not be infringed, except by state and local governments," nor does it say, "shall not be infringed, unless you're a felon or have a mental illness." It's very blunt when it says, "shall not be infringed." There are no caveats. Once the unconstitutional Gun Control Act of 1968 was passed, making it illegal for felons to own guns, government has found many more ways to make felons out of millions more Americans. Isn't that convenient? How safe will a military veteran with PTSD be if we're told that people with mental illnesses can't own guns? It is our responsibility and duty to stand up against tyranny and not to allow government to create some form of 2nd class citizen who has their rights revoked in the interest of *feel good* policies that can't possibly prevent bad people from doing bad things. Only law abiding citizens follow laws. People who commit evil acts don't check to see if the law allows it first. Why should people who have served time in prison or someone who struggles with wartime memories be prevented from protecting themselves or their families? How many school shootings have been done by felons with illegally obtained guns? None that I know of and yet the shootings still happened and by people who passed unconstitutional background checks.

The left has done a great job of indoctrinating people, so that blind ideology replaces reason. Leftists actually favor the government disarming the populace, ignoring the history that has proven this to be one of the first steps of genocide every time. They ignore the definition of words and the sentence structure of the 2nd Amendment to come up with the fantastical claim that the 2nd Amendment only allows people who are part of a government controlled militia to have guns. The 2nd Amendment doesn't say, "the right of the militia to keep and bear arms, shall not be infringed." The most radical among leftists will claim that the 2nd Amendment can only apply to muskets, since that is all we had when the Bill of Rights was ratified. Well, the truth is, no, muskets weren't all we had, but that point is moot. The 2nd Amendment doesn't say, "the right of the people to keep and bear muskets, shall not be infringed." Private citizens, not government, owned the war ships when the Revolutionary War began. Private citizens still can, although they'd cost a lot. The Constitution still allows Congress to grant letters of marque for privateers.

Leftists often accuse conservatives of disliking the *militia part* of the 2nd Amendment. Nothing could be further from the truth, because we are able to read. It recognizes the fact that a militia is necessary to the security of a free state and a *well regulated* militia, at that! Who can argue with that? We have several hundred well regulated militia in the United States. Notice it doesn't say "government regulated" or "government controlled." Since long before the time of the Revolutionary War, militia regulated themselves. Being well regulated was a common term, which meant that it was to be kept in good, working order. The men in the militia were to be kept trained to respond when called upon and they were to maintain their own arms in good working order and stay supplied with the proper ammunition. It was a pretty simple concept, which still applies today, but in an effort to thwart the 2nd Amendment, the left takes it upon itself to try to redefine words. They try to interpret the 2nd Amendment in such a way as to say that it requires government regulation of militia. They use the term "interpret" to describe their blatant misreading of the 2nd Amendment, claiming that the Constitution is a living document, meant to change with time. If that is the case, and it can mean anything you want it to, why was it ever written down in the first place? Why write down your mortgage or any contract for that matter?

The 2nd Amendment sets no requirement for the people to be in a militia. It notes that militia are necessary for freedom, and keeping the militia well regulated is the key. Militia are made up of people and are not a regular or standing army, so it is incumbent upon the people to keep and bear arms in accordance with their God given right. The right of the people doesn't change with regard to their militia membership or lack thereof. The 2nd Amendment says no such thing. It doesn't even come close to setting any kind of requirement on the people. This is the problem with leftist interpretations. They make things up, pulling baloney out of thin air and convince themselves of utter nonsense, then expect the rest of us to buy their hokum.

The 2nd Amendment makes no limitations on the types of arms the people can keep and bear. Our founding fathers overthrew the most powerful government in the world at their time. They wanted the people to be better armed than the government which served them. The notion that only the government should have weapons of war and that the people don't need such things is ludicrous. When we're told that we don't need machine guns, we have to stop reacting by saying things like, "machine guns are illegal already." Every law that says machine guns are illegal is unconstitutional and we should fight those laws, not capitulate to them. It's also false to say that people can't own machine guns. We can, we just have unconstitutional requirements put on us, such as having to register them. Also, when told that we need universal background checks, we have to stop replying with, "we already have background checks," or "there is no gun show loophole, gun show vendors do background checks too." No, we need to repeal the 1993 Brady Bill and get rid of background checks altogether. They not only violate the 2nd Amendment, but also the 4th[107] and 5th Amendments. Where is their warrant? Why are you forced to incriminate yourself? We must stop compromising liberty away one piece at a time. The 2nd Amendment is meant to ensure that *we the people* are more powerful than government. It is not there to enable hunting. It is there for the sole purpose of protecting freedom, mostly from oppressive governments whether they be foreign or domestic. It is illogical to recognize any power of any level of government to sell us permission to exercise our rights in the form of permits or to allow that government to decide who can bear arms and which arms.

Whether or not you join a militia is up to you. Work with other militia members to keep it well regulated if you do. Well regulated militia are necessary to the security of a free state. It wasn't the army who came to the rescue at the Bundy Ranch when freedom was under attack, it was militia and they were well regulated, especially with the assistance of modern social media.

Keep and bear arms! It is your right. You do not need permission. Laws that say you can't bear arms are unconstitutional. Work to repeal or nullify those laws. They infringe on your right. The right of the people to keep and bear arms, *shall not be infringed!* You can't be expected to take on powerful government agencies on your own, so join groups that give strength in numbers and make these issues count at the ballot box. Remember, just because a government wields power doesn't mean they have the legal or

---

[107] See page 250

constitutional authority to do so. It only means they are stronger than you. That is why the founding fathers saw it necessary for the people to be armed better than government. They already saw what happens when government wields too much power. When the TSA frisks you and asks you questions in airports in direct violation of your 1st, 2nd, 4th, 5th, and 10th Amendment rights,[108] they do so without any legal authority. They get away with it, because they are more powerful than you. If we the people stood against it in mass, their power would be nullified. Their power requires willful compliance by the masses. Each of us goes through the TSA line as an individual, knowing that the masses aren't going to rise up against the infringement on our rights, so the best way to tackle this tyranny is through the Congress and our courts. Had four people maintained their 2nd Amendment rights on September 11th, 2001, we could have had a happier story to tell of that day. There is never a good reason to give up your rights, as we see with every mass shooting and most gun violence that occurs in the United States. What they almost all have in common is that they occur in gun free zones or gun free cities. We have a lot of work to do in order to shut down the TSA, but that doesn't mean you ever have to become a victim in any other gun free zone. It's only a gun free zone if you let it be and if you do, it's only a gun free zone until it's not. Criminals don't follow laws or care what signs say.

The gun control leftists have never provided a solution that would prevent crimes. Their solutions only affect law abiding citizens. The majority of us go along with the laws, because that's what we're taught to do. If they ban something, we quit doing it. Countless people lost their jobs and businesses because of bars closing across the country do to smoking bans. The few bars which nullify these bans by ignoring the law actually do well. thousands of bars have closed, because they dutifully followed the smoking bans. Even with the loss of livelihood, most law abiding citizens march in lock step to follow the law. Gun control laws are no different and only affect those who have no intention of committing crimes. However, the people are fed up with gun control. People are no longer going along to get along with the assault on our 2nd

---

[108] See pages 249-251

Amendment rights.   Connecticut recently passed draconian gun control laws requiring the registration or turn in of so called *assault weapons*. The people said, "No!" Even the police said that they will not attempt to enforce that. Washington State passed laws requiring background checks for any gun trade or sale between two people. The people answered by holding a massive gun trade on the Capitol steps in direct violation of the unconstitutional law. If any of you gun control NAZIs out there want our guns, you are just going to have to come get them yourselves!

Arm yourself and your family. Take part in training classes and go to the range to practice shooting. It's great fun and it never hurts to brush up on your skills. That's what being well regulated is all about. Be a well regulated family! Guns, ammo, and all sorts of shooting activities also make fantastic gift ideas, for birthdays, Christmas and even Valentine's Day! Have fun and stay safe!

A BLACK LIFE FINALLY MATTERS IN CHICAGO! OR DOES IT?

POSTED NOVEMBER 4, 2015

Gun Grabbers gain a victory with the death of 9 year old Tyshawn Lee! Chicago's gun free environment served up another death and a grave for anti-gunners to dance on while they blame guns. Of course we all know that Chicago isn't gun free, it's only gun free for law abiding citizens who want to protect themselves from thugs. There is just one problem. This particular victory for the left's anti gun crowd comes at the expense of the Black Lives Matter movement's attempt to keep black on black crime out of the main stream media.

For the first time since the 1929 Valentine's Day Massacre, a Chicago murder has hit the national news. Also a first, a black life matters that isn't a thug killed by a police officer in the line of duty during the commission of a crime, or similar situation. Let's see if the Black Lives Matter crowd are as ambitious to solve the murder of an innocent black kid as they are to lie about hands being up when the thug Mike Brown was shot. Let's see if they're as keen on finding the murderer of Tyshawn as they were to send a patsy to murder Deputy Darren Goforth in Texas, who was just filling up his squad car with gasoline.

There isn't a lot of information out there about the gunning down of Tyshawn. The prevailing question seems to be whether or not he was targeted or caught in the cross fire. Well, let's think about that for a second. The police report says that an unknown number of people were gathered in the alley that Tyshawn was shot in. The number is unknown, but the term *gathered* implies at least a small crowd. There is no mention of a number of people being shot. Tyshawn was shot several times in the upper body, back and head. He's a *small*, 9 year old kid. If all the shots hit him and no one else, I think it's safe to conclude that he was targeted and move on to solving the crime.

Another assumption that is probably safe to make is that the unknown number of people who were gathered in the alley know exactly who did the shooting. If black lives matter, these people would come forward and help the police identify the savage thug who shot Tyshawn. There would be no need of a reward, they would do the right thing. There *is* a reward being offered and the number keeps going up. I've seen the reward for information leading to an arrest go from $11,000 to $17,000 and then to the $20,000. The fact that the media reported this non-cop involved shooting of an black person who was actually innocent gave me hope that black lives are going to actually start to matter. But apparently it's going to cost more than $20,000 to make Tyshawn's life matter to any witnesses of the shooting. Maybe it's premature to call this the first black life that mattered in Chicago.

One person named Lakesha Alexander, who was interviewed by the media said, "I was angry, I was upset, I was hurt – all at the same time. There is no one here protecting these kids." Well, whose fault is that Lakesha? You have allowed your state to systematically disarm you and take away your ability to defend yourselves and your children. You have abandoned your God given right to self defense in exchange for a false sense of security, which we all know does not exist. You people of Chicago don't have to allow your city or your state to disarm you and leave your kids vulnerable. Someone could have been there to defend poor Tyshawn, but there wasn't. If you people are angry, upset, and hurt over kids not having any protection, you need to direct that anger right at the bathroom mirror.

It serves the left's best interest to cover up all of the black on black crime (unless we are assuming the killer was a white guy) in order to perpetuate the Black Lives Matter premise that the only danger to black people is police. The particular heinous nature of this attack upon a 9 year old kid left the media with no choice but to report it. The only way they'll get any leftist mileage out of it now is to throw this bone to the Moms Demand Action for Gun Sense In America crowd, so they can dance on the grave and blame the gun. How much higher does the reward have to get to make Tyshawn's life matter more than the thug's who shot him?

FRANCE IGNORED EVERY WARNING AND WAS PREDICTABLY ATTACKED!

POSTED NOVEMBER 14, 2015

Paris, France came under attack by muslim terrorists on the night of 13 November, 2015. This isn't about what happened. You can find out what happened on various news sites if you don't already know. I am going to tell you WHY it happened. The talking heads in media will wonder why it happened for days, but I am going to tell you why. I am not hiding behind a shroud of political correctness. In a nutshell, it happened, because the Koran tells muslims to kill infidels, so that's what muslims do.

When Charlie Hebdo was attacked in France on January 7th, 2015, we hoped that it would be a wake-up call for France, the rest of Europe, and everyone else. Apparently not. We warned France that this would happen again and it would get worse if they didn't allow their citizens the right to protect themselves and if they didn't stop treating Islam with politically correct kid gloves. It's one thing if France wants to keep their people unarmed, so they are defenseless sheep. The people of France seem to prefer being defenseless anyway. However, if France wants a flock of sheep for a nation, they should probably stop importing wolves.

Twelve died and eleven were wounded when muslims attacked Charlie Hebdo cartoonists with machine guns. The French and the rest of Europe were quick to try to appease islam. All over Europe they are allowing Sharia Law to take root. Muslims are pouring into Europe by the 100's of thousands, labeled as refugees and not vetted at all. The vast majority of them are young, military aged men. If they were actually refugees and left all of their women and children behind, I'd call them cowards, but they aren't refugees. They are wave after wave of muslim invaders. For 1400 years muslims have been trying to invade Europe and slaughter infidels with over 270,000,000 killed in the name of Allah so far. When are the rest of the world going to come to their senses and stop treating Islam like a religion of peace?

Now, in a coordinated attack, muslim savages have attacked and murdered innocent people all over Paris, France. The death count keeps rising. 153 have been counted as dead while I write this. The Press marvels at how coordinated this was and how well planned. The talking heads are baffled. When the fish are in a barrel, shooting them doesn't take much planning. All it took was a group of muslims saying, "Ok, Ahmed, Muhammed, Sayid, Habib, and Abdul... at 8 O'Clock, start shooting everywhere." The media will wonder for days how such elaborate planning can have been done under the noses of law enforcement and how no one ever saw this coming. We did see this coming. Those of us on the right have been sounding the alarm bells for years. Islam is evil and can't be appeased.

I am tired of the Islamic sympathizers on the left enabling muslims to continue their killing sprees! After Charlie Hebdo, we sympathized with the French people whose government disarmed them, leaving them vulnerable, while at the same time continued to allow more muslims to immigrate into France. We called out for France to lift their ridiculous gun control laws and allow the people their God given right to defend themselves. We have repeatedly warned them of the danger they were putting themselves into by allowing an invasion of muslim savages. They didn't listen.

Our wakeup call didn't just go unheaded, it was castigated! We were accused of being insensitive for advocating that the French people be allowed to defend themselves. We were called *racists* for denouncing murderous muslims for their evil acts. We were attacked by the left for being intolerant and told that it was too soon to bring politics into the conversation while 12 people lay dead. Well, those 12 people aren't waking up and neither is France. It's the left wing politics that enabled this savagery. Which is more compassionate, crying over dead bodies or wanting to prevent more dead bodies? The *faux* compassion of those who want to silence us hasn't solved anything.

The French Government has gone out of their way to ignore the lessons of Charlie Hebdo and by their actions have practically endorsed the attacks at the Bataclan Concert Hall, the soccer stadium the President of France was at, restaurants, and several other places all over Paris. They haven't verbally endorsed the attacks, of course, but they have done far more to enable them than to prevent them. If one didn't know better, just from appearance, it would be hard not to conclude that the French Government is allied with ISIS.

Just as was the case after Charlie Hebdo, it took just one tweet[109] on Twitter to cause an avalanche of liberal, muslim sympathizing, cry babies to fling insults back at me. I was called names, cussed at and accused of being *extremely distasteful* by dozens of brainwashed, liberal simpletons. I think it is far more distasteful for the French Government to continue allowing murdering savages into their defenseless country. I think it's more distasteful for French citizens to have to clean up the carnage in the aftermath of a bloodbath. I think it's more distasteful to cover up for and absolve the evil cult of islam every time the Koran is followed to the letter and more innocent people die.

What is it going to take to wake people up? Norway deported 70,000 muslims and crime dropped 31%. Switzerland mandates gun ownership and they aren't having terrorist attacks. There may yet be hope for Germany, Denmark, Holland, Sweden, England and other European countries if they learn from this incident instead of following the example of France. France has done what France does best. France surrendered.

To learn more about Islam, read my previous post – Islam: The Religion of Peace.[110]

---

[109] https://twitter.com/A_M_Perez/status/665324805462212609

[110] See page 69 – Islam: The Religion of Peace.

HAPPY THANKSGIVING!

POSTED NOVEMBER 26, 2015

I want to wish everyone a very Happy Thanksgiving!

Let us remember why we celebrate it and give thanks to God for all of the wonderful things we have in life as Americans! Life is full of ups and downs, but when we take the time to be thankful for our blessings, we realize that there are more of them than we thought.

America was founded as a land of opportunity, not a land of freebies. It is not handouts from others that we are thankful for. Our blessings are rooted in our ability to turn our own hard work into success! We are more thankful for what we're able to give than for what we receive. Many have struggled, fought, and even died to leave us with the freedom to reach for our goals and improve our own conditions. Even in the face of an opposition that seeks to destroy the liberty and opportunity we have grown to enjoy, we persevere. We must not become complacent and take our freedom for granted, for that is when we will lose it. Through divine inspiration, God made America possible, but free will can either preserve her or destroy her.

Our enemies are no longer outside of our gates. We have a corruption within. Our faith and our resolve must be stronger than ever if we are to continue to prosper and have the most wonderful country on Earth. Thank God, not only for your place in America, but also for your ability to be part of what makes America great! Do your part to ensure that our children's children can be just as thankful to be Americans. Stand strong and don't let those who despise freedom gain ground. Together we can make America even better by returning her to those values which made her great and for which we are so thankful for!

God bless everyone and have a safe, happy, and healthy Thanksgiving Day!

Now get stuffed!

BLAME RIGHT WINGERS! BLAME GUNS!

POSTED DECEMBER 2, 2015

In a nation of 320,000,000 people we occasionally have horrible, tragic shootings. The first thing we hear from the left is that a right wing nut job committed the deed. Before any facts come out and sometimes before we even know the identity of the shooter, all that matters to the left is that they take control of the narrative immediately and blame right wingers. In almost every case they are wrong, but they don't care about that. The facts which prove them wrong won't come out until the story is buried and other more current events are in the headlines. Their goal is not the truth, it is to capitalize on shock value to push their agenda.

Their agenda is to disarm Americans by any means necessary, but they know they don't have the manpower or firepower to do it by force, so they use propaganda, scare tactics and "the children" to try to sway public opinion, as was done in Australia, where the people voluntarily handed in their guns to their masters who have guns.

Time after time, a shooting will occur and while the people on the right mourn the tragedy, and send money to charities for the victims and their families, the left does nothing but blame the right wing and the value we hold over our constitutional rights, especially the 2nd Amendment[111]. As public opinion moves swiftly away from favoring gun control and more people value freedom and the right to bear arms, the left has become quicker and more openly rabid in their attacks on the right wing when a tragedy occurs. They know they are losing, so it's driving them insane, which is only working against them. Their reactions are as predictable as the sun coming up in the morning.

We can look at the last few shootings that occurred and see how the left reacts every time. Dylann Roof shot up a church in Charleston, South Carolina, killing 9 people including Pastor Clementa C. Pinckney. In mere minutes the left was all over social

---

[111] See page 250

media accusing Dylann Roof of being a right wing nut job who could never have done such a thing if we had more gun control and universal background checks. They accused the right of wanting to give guns to everyone! The left immediate dug up a picture of Roof holding a Dixie Flag. Of course the flag got blamed as well and became their evidence that Roof was a right wing nut job. Well, first of all, we don't want to give guns to everyone, we want everyone to have the right to go buy their own. If you buy your own gun, you won't have to worry so much when a crazy person gets theirs. No law will stop the crazy person from getting their gun. Second, even though all background checks are unconstitutional, we have them and Dylann Roof had undergone them several times and passed, destroying any premise that a background check prevents tragedies. Lastly, more pictures were found of Dylann Roof and in some he was burning an American Flag. Conservatives never burn American Flags. To accuse Dylann Roof of being a Conservative when he doesn't even suggest it himself is asinine and purely an agenda driven lie on the part of the left. Well, it didn't work. We still have our guns and gun control laws continue to be repealed.

The case with Dylann Roof was particularly beneficial to the left, because they were able to use it to stoke racial division. They attacked the Dixie Flag and even had it removed from the Capitol grounds, because they claimed it was motivation for Roof's murder spree. The media buried the fact that Pastor Clementa C. Pinckney was also a South Carolina state legislator who voted to fly that flag on Capitol grounds. He also voted for the law which made it possible for him to disarm his parishioners, so that they had no prayer of fighting back against Roof's attack. Everything about the left's accusations was a lie, intent on attacking the right, our 2nd Amendment rights, and liberty. The inconvenient truth though was that Pinckney supported the Dixie Flag as many southern blacks do, but didn't support his own right to self defense. RIP Pastor Pinckney.

Before the smoke cleared in the Umpqua Community College shooting in Oregon, the left was blaming guns and right wing nut jobs. The shooter's identity, Christopher Harper-Mercer, came out right away, so immediately his almost empty MySpace page was found. The left immediately jumped on the fact that he was supposedly a self proclaimed conservative, ignoring the fact that his only friends were tied to Islamic terrorism and his pictures were all in support of IRA terrorism. The left swallowed his claim to be a conservative without a second thought, even though Mercer claimed to be a zombie killer and eater of brains on the same page. The left wing media ignored Mercer's public admiration for Vester Flanagan, the Black Lives Matter, homosexual deviant, who killed Alison Parker and Adam Ward, two Virginia journalists. Vester Flanagan was as left wing as they come. Christopher Harper-Mercer also passed an unconstitutional background check, as did Vestor Flanagan, aka Bryce Willams.

Mercer questioned his victims on their religious faith, so he could pick out the Christians to kill. Which side hates Christianity, the left or the right? What enabled Mercer to kill so many was Umpqua Community College's disregard for Oregon State Law with their Gun Free Zone School Policy. While the law allowed students to ignore this policy, as does the 2nd Amendment, the students were too stupid to know that and most likely embraced the gun free policy themselves until it was too late. Again gun free zones failed and every fact was ignored while the left blamed the shooter for being a right wing nut job. Nothing could have been further from the truth.

The most recent shooting was done by Robert Dear in the Colorado Planned Parenthood facility. At least that is the location his shooting spree ended. We don't know the details. All it took was for Planned Parenthood to be named as the location of the shooting for the left to accuse right wing nut jobs. Never mind the fact that we hardly have any facts on this case, even a week later. The left claimed that the nut job said, "no more baby parts!" Ok, let's say that he did. When nut jobs go shooting people are we supposed to take them at their word now? Are we seriously supposed to believe that left wingers don't create false flags to give credit for their actions to the right wing? President Barack Hussein Obama and Attorney General Eric Holder got caught creating a huge false flag for precisely the same reason, to give guns and gun owners a bad name, in Operation Fast and Furious. The left is always creating false flags by committing atrocities and blaming the right. For the sake of argument, let's just say that Dear did say, "no more baby parts" and meant it. Would that make him a conservative? To answer that, let's look at the rest of the facts that have come out so far.

We know that Robert Dear is registered to vote as an independent and as a woman. We know Dear has been married and divorced at least 3 times and is a known wife beater. We have police reports as evidence. We know that he is religious, but believes that he doesn't have to follow the Bible and can do anything he wants, because Jesus will forgive him. We know he has a history of violence and openly cheating on his wives. We know from his web browser history that he frequented marijuana web sites. We know he moved to Colorado because they legalized marijuana.

Does being a religious, pot head make Robert Dear a right winger or Constitutional Conservative who devoutly cherishes our rights, our freedoms, and our nation? Surely no left winger is going to be so bold as to make the claim that democrats or left wingers can't be Christian. Maybe most left wing Christians don't act like it, but are they really going to make the claim that there are none? So far, being Christian is the only thing we really know about this Robert Dear's affiliations or beliefs. He's a self described Christian who doesn't think he has to follow the Bible. We really don't know much else about his political opinions or if he has any. Conservatives certainly aren't accusing him of being a left winger, because we really don't know. My personal opinion is that it takes intelligence and effort to be a conservative. You have to really be grounded, know what you stand for and why. So if you can't be definitively classified as a right winger who believes in traditional American Values, then you're a left winger. I don't believe in moderates. If you aren't a right winger you are at the very least, a tool of the left.

Regardless, we on the right want innocent people to be able to protect themselves. We don't have knee jerk reactions to blame the leftist ideology of the shooter before the facts come out. We want to learn the facts and serve justice to the guilty. Liberals on the other hand, don't need information, they have an agenda. They don't even want the facts. They want to control the narrative before the facts have a chance to surface. Blame the right wing. Blame guns. Every shooting is an opportunity for liberals; a means to an end for statist control over our lives.

I am tired of the lies, the propaganda, the spinning of stories and the fear mongering from the left. Conservatives don't run around shooting innocent people. It takes a certain kind of mindset to be conservative, one which values individual freedom. You leftists are going to have to do far more than continue lying if you want our guns. You're going to have to send guys with guns to take our guns or be brave enough to try it yourselves.

MUSLIMS & LIBERALS TAG TEAM TO ATTACK AMERICANS

POSTED DECEMBER 4, 2015

Muslims killed 14 people and injured 17 in San Bernardino, California on December 2nd, 2015. The reason for their attack was because Muhammed ordered it in the Koran. People need to abandon the notion that there are moderate muslims. Muslims are muslims and that's it. The Koran gives the same evil message to all muslims.

Immediately following the onslaught the media began trying to spin it to their advantage to push liberal agendas, such as gun control and Islam being a religion of peace. The shooters wore masks yet we had speculation that they were white men. CNN reported that the shooting occurred near a Planned Parenthood location, obviously stoking the flames the media started with the Colorado shooting that ended in a Planned Parenthood butcher shop. They tried to advance the premise that another right wing nut job was against selling the parts of murdered babies.

It wasn't long before police scanners picked up word that one of the shooters was killed and turned out to be an Arabic woman. Then we got the name of the other shooter, *Sayed Farook*. All of the mainstream media other than Fox, tried steering the narrative away from this being a terrorist attack. CNN is still claiming that this may be a case of *workplace violence*. There was some confusion for a while as to how many shooters there were, how many were downed by police officers and which was which, but in the end we know that they were a muslim couple named Sayed Farook and his wife Tashfeen Malik. Tashfeen is from Pakistan.

Over 24 hours later, ABC News reporter David Muir is asking the question, "were they radicalized?" No David, they were muslim. Muslim = muslim. I am so sick and tired of the term *radical* being used to describe *normal* muslim behavior, as demanded by the Koran. ABC is also giving advice on what to do if you are caught in a shooting event. They recommend spraying a fire extinguisher for a smoke screen, running, and hiding. Liberals are complete imbeciles. No ABC… the correct response is to shoot back!

Most of our politicians had something to say about the shooting. I'll paraphrase what I heard a few of them say on various news networks throughout the day. Barack Hussein Obama's response showed absolutely zero concern for the victims of the attack or the reason behind the attack. He dismissed the attack as a case of workplace violence and called for stricter gun control and unconstitutional background checks on people who are on the No Fly List. The No Fly List is an unconstitutional way that a bureaucrat can revoke an American's rights without due process. Without being charged with a crime or being able to defend yourself in front of a jury, you are convicted. Now Obama wants to use this conviction, that you probably don't know you have, against you to revoke your 2nd Amendment[112] right.

Donald Trump at least had a moment of silence in respect of the victims and acknowledged the problem is a muslim problem. He questioned why Obama can't ever bring himself to say the words *radical islamic terrorism*. He said that there is something wrong with Obama that we don't know about. Ted Cruz said that this is more proof that we are at war.

Hillary Clinton, also incapable of uttering the words *radical Islam*, came out in defense of muslims, saying that they were just as upset about the shooting as we are. Really Hillary? Where are all of these upset muslims? CAIR (Council on American Islamic Relations) came out with a press conference designed to shift the blame from muslims, but showed no remorse whatsoever. CAIR is classified as a terrorist organization and should be shut down and all of their leadership arrested. CAIR recently lost a federal case[113] in which they were suing a gun shop owner in Florida who banned muslims from his store.

---

[112] See page 250

[113] http://www.wnd.com/2015/11/muslim-free-zone-gun-shop-wins-case/

Whenever there is a mass shooting of any kind, the left is always ready to dance on the graves of the victims and take advantage of the situation to push their agenda. Harry Reid took this opportunity to attach federal gun control legislation to a Republican bill in the Senate for repealing Obamacare. Do we really think that Reid or any of the democrats would vote to repeal Obamacare if they got some form of gun control to go along with it? That's quite a noodle scratcher. Obamacare is so destructive to our entire economy that it almost makes it worth a shot. I said almost, so don't attack me! Any form of gun control is unconstitutional, whether it is at a federal or state level, so if it did happen, the best response from the American people would be to nullify it by ignoring it. Most sheriffs in the country have already promised to do just that!

The fact of the matter is that California and San Bernardino have very strict gun control. Every one of the victims of this muslim terrorist attack was disarmed, precisely as the left demanded. Not a single one of them was capable of shooting back. All of the stories from the survivors were about hiding. All tales were of hiding behind walls, hiding behind cars, tucking their heads between their legs and kissing their behinds goodbye. The victims applied the ABC News Terrorism Response Plan, by the book, just as the French did.

America needs to wake up! We aren't in a war on terror. We aren't in a war on workplace violence. We're in a war on Islam. It does us no good to avoid admitting that, because all of Islam knows it. They are certainly at war with us. We can spare no effort at putting a stop to Obama's plan to import hundreds of thousands more muslim *refugees*. Rather than debating on the number of *refugees* we should allow into the U.S. and how we can vet them, we need to turn the narrative to a debate on how many we can **deport**. We need to deport the muslims who are in our country now.

Islam is evil. Every muslim participates in the core principle of Islam, which is Jihad. Jihad has three stages. The first stage is when they infiltrate by lying about being peaceful. This is their doctrine, not an opinion. The second stage occurs when they have large enough numbers to start acting violent and stirring unrest. The third stage is when they gain a majority and completely wipe out the opposition and take over. They have done this to every middle eastern country but Israel to varying degrees and they are well into the 2nd stage of Jihad in most of Europe. We need to nip this in the bud right now and get rid of them. Millions of non-American muslims are in our country right now and have no right to be here. We have every right to protect ourselves and our sovereignty. The evil that is Islam, must be neutered in America. Would I support shutting down mosques? You bet I would! Even if we fool ourselves into believing that Islam is a *religion* and not a political system or cult, the 1st Amendment[114] never has protected religion from State governments, only from Congress.

As individuals you can make demands of your congressman, governors, and state legislators to deport these animals. As Americans, I don't care where you are or what your local laws say, you have the **Right to Bear Arms** and I highly encourage you to do so! Protect yourself from this evil and protect your loved ones. No time is better than the present to sign your family up for a basic, small arms self defense class. They're fun and educational. As any Boy Scout can tell you, be prepared! Don't be the next victim.

---

[114] See page 249

OBAMA BLAMES AMERICA IN HIS SPEECH.

POSTED DECEMBER 7, 2015

74 years ago, America was attacked by 353 Japanese planes and some midget torpedo submarines. 2,403 people were killed. Even a liberal like Franklin Delano Roosevelt had no problem naming the enemy. Japs! That's right, Japs. We weren't crippled by political correctness back then and could call a spade a spade. We didn't have a population of pansies who squirmed if we insulted our enemy. Patriotism was considered a virtue.

In less than 4 years, the United States ended the war in the Pacific by dropping two nuclear bombs on the Japanese cities of Hiroshima and Nagasaki. We weren't crying about collateral damage, we were winning. Crushing the enemy is how you win wars.

Now we face a bigger enemy, which has a seething hatred for America and the rest of the world. That enemy is Islam. There is no parsing it. It's not just a radical element of Islam, it's all of Islam and their own Koran demands the jihad and caliphate they are waging against us. We have a president who can't even bring himself to utter the words *radical islam*, which would at least give some identity to our enemy. After we were just attacked by two more muslims, in San Bernardino California, our Sissy in Chief addressed the nation with a 14 minute speech.

Obama began his speech by saying that the 14 people who died were celebrating the holidays. *No, Hussein, they were celebrating Christmas. Christmas. Can you say Christmas?* Obama went on to say that the victims were brutally murdered and injured by one of their co-workers and his wife. He stressed the word *co-workers*. Obama said that so far we have no evidence that the killers were directed by a terrorist organization. Obama is completely mad. This was not *workplace violence*. This was jihad. Everyone but those in the Obama Administration knows why these two muslims killed 14 people. Obama begrudgingly admitted that it was an act of terrorism, but he would not say that it is islamic terrorism. He danced around it. He did say they were radicalized. *No, they're just regular muslims following the teachings of Muhammed in their Koran.*

Obama said that we have been at war with terrorists since they attacked us on 9/11/2001 and in the process we have hardened our defenses from airports to financial centers. Yeah, what good has that done? We strip the rights of Americans who walk into an airport and we have had more attacks on our soil since we began doing that. All of these domestic attacks were under Obama's watch.

He ran off a list of things America has done to fight terrorism, such as killing Osama Bin Ladin and decimating Al Qaeda's leadership. I don't think he knows what *decimate* means. Besides, who cares about Al Qaeda? What difference does it make what name muslims call their organization this week? Hamas, Al Qaeda, Taliban, ISIS, ISIL, Daesh, etc. They're all the same.

Obama claimed that we have become better at stopping the complicated plots like what happened on 9/11, so terrorists have turned to less complicated acts of violence such as mass shootings which are all too common in our society. He said that it is this type of attack that we saw at Fort Hood in 2009, *(No, Obama, that was a muslim attack)*, in Chattanooga earlier this year, *(wrong again, that was a muslim attack)*, and now in San Bernardino, *(nope, muslim attack again)*. He then blamed the internet for erasing the distance between countries allowing terrorists to poison the minds of people like the Boston Marathon bombers *(no guns used there Obama)*, and the San Bernardino killers. *Wait, in less than 3 minutes Obama went from saying that the San Bernardino killers weren't influenced by any terrorist organizations to now saying that they were and it's the internet's fault.*

Barack went on to say that we will destroy ISIL and any other organization that tries to harm us. *The organization is called Islam. I thought ISIL was contained?* He said that our success won't depend on tough talk, abandoning our values, or giving into fear. *Talk is all he's done, he doesn't share our values, and fear mongering is all the left does in an effort to scare us into giving up more rights, including our right to bear arms.* He continued with his tough talk to tell us how the military was taking out ISIL leaders and infrastructure and our allies are adding to our military campaign. Next he said that we will continue to provide training and equipment to Iraqi and Syrian forces. *What? Are we ever going to stop arming our enemies? Whose arms does Obama think ISIS is wielding now?*

He said that we are working with muslim leaders in other countries and here at home to counter the vicious ideology that ISIL promotes online. *Really Obama? Where? Which leaders? Where can I find the counters to ISIL's ideology from muslim leaders?*

Here at home, Obama said that we have to work together and that there are several steps that Congress should take right away. This is where Obama blames and attacks Americans. He said that Congress should make sure that no one who is on a no fly list should be able to buy a gun. *So **without any due process**, your rights can be stripped, because some bureaucrat typed your name into a database, or someone else's name that happens to be the same as yours.* Next he said that we have to make it harder for Americans to buy powerful assault weapons. He called this a gun safety measure. *It's your fault American, because it's too easy to buy guns. We should make it harder to get guns, so terrorists can't get guns. That worked so well in France. 130 dead.*

He then said that we need tougher screening for people who come to America without a visa. *What are they doing coming to America without a visa in the first place? We should require visa's for anyone traveling to America.* Obama then called on Congress to vote to show that we are really at War with ISIL, so we can fight them. *What? The only one who doesn't know we are at war and who has pulled our troops out of Iraq and handed ISIS all of our weapons and equipment is Barack Hussein Obama. The only one releasing our enemies from GITMO is Barack Hussein Obama. The only one giving 100s of billions of dollars to Iran and allowing them to nuke up is Barack Hussein Obama.*

In the next breath he said that we should not be drawn into a long and costly ground war. He said that occupying foreign land is what strengthens the enemy and allows them to recruit and that the strategy we are using now, such as air strikes is what works best. *How did we ever elect this buffoon?* He said that allowing local forces to regain control of their own country is how we will achieve a more sustainable victory. *We tried that in Iraq, Obama, remember? That's what gave birth to ISIS.*

Obama said that we cannot turn against one another by defining the war as being between America and Islam. *So, bury your heads in the sand, folks, because Obama said so.* He said that ISIL accounts for a tiny fraction of the more than a billion muslims including millions of patriotic muslim Americans who reject their hateful ideology. *Where? Can someone please point out these patriotic muslim Americans for me?* He called out for these *unseen* muslim leaders to reject the hateful ideology that groups like ISIL promote and to speak out against those interpretations of Islam, which are incompatible with religious tolerance, respect and human dignity. *So that means they would have to denounce the Koran, because that is precisely what it promotes.*

Obama said that it is our responsibility as Americans to reject discrimination. It is our responsibility to reject religious tests on who we admit into this country. He called it a betrayal of our values. *No, Obama, the one betraying our values is you. America is the target of Islam. There are no values in Islam that are compatible with our Constitution. It's high time the American people stood up and boldly recognize who the enemy actually is.* He said that muslim Americans are our friends, neighbors, coworkers and sports heroes and even our men and women in uniform, who are willing to die in defense of our country. *Like Nidal Hasan who killed 13 at Ft. Hood.*

He said that our country was founded on the principle of human dignity and that no matter what religion you practice you are equal in the eyes of God and the eyes of the law. *My Bible doesn't say that God sees everyone of every religion equally. Perhaps Obama should tell muslims that, because their doctrine is that you convert and worship allah, or die.* He went on to say that we should not forget that freedom is more powerful than fear. *This after he fear mongered us about assault weapons and threatened our freedom regarding our right to bear arms.*

He ended by saying that as long as we come together around our common ideals as one nation and one people, he has no doubt that America will prevail. *Most of us are, Obama, it's just that you don't share our common ideals. You share the ideals of our enemy. It is sick that your response to America being attacked, is to blame Americans, our freedom, our rights, and our recognition of the enemy.*

Barack Hussein Obama needs to be impeached. He has no right to stand there and lecture the American people every time we get attacked by our enemies. I don't care if Joe Biden ends up as president for the next year. At least Biden isn't a muslim.

JUSTICE DEFEATS WITCH HUNT WITH MISTRIAL FOR OFFICER PORTER

POSTED DECEMBER 17, 2015

The Black Lives Matter savages of Baltimore don't want justice, they want blood. For the six police officers being tried for murder in the Freddie Gray case, there is only one jury decision that will make them happy: *guilty*. If justice is truly what they sought, they wouldn't be upset by a hung jury. At least a hung jury shows that a trial is fair and not a witch trial. Isn't fairness a good thing? We know we have witch trial prosecutors, but at least a hung jury earns credibility for being impartial. Baltimore residents should be thrilled that they can claim impartiality, and not blood lust is the driving force in the court room.

William Porter was charged with lesser crimes than the other police officers charged in the case. His charges were only for involuntary manslaughter, second degree assault, reckless endangerment and misconduct. Prosecutors and the Baltimore Looting and Rioting Society, AKA Black Lives Matter, Baltimore, had their fingers crossed that he would be the easiest one to convict. This would set the stage for the dominoes to fall, taking the other five police officers down for more serious charges.

It should be noted that all William Porter was really accused was not putting Freddie Gray in a seat belt, a brand new requirement for police officers in Baltimore on the day Freddie Gray was arrested. Gray was pursued for running away from a cop who had done nothing more than make eye contact with him. If you and a police officer look at each other at the same time and then you bolt off in a panicked flight from the officer, it's going to result in a chase. That's common sense, something Freddy Gray did not possess, which is made clear by his arrest record[115].

---

[115] http://heavy.com/news/2015/04/freddie-gray-arrest-record-criminal-history-rap-sheet-why-was-freddie-gray-arrested/

Gray was a repeat criminal. Arguments can be made whether or not the laws he broke should be laws in the first place, but he still broke them. His final arrest after fleeing from police was only for carrying an illegal switch blade knife. The 2nd Amendment[116] clearly protected Gray's right to carry any knife he wants. Many laws, drafted and passed by liberal democrats, are designed to create a criminal class of repeat offenders. There are a lot of motivating factors for creating more criminals.

Creating criminals provides an income source for the city and state. Fines add up fast! Private prisons with powerful lobbyists make a lot of money *housing* millions of criminals who never hurt a soul. Attorneys rely on the criminal element for their bread and butter. Fewer criminals would mean less money for lawyers. The unconstitutional Gun Control Act of 1968 made it illegal for a felon to own a gun, so the more ways the government can turn you into a felon, the better chance they have of disarming you! We all know how badly the left wants citizens to be disarmed.

Police officers do not write the laws and are trained and paid to enforce them. Most police officers are honorable men and women who do their jobs well. Even if a law preventing a citizen from carrying a knife is unconstitutional, it's not the job of the police to determine that. Freddie Gray would have benefited from learning more about his constitutional rights and fighting for them legitimately. The very people that Freddie Gray and his fellow Black Lives Matter deadbeats voted for, are the ones who made it illegal for Gray to be carrying the knife. If these deadbeats voted smarter, they would have fewer laws to break. They would be freer Americans and spend more time with family and less time in prison.

Probably the funniest outcome of a hung jury is that the prosecution's plan to arm twist William Porter into testifying against his fellow officers in their trials has been thwarted. The next trial for Officer Caesar Goodson for second degree murder is scheduled for January 2016. They won't be able to take advantage of William Porter as a witness now! There is even talk of being unable to proceed with Officer Goodson's trial without having Officer Porter to exploit, so

---

[116] See page 250

they need to delay Goodson's trial until they get a do-over of Officer Porter's trial.

I have always found it unsettling that a hung jury is treated as a mistrial. It is not as if the trial had anything wrong with it. They simply could not prove Officer Porter guilty. If you are innocent until proven guilty, why should it take a unanimous jury decision to prove one's innocence? Porter has so far, not been proven guilty, so remains innocent in the eyes of the law. A mistrial should be an irregularity with the trial itself, such as jury tampering, bribing a judge, introducing illegally obtained evidence, or something of that nature. A mistrial shouldn't be, *"oops, we couldn't find the defendant guilty the first time!"*

Black Lives Matter are raving lunatics. Officer Porter and two of the other five police officers involved are black. Seven of the jurors were black. Most of Baltimore is black. Everything about the way Baltimore is run was created by blacks and run by blacks, so they can rule over the blacks who keep voting for more of the same. Large groups of blacks blame police and whites for the trouble they bring on themselves by voting for it. Their anger is stoked and their and misinformation is provided by the likes of Jesse Jackson and Al Sharpton, who profit from race baiting. Keeping blacks uneducated and angry is a very profitable business.

If blacks learned more about conservatism, the Constitution, and their rights, maybe they would stop voting for their own subjugation. Blacks vote themselves into slavery. They do so after being convinced that they are voting for free stuff. They vote for welfare, food stamps, WIC checks, and HUD homes, which are a very small price for government to pay to house the mothers and children of all the black men they throw in prison. Taxpayers pay for the freebies and the prisons. Government grows and prison owners buy yachts. Wake up, black people! If Black Lives Matter, act like it!

MITCH LANDRIEU FIXED THE CIVIL WAR!

POSTED DECEMBER 19, 2015

Liberals never stop trying to ban anything American. This is especially true when it comes to history, culture and tradition. Mayor Mitch Landrieu of New Orleans signed an ordinance to have four historical Civil War monuments removed. The statues are of Confederate President Jefferson Davis, General Robert E. Lee, General P.G.T. Beauregard, and a monument that was dedicated to the Battle of Liberty Place.

The Battle of Liberty Place was in 1872, seven years after the end of the Civil War in 1865. A group of 5,000 white Democrats known as the White League overthrew the Republican majority government in New Orleans and occupied the New Orleans State House until President Grant sent troops to take it back. Mitch Landrieu of course, is a democrat and follows the Democrat playbook. He will do whatever it takes to either blame Republicans for past Democrat sins or he will erase them from history.

After signing the ordinance passed by the New Orleans City Council to remove the four monuments, Landrieu said, "We, the people of New Orleans, have the power and we have the right to correct these historical wrongs." No historical wrong is being corrected, because history already happened and Landrieu's lack of a time machine makes him a liar. No, he isn't correcting anything. He's burying history.

It's true that the winners write the history, which is why we are taught in schools that the Civil War started over slavery and that the North were the *good guys* and the South were the *bad guys*. We don't get both sides. We don't hear that Lincoln publicly supported an Amendment to the Constitution to make slavery permanent. We aren't taught that he suspended habeas corpus by usurping power that the Constitution reserves only for Congress. We aren't taught that the southern states seceded even after being offered permanent slavery on a silver platter. No, we're supposed to think that slavery was the issue being fought over in the Civil War. Those in power in the Federal Government, especially on the left, can't afford for We the People to get uppity about states' rights again. That's a subject they don't ever want us talking about. We're taught one side of history and one side only, but to erase history altogether is even worse.

Landrieu said, "We must reckon with our past. With eyes wide open, we should truly remember history and not revere a false version of it." He says this while tearing history down, bulldozing it out of sight and out of mind. He is shutting the eyes of the people, so that no one can remember history at all. We should forget about the 620,000 who died in the civil war, roughly half of all American war deaths the United States has had from 1775 to 2015. We should especially forget about the 258,000 Southerners who died fighting in the Civil War. Fallen Southerners are a false version of history according to Mitch Landrieu.

However you feel about the Civil War and whichever side your loyalties lie on, even today 150 years later, the truth is that the Civil War did happen. If we forget history, we may be destined to repeat it. The Federal Government tramples on the rights of States today, far more than anyone could conceive of in the 1860's. The left seems to be working very hard to create divisiveness in America in any way they can.

We have leftist race baiters who are doing everything within their power to stoke hatred based on racial tension in minority communities with groups like Black Lives Matter and even La Raza (Spanish for *The Race*). At the same time, we have a government who is allowing illegals to cross our border in the 10's of millions, even providing them buses to get here. They are also importing millions of muslims who hate everything our country stands for, but who won't complain about receiving their welfare checks, food stamps and government housing. While purposefully dividing us liberals wage a constant battle against the constitutional rights of Americans. They infringe on our 2nd Amendment[117] rights, search us without warrants in airports, and convict us without due process via bills of attainder, by adding us to no fly lists. Those are just a few examples.

---

[117] See page 250

The left is doing everything they can to thoroughly destroy American values and our way of life.

We cannot afford to forget history. We can no longer count on the public education system to teach history to our children. They teach Social Studies, a liberal indoctrination in the way we are supposed to behave as a society. Individual responsibility and personal opinions are frowned upon. Public education teaches us to be hive minded.

There is a glimmer of hope with regard Mitch Landrieu's desecration of history in New Orleans. This didn't come unexpectedly, so it only took one day for a huge federal lawsuit to be filed to put a stop to the removal of the monuments, starting with a temporary injunction and restraining order and moving on to a permanent injunction. The case looks very promising, because it doesn't appear that the city has ownership of the monuments or the authority to remove them. We shall see. The city wants to tear the monuments down immediately, in just a few days, so the dirty deed will be done before anyone could do anything about it. They would have gotten away with it had the law suits not been prepared in advance.

Watch out for this kind of thing in your states and cities. Don't feel complacent if your local government has a majority of Republicans, because many of them will go along to get along. The mere thought of bad press will cower most Republicans in to complying with liberal demands. Be ready to hold them accountable and always remind them of why they are in office. Remain vigilant and intolerant of historical and cultural destruction. Learn and remember history, both good and bad. We learn lessons from both, so we can sustain the good and avoid repeating the bad.

MERRY CHRISTMAS!

POSTED DECEMBER 24, 2015

Merry Christmas Everyone!

I hope and pray that this Christmas brings you warm blessings! Remember, Christmas is a celebration of the birth of our savior, Jesus Christ and is not just about presents and trees! That said, it is also a time for giving, which is far more rewarding than receiving! Try to find at least one person this year who is in need, whether you know them personally or not, and give them something to bring a little cheer into their life. Consider giving to a wounded veteran. Your local American Legion, Disabled American Veterans (DAV), AMVETS, or other similar organization is sure to know of many veterans in your area who could use a hand.

America has a long tradition of celebrating Christmas. From the beginning, the importance of Christmas stood out for America. While fighting for our independence, George Washington went through one of the most blessed and the of the most trying Christmases in our nation's history.

Having suffered repetitive defeats for a year and a half against the most powerful army in the world, it was Christmas Day of 1776 when George Washington took his rag tag army of volunteers across the Delaware river in a surprise attack against the Hessians in Trenton, New Jersey. The German Hessians had been warned by spies, so Washington's attack should have failed. The Germans were over confident and didn't believe the attack would come, so they celebrated Christmas by getting drunk. George Washington caught them by surprise and in a very short battle, his 2400 men overwhelmed the 1500 Germans and took most of them prisoner. It was one of the most pivotal battles of the Revolutionary War and lead to a string of victories in the Revolutionary War.

The following Christmas of 1777 wasn't so blessed and marked some of the toughest hardships Washington and his armies ever had to endure. Washington's army was out of food, supplies, and even clothing. My words can't do justice to the misery the men suffered, so I will leave you with the words of George Washington himself, describing the conditions at Valley Forge. In a plea for help, he wrote this letter to the Convention of New Hampshire. The letter was also sent to the State Houses of every other state except Georgia.

When you are celebrating with your family and friends this Christmas, exchanging gifts in front of a lit up Christmas tree, cozy in the warmth of a fireplace, remember what it took on Christmases past to bring you this luxury. Remember the honor, the bravery, and the pain and suffering it took to earn the freedom that we take for granted. Please take the time to read George Washington's account of Christmas time at Valley Forge. Have and appreciate a very Merry Christmas!

George Washington to [The Convention of New Hampshire]
Valley Forge, [Pennsylvania], December 29, 1777.
Letter signed, 5 pages.
Head Qrs: Valley Forge Dec 29th: 1777
Gentn:

I take the liberty of transmitting you the Inclosed Return, which contains a state of the New Hampshire Regiments. By this you will discover how deficient, – how exceedingly short they are of the complement of men which of right according to the establishment they ought to have. This information, I have thought it my duty to lay before you, that it may have that attention which it's importance demands; and in full hope, that the most early and vigorous measures will be adopted, not only to make the Regiments more respectable but compleat. The necessity and expediency of this procedure are too obvious to need Arguments. Should we have a respectable force to commence an early Campaign with, before the Enemy are reinforced, I trust we shall have an Opportunity of striking a favourable and an happy stroke; but if we should be obliged to defer it, It will not be easy to describe with any degree of precision what disagreable consequences may result from It. We may rest assured, that Britain will strain every nerve to send from Home and abroad, as early as possible, All the Troops it shall be in her power to raise or procure. Her views and schemes for subjugating these States, and bringing them under her despotic rule will be unceasing and unremitted. Nor should we, in my opinion, turn our expectations to, or have the least dependance on the intervention of a Foreign War. Our wishes on this head have been disappointed hitherto and perhaps it may long be the case. However, be this as it may, our reliance should be wholly on our own strength and exertions. If in addition to these, there should be aid derived from a War between the Enemy and any of the European Powers, our situation will be so much the better. If not our Efforts & Exertions will have been the more necessary and indispensable. For my own part, I should be happy, if the idea of a Foreign rupture should be thrown entirely out of our Scale of politicks, and that it may not have the least weight in our public measures. No bad effects could flow from it, but on the contrary many of a salutary nature. At the same time I do not mean that such an Idea ought to be discouraged among the people at large because the event is probable.

There is one thing more to which I would take the liberty of solliciting your most serious and constant attention; to wit, the cloathing of your Troops, and the procuring of every possible supply in your power from time to time for that end. If the several States exert themselves in future in this instance, and I think they will, I hope that the Supplies they will be able to furnish in aid of those, which Congress may immediately import themselves, will be equal and competent to every demand. If they do not, I fear, I am satisfied the Troops will never be in a situation to answer the public expectation and perform the duties required of them. No pains, no efforts on the part of the States can be too great for this purpose. It is not easy to give you a just and accurate idea of the sufferings of the Army at large – of the loss of men on this account. Were they to be minutely detailed, your feelings would be wounded, and the relation would probably be not received without a degree of doubt & discredit. We had in Camp, on the 23rd Inst. by a Field Return then taken, not less than 2898 men unfit for duty, by reason of their being barefoot and otherwise naked. Besides this number, sufficiently distressing of itself, [4] there are many Others detained in Hospitals and crowded in Farmers Houses for the same causes. In a most particular manner, I flatter myself the care and attention of the States will be directed to the supply of Shoes, Stockings and Blankets, as their expenditure from the common operations and accidents of War is far greater than of any other articles. In a word, the United and respective exertions of the States cannot be too great, too vigorous in this interesting work, and we shall never have a fair and just prospect for success till our Troops (Officers & Men) are better appointed and provided than they are or have been. We have taken post here for the Winter, as a place best calculated to cover the Country from the Ravages of the Enemy and are now busily employed in erecting Huts for the Troops. This circumstance renders it the more material that the Supplies should be greater and more immediate than if the men were in comfortable Quarters.

Before I conclude, I would also add, that it will be essential to inoculate the Recruits or Levies, as fast as they are raised that their earliest services may be had. Should this be postponed, the work [5] the work will be to do most probably at an interesting and critical period, and when their aid may be very materially wanted.

I have the Honor to be with great respect Gentln.

Your most Obed Servt

Go: Washington

Thank you to The Gilder Lehrman Collection for the text of George Washington's letter[118].

Learn more from the Gilder Lehrman Institute of American History![119]

---

[118] http://www.gilderlehrman.org/history-by-era/war-for-independence/resources/george-washington-from-valley-forge-urgent-need-for-me

[119] http://www.gilderlehrman.org

BUNDY VS BLM STANDOFF 2.0

POSTED JANUARY 3, 2016

A situation similar to the one which occurred at the Bundy Ranch in Nevada is now taking place in Burns, Oregon. The Bundys were the last holdouts of over 50 Ranching families who were run off their land by burdensome federal regulations and taxes. This was all part of a scheme by Harry Reid to make a land deal with the Chinese to build solar power farms. The Bundys held out and after the unconstitutional Federal Bureau of Land Management (BLM) used SWAT teams to round up the Bundy cattle, a large group of militia formed from all over the country and forced the federal government to back off and return the cattle.

In Burns, Oregon, father and son ranchers, Dwight and Steven Hammond, came under assault by the federal government in a slightly different way. Like the Bundys, they leased federal land for grazing around their ranch. The unconstitutional way that the federal government grabs up land and then leases its use back to We The People is the subject of long debate.

The Hammonds purchased their ranch in 1964 along with leases and water rights on public lands around it. The federal government bought up all of the other ranches in the area in the 1970s and handed the land off to the Fish and Wildlife Service. They have been after Hammond's land ever since. The Hammonds have suffered almost 5 decades of harassment from the federal government in various forms, such as The Fish and Wildlife Service barricading public roads the Hammonds used and fencing off their water supplies.

The Hammonds had problems with wild fires and invasive plant species. They addressed these problems with controlled burns, to mitigate the risk of wild fires and invasive plants going out of control. The federal government brought charges against them. Everyone is thinking they were arson charges, never mind the fact that arson is not a crime that Article 1, Section 8[120] of the Constitution allows

---

[120] See page 237

Congress to legislate. The Constitution leaves almost all domestic criminal justice to the states.

The Hammonds weren't charged with arson by the federal government. First, they were immediately arrested and charged with various crimes, such as arson by the State of Oregon. It was determined that the charges didn't warrant prosecution and all charges were dropped. *Five years later* the federal government charged the Hammonds with **terrorism** under the Federal Anti-Terrorism Effective Death Penalty Act of 1996! Yes, they are charged with terrorism for helping Smokey The Bear.

The terrorism charge carries a 5 year minimum sentence, but the federal judge on their case gave them shorter jail terms, saying that long of a sentence would "shock the conscience." He also said it violated the 8th Amendment[121] by being cruel and unusual. Dwight Hammond served 3 months and his son Steven served a year, because he was convicted of multiple counts. They were both given 3 years of supervised probation after their sentences.

After they served their shorter sentences The 9th Circuit Court of Appeals unconstitutionally threw out the shorter sentences and mandated the 5 year minimum sentence. The Hammonds were also ordered to pay the BLM $400,000. They've paid half if it and were ordered to pay the remainder by the end of 2015 or lose their ranch. This is double jeopardy. They had already served the sentences they were given for the crimes of *terrorism* they were found guilty of.

Ammon Bundy learned about the situation and he met with the Hammonds to offer support. The Hammonds were planning on simply turning themselves in on January 4th, to comply with the second sentencing for the *terrorism* crimes they already served time for.

On Saturday morning of January 2nd, 2016, a peaceful protest was held in Burns, Oregon in support of the Hammonds. Afterward, 150 militiamen along with Ammon Bundy and two of his brothers split off and went to the Malheur National Wildlife Refuge and occupied the Federal Headquarters there, which is used by The

---

[121] See page 251

Bureau of Land Management. This was a peaceful occupation, of course. The leftist rancor over this issue, calling it terrorism, is outlandish and ignorant. Unlike the left wing "Occupy Wall Street," no one is being raped or urinated on.

The Hammonds still plan on turning themselves in at this point, but the Bundys and militia intend on continuing to occupy the National Wildlife Refuge Headquarters Building as well as taking over the BLM Fire Department building, which is currently vacant. They are making the stand to put a stop to the tyranny that is plaguing the residents of Harney County. They have exhausted every possible legal means to seek redress and have had every application and petition to law enforcement, sheriffs and all levels of government flatly ignored. The people just want to be free and left alone to prosper as they have for over 100 years, without the shackles of federal tyranny being clamped upon them.

Ammon Bundy is calling for more people to come join them in Harney County. In this Video[122], Ammon Bundy says, "I am asking you to come to Harney County, to make the decision right now, of whether this is a righteous cause or not, whether I am some crazy person or whether the Lord truly works through individuals to get His purposes accomplished. I know that we are to stand now and that we are to do these things now or we will not have anything to pass on to our children. That they will be placed under the same exact measures that the Hammonds have been placed under. And I ask you now, to come to Harney County to participate in this wonderful thing the Lord is about to accomplish. And I say those things to you and I'm grateful to have such great friends and I look forward to seeing you. Thank you.

If you haven't already, please view the video. For a far more detailed timeline of the unconstitutional actions taken by the federal government against the Hammonds over the last half a century, go here: The Conservative Tree House[123].

---

[122] https://www.youtube.com/watch?v=M7M0mG6HUyk

[123] http://theconservativetreehouse.com/2016/01/03/full-story-on-whats-going-on-in-oregon-militia-take-over-malheur-national-wildlife-refuge-in-protest-to-hammond-family-persecution/

UPDATED JANUARY 4, 2016:

Reporters get tour of the Malheur Refuge buildings that are being occupied. Notice the respect they have for the property compared to all of the liberal occupations of public property, which were strewn with litter, vandalism, urine, and feces. KOIN 6 Reporter gets Tour of Maheur Wildlife Refuge Buildings[124].

UPDATED JANUARY 24, 2016:

Three weeks into the occupation of an empty lodge in the middle of the forest, Ammon Bundy and is fellow ranchers still haven't burned down any buildings, set cop cars on fire, thrown molotov cocktails, blocked traffic, looted stores, raped anyone, or murdered civilians and cops. If they are supposedly terrorists, they have a lot of savagery to commit before they catch up with Black Lives Matter or the Occupy Wall Street deadbeats.

As it stands now, Ammon Bundy says that he is willing to talk with FBI, but still doesn't recognize their authority in the matter and considers it an issue for the sheriff to solve. The federal government is the problem, not the solution.

Oregon's Governor, Democrat Kate Brown, is complaining that the occupation has cost Oregon tax payers half a million dollars. No Kate, the FBI and BLM occupation of Burns, Oregon is what costs you money. The ranchers haven't sent you a single bill or caused one bit of damage to any property that would cost tax payers a dime. Want to save money, send the FBI and BLM home. But that's not how Kate sees it. She asked Attorney General Loretta Lynch and FBI Director James Comey to "to end the unlawful occupation of the Malheur National Wildlife Refuge as safely and as quickly as possible." In other words, a State Governor is deferring her authority to unconstitutional agencies and asking them to come in guns blazing. This woman is sick and Oregon residents should recall her. She wasn't even elected and replaced John Kitzhaber who

---

[124] http://americanpowerblog.blogspot.com/2016/01/militia-occupation-update-koin-6.html#.VonnxA6ccpw.twitter

resigned over a scandal involving allegedly abusing his power to benefit his wife's business.

Ammon Bundy responded to the unconstitutional request of the Governor by saying, "It just again shows the ignorance of some of our elected officials. It's just amazing that she would just disregard the Constitution to the point where she would think it would be OK to give the federal government that authority to come in and take some dynamic action or something like that."

It should be noted that during Bundy's occupation of the Wildlife Refuge, his group has been performing repairs on the Malheur National Wildlife Refuge property and structures, addressing fire hazards in the firehouse, and assisting local ranchers with maintenance. Their actions have been the exact opposite of any liberal rally or demonstration in U.S. history. Never has there been a location that was left in better condition by liberals who have demonstrated there. Accused of being terrorists by the left, all this group has done so far is peaceably assemble on vacant public land. Exercising this right and their right to bear arms outrages the left, because they simply do not understand what rights are or why we have them. Liberals are allergic to liberty.

UPDATED JANUARY 27, 2016:

Ammon Bundy and 7 others were arrested and one rancher, Robert "LaVoy" Finicum was killed in an FBI operation when they were pulled over while traveling to a meeting in Burns Oregon. The details are sparse, but what is clear is that Ammon's brother Ryan was also shot in the arm. The arrested ranchers are charged with "conspiracy to impede officers of the United States from discharging their official duties." In other words they are charged with committing no crime other than not wanting to be harassed by the FBI and BLM who couldn't find a crime to charge them with.

Ammon Bundy said that Finicum was shot three times while peacefully complying and with his hands up. There were six witnesses. It appears that the only guns discharged were those of the FBI.

Robert "LaVoy" Finicum leaves behind a wife, 11 children, and 50 foster children.

U.S. Sen. Jeff Merkley (*Democrat*-Oregon) congratulated the FBI and said, "I am pleased that the FBI listened to the concerns of the local community and responded to the illegal activity occurring in Harney County by outside extremists." Oregon should be ashamed of electing this man to the U.S. Senate who is pleased that a man is now dead who was guilty of no more than peaceable assembly.

When the L.A. Times infomed Cliven Bundy, Ammon and Ryan's dad, he said, "Isn't this a wonderful country we live in? We believe that those federal people shouldn't even be there in that state, and be in that county and have anything to do with this issue. I have some sons and other people there trying to protect our rights and liberties and freedoms, and now we've got one killed, and all I can say is, he's sacrificed for a good purpose."

UPDATED JANUARY 29, 2016:

Here is the link to the video where Lavoy is shot. He obviously has his hands up exiting the vehicle. He appears to succumb to a gut shot and turn around and head back, but is taken down quickly. To claim he is grabbing a gun is really reaching for moon beams, because if that were the case he would be facing off one of the agents, but he doesn't. Stumbling through snow, he is attempting a 180 degree turn to head back the way he came. He is grabbing several places on his body as he is taken out. Not a gun grabbing maneuver. Only people who have never pulled a gun from a holster can see a gun grab from this video. I have never seen a right handed person with a holster over his pancreas, which is the first place on his body that Lavoy appears to grab. It must also be noted that so far there is no claim by the FBI that Lavoy was even armed.

Watch the video. The shooting starts at about 9:20[125].

125

https://www.youtube.com/watch?v=aAGxDWKrjPQ&feature=youtu.be

UPDATED FEBRUARY 13, 2016:

After 40 days and 40 nights of Peaceable Assembly in an empty lodge on public land, the last four people surrendered. David Fry was the last to come out and give himself to the FBI. Gavin Seim, Kris Anne Hall, and Reverend Frankling Graham helped to facilitate the surrender by live streaming it, to ensure the FBI remained peaceful. The media is reporting them as anti-government activists, but nothing could be further from the truth. They only want government to follow the Constitution and the law. What is wrong with that?

It should be noted that it is unconstitutional for the federal government to own this land. They can own territories, but not land within states unless purchased with the consent of the state legislatures for certain reasons outlined in Article 1, Section 8, Clause 17[126] of the U.S. Constitution. Creating a park, or using the land to lease to cattle ranchers are not among those reasons. Other than Washington D.C., they can own land acquired from states only for Forts, Magazines, Arsenals, Dock Yards, and other needful buildings. A needful building might be something like a U.S. Post Office or Army recruiting center. Not a lodge for operating control of millions of acres of park land the federal government can't legally own.

Ammon and Ryan Bundy have vowed to take the federal government to court. Among those in jail with them is online journalist Pete Santilli who visited the site to report on the situation. Apparently freedom of the press is no more protected from the tyranny of the federal government than peaceable assembly is.

Also arrested was Cliven Bundy, the patriarch of the Bundy family from Nevada. It's not clear why he was arrested. He is charged with conspiracy and extortion. Baseless charges where no real charges could be found. The 25 ranchers who were peaceably assembled at Malheur, minus LaVoy who was killed in the ambush, are all charged with interfering with an investigation. In other words, they peaceably assembled on public land and didn't want to forfeit their 4th and 5th Amendment[127] rights. In the absence of any actual

---

[126] See page 238

[127] See page 250

crimes they could be charged with, their crime is not allowing the FBI to figure out a crime to charge them with.

UPDATED MARCH 10, 2016:

The FBI agents involved in the ambush and killing of LaVoy Finicum are now under criminal investigation by the Justice Department. Video footage being taken from passengers in the car with LaVoy, which includes audio brings new light to the story. With his hands already in the air as LaVoy exited the vehicle, an FBI agent shot the rear window of the car out through the roof. Multiple shots were fired at the vehicle and its occupants before LaVoy was finally taken down. Claims that LaVoy got shot, because he was reaching for his gun, no longer hold water. It's now clear that if he were reaching for a gun, it was in self defense. It's still not clear that he was even reaching for a gun though and not just stumbling through thick snow. This video blows away any arguments the "tolerant" leftists had for cheering on LaVoy's death.

Watch new Video from inside the car[128].

Slow Motion video of the gun shot through the roof, shattering the back window with LaVoy's hands high above his head[129].

128

https://www.youtube.com/watch?v=YWLHiU8gYWY&feature=youtu.be

[129] http://videos.oregonlive.com/oregonian/2016/03/slow-motion_video_of_gunshot_f.html

MUSLIM SHOOTS PHILLY COP! MEDIA CONFUSED

POSTED JANUARY 9, 2016

While Obama continues to import more muslim terrorists into the United States, calling them peaceful widows and orphans, Islam continues to refute him by revealing itself for what it is.

Philadelphia police officer, Jesse Hartnett was on routine patrol in his squad car, when out of nowhere, Jihad reared its head in the form of a typical, angry muslim. The muslim, by the name of Edward Archer, ran up to the cop car shooting at the car with a 9mm Glock that was stolen from another police officer's home in 2013. He reached into the driver's side window and shot Officer Hartnett at point blank range. Three of the bullets went into Officer Hartnett's arm. He was wearing a bullet proof vest, so wasn't otherwise hurt.

Officer Hartnett, with a dangling left arm, immediately jumped out of the car and pursued Archer and returned fire, hitting him. Archer's bullet wound is the reason he was caught. Considering Hartnett's condition and being caught by surprise, his actions should bring him commendation as a hero.

Once in custody, the muslim, Edward Archer admitted to the shooting and said, "I follow Allah. I pledge my allegiance to the Islamic State, and that's why I did what I did." The Islamic State is ISIS, the Islamic terrorist organization that Obama claims has nothing to do with Islam. The liberal talking heads on various news outlets were claiming that Archer was not a member of any actual group. Yes, actually he is. The group is called Islam. Islam is Islam. Islam's main goal is to convert everyone else to Islam or kill them. It's a world wide caliphate. Jihad is the core principle of Islam for meeting this goal. All muslims participate in Jihad. It comes in three stages. 1: stealth, 2: defensive, and 3: offensive, depending on the muslim population in the area.

We recognize stealth Jihad as "Islam, the Religion of Peace." These are the muslims who are friendly and tolerant. They have to be when they are greatly outnumbered. This is how the Koran instructs them to gain acceptance by society. Defensive Jihad is when they start becoming offended by everything, such as the muslims in Switzerland who are now demanding the cross be removed from the Swiss flag. Next comes offensive Jihad. This is when muslims start killing everyone. Obama calls this "workplace violence" and blames America and guns.

In America, the muslim population is so low that they have been in Stealth jihad for the most part, but a weak Obama administration and a media who makes excuses for Islam has made it politically incorrect to insult Islam. Muslims don't have to be as stealthy when we wear blinders, so offensive jihad crops up in random attacks, such as Archer shooting Officer Hartnett and the San Bernardino shooting. We are making stealth Jihad unnecessary with political correctness. They normally can't start killing people when they are vastly outnumbered, because a smart society would quickly put them down. In our case, the more violent muslims become, the more America blames itself and invites in more muslims. Islam has never had it this easy.

If you have friends who are muslims, they are liars. They might be your friends, but you certainly aren't theirs. They are conducting phase 1 Jihad. Their friendship and peaceful nature is a lie called Taqiyya and is instructed by the Koran. Their job is to gain your acceptance, so you are open to accepting more muslims into your community.

So far, there have been statements made by at least two Philadelphia City officials. Police Commissioner Richard Ross called the attack an attempted assassination and said that Officer Hartnett's survival was absolutely amazing and nothing short of miraculous.

Jim Kenney, the newly elected democrat Mayor of Philadelphia described Archer's attack as abhorrent and terrible, saying that it had nothing to do with the teachings of Islam. "This is a criminal with a stolen gun who tried to kill one of our officers," he said. "It has nothing to do with being a Muslim or following the Islamic faith." *What?*

People of Philadelphia, one of your finest has just been attacked and shot by a savage muslim in an *admitted* act of Jihad and your mayor's first reaction is to defend Islam! What does Jim Kenney know about the teachings of Islam? You need to recall this piece of garbage you elected as a mayor. What city should your mayor be loyal to, Philadelphia or Mecca? Shame on Mayor Jim Kenney and shame on Philadelphia if you don't fire this meathead. Democrats can't run to a microphone fast enough to make excuses for Islam, every single time a muslim commits violence.

The media is tripping over itself trying to explain away the Islamic connection from a muslim shooting a cop and admitting it's jihad. They are discussing topics like, "how muslim is he?" They are claiming that he might have a head injury from high school football, so the voices in his head made him shoot the cop. If he didn't shoot Hartnett because he's muslim, then that maybe he did it for Black Lives Matter, as they are running around killing cops too. No, Black Lives Matter wasn't behind the shooting this time. The media is looking for any excuse, but the obvious. He's a **muslim**! He did exactly as the Koran instructs. That's it! The muslim heathen said it himself!

Fellow Patriots, I urge you to arm yourself. We are going to see a lot more Islamic violence before it ever gets better. This is still the beginning. You need to protect yourself and your family. You may be in an unfortunate situation where you are the only hope for people you don't even know. Buy guns, learn to use them safely. Take self defense courses and practice. The upside is that it will be fun!

OBAMA'S FINAL SOTU – DIRECTOR'S CUT!

POSTED JANUARY 13, 2016

My synopsis of the very last State of the Union Address from Barack Hussein Obama should save you the Excedrin needed to watch it yourself by cutting through the bull!

Obama began his final State of the Union address by saying that he understands that being an election season, expectations for what we will achieve this year are low. Then he thanked Speaker Ryan for passing his budget (*giving him everything he wanted*). So he hopes we can work together this year on some bipartisan priorities like criminal justice reform and helping people who are battling prescription drug abuse and heroin abuse. *Where does the Constitution give the federal government authority in the area of drug abuse? It gives almost no authority for domestic, criminal justice.*

He said that he wants to go easy on the traditional list of proposals for the year ahead. Then he listed his proposals for the year ahead. Helping students learn to write computer code. *None of the federal government's business.* Personalizing medical treatments for patients. *None of the federal government's business.* Fixing a broken immigration system. *I wonder who broke that, Obama?* Protecting our kids from gun violence. *None of the federal government's business.* Equal pay for equal work. *None of the federal government's business.* Paid leave. *None of the federal government's business.* Raising the minimum wage. *None of the federal government's business.*

He went on about how America has always gone through change and there are always those who fight against it and claimed that we always emerge stronger and better than ever before. What was true then can be true now. *Can be? Shouldn't it already be? We have had change shoved down our throats for 7 years, we should be ecstatic now. When does the emerging stronger and better start?*

He said that this is how we recovered in the last 7 years from the worst economic crisis in generations. Really? The worker participation rate is the lowest it's been since the Great Depression if not lower. Half the country is receiving one form of unconstitutional federal subsidy or another. Hearing about this mythical recovery grows tiresome. For all of you who are unemployed, don't believe your eyes, Obama said you are recovered now. Cheer up.

He said that's how we reformed our health care system and reinvented our energy sector. The price of health insurance skyrocketed, so people can't afford it and have to pay fines for not buying insurance. Also, in Obama's own words, electricity rates necessarily skyrocketed.

He continued, by saying that's how we gave more care and benefits to our troops coming home and our veterans. *As the VA got caught in a scandal to purposely avoid treating veterans under Obama.* That's how we secured the freedom in every state to marry the person we love. *We? No, The Supreme Court unconstitutionally threw out state laws that* **we secured.** He said that such progress is the result of choices we make. *The people chose to outlaw gay marriage, Barack. What happened to those choices?*

Obama said regarding the future we have four questions that we as a country have to answer. First, how do we give everyone a fair shot at opportunity and security in this new economy. *Ooooh! Ooooh! I know! Butt out! The constitution enumerates no authority for federal involvement in our security and they are the only ones standing in the way of people having fair opportunity.* Second, how do we make technology work for us and not against us? Especially when it comes to solving urgent challenges like climate change. *Oh! Can I take this one too? Same answer as the last question. Butt out! This isn't the charter of the federal government.* Third, how do we keep America safe and lead the world without becoming its policeman? *For a start, let's not import terrorists. Then let's close the borders. Wow! These questions are easy!* Finally, how can we make our politics reflect what's best in us and not what's worse? *Perhaps you could stop lying? Next, shut down the Department of Education and allow local communities to teach their children American History instead of Social Studies.*

Obama wanted to start with the economy and a basic fact. He said that the United States of America, right now has the strongest, most durable economy in the world. We're in the longest streak of private sector job creation in history. More than 14 million new jobs, the strongest two years of job growth since the 1990s, an unemployment rate cut in half. *No, what was cut was the counting of those who no longer qualify to collect an unemployment check, even though they never found work.* *He went on and on with more lies about how great our economy is while cutting our deficit by three quarters.* *Congress kept clapping.* Obama blamed American anxiety on technology automating jobs, the global economy making it easy for companies to relocate overseas and more wealth being concentrated at the top. *Raise the minimum wage to $15.00 and see how many robots replace workers! It is not easy to relocate overseas, but our burdensome taxes and regulations make that difficult move more appealing than staying here.*

He said this has made it harder for people to pull themselves out of poverty, for young people to start their careers, and tougher for workers to retire when they want to. *But wait, I thought we cut unemployment in half and this was the best economy ever? Which is it, Obama?* He said that there are areas where we broadly agree. We agree that real opportunity requires every American to get the education and training they need to land a good paying job. *No, we don't agree. What you want, Obama, is for me to pay for someone else's liberal indoctrination.* He said we need to provide Pre-K for all and offer every student the hands on computer science and math classes that make them job ready. And we have to make college affordable for every American. *College was affordable before the federal government got involved handing out unconstitutional grants and loans, creating the dirtiest system of graft there is.* He said, now we have to cut the cost of college, providing two years of community college at no cost is one of the best ways to do that. *Really? Who pays for this?*

Obama said that we need basic benefits and protections that provide a basic measure of security. *No we don't. Leave me alone. I want nothing from you.* He said Social Security and Medicare are more important than ever, we shouldn't weaken them, we should strengthen them. *Of course, you have to keep the people dependent on you if you want their votes.* He said that filling the gaps between employer based healthcare between jobs and into retirement is what is so important about Obamacare and that businesses have created more jobs every month since it has become law. *Yes, by laying off full time workers and hiring more part time workers in their places, so they can avoid having to deal with Obamacare.*

He said that a lot of disagreements are in what role the government should play in making sure the system is not rigged in favor of the wealthiest and biggest corporations. *No role. That is exactly how much role it should play.* I believe a thriving private sector is the lifeblood of our economy. *After he just got through touting Obamacare, which confiscated 1/6 of the private economy.* I think there are outdated regulations that need to be changed. There is red tape that needs to be cut. *The Congress cheered as Obama went into campaign mode.* But... After years now of record corporate profits (*camera pans to Bernie Sanders*) working families won't get more opportunity or bigger paychecks. Just by letting big banks or big oil or hedge funds make their own rules at everybody else's expense. *But I thought the economy was so great now. I am really getting confused. Is this the best economy on Earth forever and ever, or are we doomed and it's all because government doesn't control big banks and corporations enough?* Food stamp recipients did not cause the financial crisis. *No, Hussein, but making me pay for them did!* Immigrants aren't the principle reason wages haven't gone up. *Principle reason? So you admit that they are **a** reason?*

Obama claimed that this year he plans to lift up the many businesses who figured out that doing right by their workers or their customers or their communities, ends up being good for their shareholders. *Lift up businesses? What does that mean? Where is this in Article 2[130] of the Constitution?* Many of our best corporate citizens are also our most creative. This brings me to the second big question we as a country have to answer. How do we reignite that spirit of innovation to meet our biggest challenges? *Wait, I thought the second question was, "How do we make technology work for us and not against us?" He changed the questions on us! As for innovation, has Barack seen an iPhone? Does he realize that private companies are going to space?*

Not to go through a whole speech without bashing American, Barack said that 60 years ago, when the Russians beat us into space, we didn't deny Sputnik was up there. We didn't argue about the science or shrink our research and development budget, we built a space program almost overnight and 12 years later we were walking on the moon. He said that over the last 7 years we've nurtured that spirit. We protected an open internet. *No, we gave the internet away.*

---

[130] See page 239

We've taken bold new steps to get more students and low income Americans online. *Free, Free, Free! And who is paying for this? Bread and circuses!* He then explained how he is putting Joe Biden in charge of mission control to cure cancer once and for all. *The idiots in Congress cheered. Joe Biden and Paul Ryan exchanged words and smiled.*

Obama said that we need the same level of commitment when it comes to developing clean energy sources. *Has anyone in the federal government ever read the Constitution? How is any of this baloney, their responsibility? This is lunacy.* If anybody wants to dispute the science around climate change, have at it. *You will be pretty alone! Because you'll be debating our military, most of America's business leaders, the majority of the American people, almost the entire scientific community, and 200 nations around the world who agree it's a problem and intend to solve it. If this is so, why is he still trying to convince us? The Military has no choice but to say what Obama says they can say. Businesses are cashing in on the ignorance. Almost the entire scientific community? If it's settled, why not all? Could grants have something to do with it? Hmmm?*

Seven years ago we made the single biggest investment in clean energy in our history. *Companies like Solyndra, who took $500,000,000 from tax payers and went bankrupt.* He went on to lie about how great wind and solar have done and how much money they save everyone. He said they've taken steps to give home owners the freedom to generate and store their own energy. *Obama gave us that freedom? What business is it of his in the first place? When did we not have that freedom?* He said that we cut imports of oil by 60% and cut carbon pollution more than any other country on Earth. Gas under two bucks a gallon ain't bad either. *Oil prices dropping are despite Obama, not because of anything he has ever done. He has fought oil production tooth and nail, and was even held in contempt of court over banning gulf oil drilling and he has single handedly stopped the Keystone pipeline.*

I told you earlier, all the talk of America's economic decline is political hot air. Well so is all the rhetoric you hear about our enemies getting stronger and America getting weaker. Let me tell you something. The United States of America is the most powerful nation on Earth. Period. Period. It's not even close. It's not even close! *The camera panned to seven scowling generals who didn't appear to agree. The democrats cheered.* He kept repeating that it's not even close. He went on to brag about how much we spend on our military and how fine it is. No nation attacks us directly or our allies, because they know that's the path to ruin. *Who said anything about nations, Barack?* Survey's show our standing around the world is higher than when I was elected. People in the world do not look to Beijing or Moscow to lead, they call us. *That's why Russia has had to get involved in Syria now.*

Obama said that in today's world we're threatened less by evil empires and more by failing states. The Middle East is going through a transformation that will play out for a generation. *It's been going on for 1400 years and obviously Obama is cool with that continuing if he's spotting it another generation.* Regarding the international system we built after World War II, he said that it's up to us to help remake that system. *Like Israel?* To do that well, it means we've got to set priorities. Priority number one is protecting the American people and going after terrorist networks. *How do we do that when Obama won't even call a terrorist network by its name or admit that they are muslim?* Both Al Quaeda and now ISIL pose a direct threat to our people, because in today's world, even a handful of terrorists who place no value on human life including their own can do a lot of damage. *So, nations aren't attacking us directly, but terrorists are. Just a handful.* They use the internet to poison the minds of individuals inside our country. *That pesky internet.* We have to take them out. Over the top claims that this is World War III just play into their hands. Masses of fighters on the back of pickup trucks, twisted souls, plotting in apartments or garages, they pose an enormous danger to civilians, they have to be stopped. But they do not threaten our national existence. My God! *Does he know what he is saying? Our country is ok, it's just you civilians who need to watch out. Ok, I accept the challenge and will be buying more ammo.*

We don't need to build them up to show that we're serious. And we sure don't need to push away vital allies in this fight by echoing the lie that ISIL is somehow representative of one of the world's largest religions. *Buddhists? Hindus? Let's see, what religion is ISIS?* The democrats applauded. Obama said that we just need to call them what they are, killers and fanatics. *No, we need to call them what **YOU** are, Obama. Muslims.* He described how successful he has been at taking them all out. *As he let's them all out of GITMO.* He said that we are steadily claiming territory in Iraq and Syria. *Really? Territory we already had secured 8 years ago.* If you doubt America's commitment or mine, to see that justice is done, just ask Osama Bin Laden. *I'd prefer to ask Seal Team 6. What happened to them?*

Obama yammered on about all the things we can't do, which were basically a list of ways to win. He claimed that it leads to quagmire. He said that fortunately there is a smarter approach. We will mobilize the world to work with us. And make sure other countries pull their own weight. That's how we're helping that broken society in Syria produce a lasting peace. *What?* We built a global coalition to prevent a nuclear armed Iran. *What? This man unilaterally and unconstitutionally signed a deal with Iran which guarantees them nukes that we pay for.* He claimed Iran has shipped out its uranium stockpile and the world has avoided another war.

Obama went into about a 10 minute spiel about how American strength and leadership are all about us running around the world helping everyone, feeding poor, curing ebola, etc. This was all far too boring to focus on. He lead into promising to shut down GITMO, and said it is a recruitment brochure for our enemies. *No it isn't. GITMO is not a topic on ISIS recruitment brochures. Go find 100 recruitment brochures for ISIS and count how many have the word GITMO in them.*

We need to reject any politics that rejects people because of race or religion. This is not a matter of political correctness. *No kidding, shipping in more of our enemies is a matter of treason.* This is a matter of understanding just what it is that makes us strong. The world respects us not just for our arsenal, it respects us for our diversity and our openness and the way that we respect everything. When politicians insult muslims, whether abroad or our citizens, when a mosque is vandalized or a kid is called names, it doesn't make us safer. That's not telling it like it is. It's just wrong. *I'm not a politician. Can I say that islam is an evil cult with 300,000,000 dead in the name of Allah?*

We the people. Our Constitution begins with those three simple words. Words we've come to recognize mean all the people. *Wrong. We the people specifically refers to Americans. It says, "We The People of the United States..."* The future we want... all of us want... opportunity and security for our families, a rising standard of living, a sustainable, peaceful planet for our kids. All that is within our reach. But it will only happen if we work together. *...Or we shove it down your throats.* It will only happen if we can have rational, constructive debates. *Where* *we agree with liberal socialists or it won't be considered rational or constructive.* It will only happen if we fix our politics. That doesn't mean we have to agree on everything. It's a big country. Different regions, different attitudes, different interests. Our founders distributed power between states and branches of government. *Justice Ginsburg is asleep again.* And expected us to argue, just as they did. Fiercely! Over the size and shape of government. Over commerce and foreign relations. Over the meaning of liberty. *That is Obama's problem, he thinks he can redefine liberty.* A democracy does require basic bonds of trust between its citizens. *We aren't a democracy, Mr. Constitutional Professor.* He went on to lecture us about how disagreeing with each other doesn't mean the other side is unpatriotic or wants to hurt America. He just droned on and on. *Biden was drifting off. There is a lot of sleeping going on in the room during this speech.* He went on and on about politics and how it has to change. *Elisha Cummings was fighting hard to keep his eyes open. It is indescribable how long and boring Obama's final 15 minutes went, while talking about politics, voting and how hard it will be to change our brand of democracy. He made no real points. It was as if he just needed filler for the last 15 minutes and had no material. Part of his wrap up was about how courageous it is for a son to come out for who he is to his father.*

Obama said, "I believe in change, because I believe in you! The American people. And that's why I stand here as confident as I've ever been that the state of our union is strong. *The state of our sailors Iran just captured, not so much.* Thank you. God bless you. God bless the United States of America.

Well, surprisingly he didn't bring up anything about evil guns. At least, if he did, it was when I was dozing along with Ruth Bader Ginsburgh. I don't think I have ever suffered through such a boring hour in my life. An hour packed full of lies and obfuscation. Hopefully that is the last speech I ever see from this man. I doubt it, though.

Please have sympathy for my suffering through this for you and share this with your friends and family on Twitter, Facebook, or anywhere else you like.

THE ANTI-BULLY CAMPAIGN IS THE BULLY

POSTED JANUARY 21, 2016

Bullies are the real victim class among our youth today. It's time for the war on bullies to be exposed for what it is and for it to come to an end. It must sound shocking to side with bullies, but that depends on who is defined as a bully. The Anti-Bully Agenda is about a lot more than stopping playground fights during recess.

First of all, when has bullying ever been allowed in schools? Never. We aren't really talking about bullying as we knew it as children. Most of us knew bullying as weaker kids getting punched, knuckled in in the arm, tripped on the playground, an indian burn here and there and an occasional beating at the bus stop. Now bullying includes any behavior or *words* that can be considered intolerant of leftist principles, especially homosexuality.

The Anti-Bully Agenda isn't about teaching the school yard bully to behave. The primary focus behind this campaign is for children to be taught to accept and embrace homosexuality. Just take a look at all of the groups who are behind the Anti-Bullying Agenda. Groups like The Gay, Lesbian and Straight Education Network (GLSEN) are pushing homosexuality to children as young as kindergarten. Notice how *straight* comes last in the name of their cartel. Their website is a sickening list of perversions they want your children to learn about, tolerate, and embrace. You don't have to get any further than their home page to see how they tie Anti-Bullying to Pro-Gayness.

While you are at work, your children are their captive audience. They convince you that they are looking out for your kids with an Anti-Bully Agenda on their web page, but they are trying to force homosexual obedience down the throats of your children. You're only supposed to be concerned about the bully part of the message. You aren't supposed to notice that right under the topic, "No Name-Calling Week is Jan. 18-22, 2016," is the announcement that GLSEN calls for LGBTQ-Inclusive Sex Ed.

LGBT has a Q now. Will it get an F or a D next? Does the Q in LGBTQ stand for *Queer*? Can we call them *queers* now? So even during "No Name-Calling Week," it's not *name calling* to call them *queers*, since they call themselves *queers*, right? Now let's see… what does queer mean? Let's see what Webster has to say[131].

Popularity: Top 20% of words

1. a : worthless[132], counterfeit[133] *<queer money>* *b* : questionable[134], suspicious[135]

2. a : differing in some odd way from what is usual or normal *b* *(1)* : eccentric[136], unconventional[137] *(2)* : mildly insane : touched[138] *c* : absorbed or interested to an extreme or unreasonable degree : obsessed[139] *d (1) often disparaging* : homosexual[140] *(2) sometimes offensive* : gay[141] 4b

3. : not quite well

queer·ish play \-ish\ *adjective*

queer·ly *adverb*

queer·ness *noun*

---

[131] http://www.merriam-webster.com/dictionary/Queer

[132] http://www.merriam-webster.com/dictionary/worthless

[133] http://www.merriam-webster.com/dictionary/counterfeit

[134] http://www.merriam-webster.com/dictionary/questionable

[135] http://www.merriam-webster.com/dictionary/suspicious

[136] http://www.merriam-webster.com/dictionary/eccentric

[137] http://www.merriam-webster.com/dictionary/unconventional

[138] http://www.merriam-webster.com/dictionary/touched

[139] http://www.merriam-webster.com/dictionary/obsessed

[140] http://www.merriam-webster.com/dictionary/homosexual

[141] http://www.merriam-webster.com/dictionary/gay

Hmmm, that's queer. Queerness, queerly appears queerish in the queerest sense of the word.

Anti-Bullying isn't about teaching little brats a lesson in manners. It's about feminizing boys and fostering more and more homosexuality by brow beating boyhood into submission. Most boys and girls recognize *queer* at an early age. To them it is unacceptable for someone to be odd or eccentric. They tend to pick on the children who show traits that aren't socially acceptable. It's not exactly meant to be nice and no one is advocating that children physically beat each other. But "No Name-Calling Week?" Much of the taunting that we have endured at one time or another in our lives, has strengthened us. We are better off as adults having suffered some pain as children. We understand that life isn't fair and that some people are more cruel than others and we gain the skills to deal with unfriendly situations both emotionally and intellectually. Look what happens when we shelter children from reality. Sheltered kids grow older, go to college, and then start demanding *safe spaces* from free speech if people say things they don't want to hear. It's infantile and repugnant. Sheltered kids grow no spines.

These days children are being suspended from schools for wearing shirts that support the constitutional *right* to keep and bear arms, but they are being taught that boys who self identify themselves as girls have the *right* to make real girls uncomfortable, by using the girls' bathroom and locker room showers. How have we come to this? If you as a parent, let your 17 year old Brony boy go to high school wearing a pink, My Little Pony t-shirt, then he deserves to be made fun of and it's your fault as his parent that he has to learn his lessons the hard way. You can act *queer* all you like, but you have no right to force the rest of us to embrace it, so prepare yourself for mockery if you do. It's the normal kids who are acting natural.

If one child actually bullies another, especially in a physical manner, then punish him or her. It's already a crime to assault someone. There is no need for any new laws. Liberals want to manufacture a new crime which effectively outlaws Christian family values. They are attempting to equate the intolerance of immoral filth with bullying. No one is really Pro-Bullying, but know what it is you're really signing your kids up for if you fall for this Anti-Bully Campaign. Liberals always hide a twisted, corrupt agenda beneath the guise of a compelling misnomer. We must stop capitulating to the intolerance of Christian family values and normality from *queers*.

THE OLD GUARD: BLIZZARD? WHAT BLIZZARD?

POSTED JANUARY 24, 2016

"My dedication to this sacred duty is total and whole-hearted" – First line of the Sentinel's Creed.

The 3rd Infantry Regiment[142], otherwise known as The Old Guard, was founded in 1784. It is the oldest active duty regiment in the U.S. Army. In honor of their bayonet charge in the 1847 battle of Cerro Gordo, they are the only Army regiment which is authorized to carry rifles with fixed bayonets in any parade.

With three active battalions, serving in various capacities in the U.S. Army, their best known role is to stand guard over the Tomb of the Unknown Soldier. Since they began standing guard of the tomb on April 6th, 1948, they haven't left it unguarded for one second. Old Guard soldiers have stood guard even through hurricanes.

Blizzard Jonas didn't even raise a concern for the honorable soldiers of The Old Guard. The Tomb of the Unknown Soldier remains guarded without pause.

Please take a moment out of your cozy day and thank The 3rd Infantry Regiment for their unflinching resolve and honorable service.

They can be found on Facebook[143].

---

[142] http://www.oldguard.mdw.army.mil/

[143] https://www.facebook.com/oldguard

JUSTICE SCALIA DEAD!

POSTED FEBUARY 13, 2016

Justice Antonin Scalia was found dead at the Cibolo Creek Ranch, where he was a guest. His death, at the age of 79, appears to be of natural causes. May he rest in peace. He was one of a scant few in Federal Government who still respected the U.S. Constitution.

With President Obama in office, this couldn't come at a worse time. During the Republican Primary race, many have been concerned with the notion that the next President will have to appoint new Supreme Court Justices. This is a subject that Ted Cruz supporters have been beating a drum about, but which supporters of all candidates are concerned with.

With almost a year left in office, it is very possible that Obama will be choosing the next Supreme Court Justice, but rather than replacing one liberal with another, as he did with Sotomayor and Kagan, he will be replacing the most Constitutionally Conservative Justice with a Constitution hating socialist.

There is hope. If the establishment Republicans in the Sen turn over a new leaf and decide to do what is right for America for a change, they can hold out on any confirmation to the Supreme Court until the next President is sworn in next January. The confirmation process for a Supreme Court Justice used to be very quick, but in recent years has taken an average of 60 days and up to 90 days. It can take longer if the Republican Party holds the line. It only takes a majority vote of the Senate, 51 votes, to confirm a Supreme Court Justice, unless other Senate rules are put into motion.

First, the Senate Judiciary Committee takes up the debate on the confirmation. They can delay their decision, but inevitably they vote on whether or not to send the nomination to a full Senate vote. If they do, they can give a recommendation as to whether or not the Senate should confirm the nomination.

Once the full Senate has the decision to make, they debate the nomination. The debate doesn't end until someone asks for a unanimous consent to end the debate and move to a vote. However, this is deceiving, because a unanimous consent isn't even required, because of Senate rules that say they can have a cloture motion to end the debate. It used to take 60 votes to end the debate with a cloture motion, but in 2013 the Senate changed the rules to require only 51 votes. Luckily they applied that change only to votes on legislation and not on Judicial nominations, so they currently still need 60 votes to end the debate and put the nomination to a full Senate vote. If that happens, that vote only takes 51 votes. Joe Biden breaks a tie.

If the Republicans have ever wanted to do anything right for America in their entire lives, this is the time. They must not allow a single nominee for Supreme Court Justice to be voted on in the Senate until after the next President is sworn into office. It is imperative that everyone let their Senators know that they are serving their very last term in office if they allow Barack Hussein to appoint another Supreme Court Justice.

Senate Republicans have already announced that they will not confirm another Obama appointment to the Supreme Court no matter who it is. Mitch McConnell says the next President should replace Scalia. Let's make sure we hold the Senate to this.

Questions have been asked as to whether or not Obama can use a Recess Appointment. Originally I read that the Senate reconvenes on Tuesday, but this was wrong. They are in fact in a week long recess, but this is really not a huge concern. Obama has already lost a similar case in the Supreme Court, in The National Labor Relations Board vs Noel Canning. The decision was that it's up to the Senate to say when they are in recess and the recess has to be longer than three days. McConnell can simply call a pro forma session with as few as one Senator showing up to work on legislation, no matter how minor the work. It was also decided that the temporary recess appointment lasts only until the end of the next Senate session, which would put it on about March 20th. So there is nothing to worry about as far as a recess appointment goes. This is in the hands of the Senate, not Obama.

May God Bless Antonin Scalia and his family. God Bless America!

FLINT'S LEADED WATER IS FLINT'S PROBLEM

POSTED MARCH 2, 2016

Flint, Michigan, do you have lead in your water? Maybe even a little Legionnaires disease? Are you looking for a Federal bailout to solve your problem? Well, tough. It's not my job to pay for your stupidity.

You people of Flint have continuously voted Democrat and watched as those Democrats destroyed everything about your city. Your property values have plummeted and your crime rate has risen. Now you get to make lead flavored Kool-Aid for your kids and you have no one to blame but yourselves. Lead-Aid! Oh-Yeaahh!

You don't get to keep voting democrat and then shaking me down to bail you out of the disaster that inevitably comes of it. When you vote Democrat, you get what you deserve when it backfires on you. I understand that Democrats always promise you freebies. Well, when you are too lazy to earn your own way through life and are content to live off of the scraps that others throw you, then you don't get to be choosy. You get the scraps whatever they may be, even if they include poison and disease.

The most effective way to learn a lesson is to learn it the hard way. You won't learn your lesson if smarter people who don't put themselves in your situation come to your rescue every time. To actually learn your lesson and have it really sink in, you need to actually suffer the consequences of your own decisions. That's what learning it the hard way is all about. If it takes lead poisoning for you to finally get it, then drink up. Pour yourselves another glass of delicious Lead-Aid. The only way for you to really fix your problems is to clean your own house. Vote out the Democrats who keep making promises and do nothing but keep you in a state of dependency, so they can continue making the same promises every election year.

It is unconstitutional for the Federal Government to spend *my* money to come bail you out, Flint. Maybe you can appeal your case to your State government. At least you have a Republican Governor, Rick Snyder. It looks like you're being just as stupid as ever though, because the people of Flint are calling for Rick Snyder to resign, yet not calling for your Democrat, Flint politicians to resign even though they caused your problem. It is amazing how blindly stupid people can be. Rick Snyder had nothing to do with your water.

It was the Flint City Council in March of 2013 who voted to stop buying water from Detroit and get it from Lake Huron instead. Rather than wait for the Lake Huron pipeline to be completed, sometime in 2016, they switched off the Detroit spigot in April, 2014, and took water from the Flint River. Your city council did this to save money. Well guess what? You saved money. It only cost you a little lead poisoning to do it. The people of Flint complained that the water smelled bad. Your mayor at the time, Mayor Dayne Walling, Democrat, said on June 12th, 2014, " "It's a quality, safe product. I think people are wasting their precious money buying bottled water."

Now if you don't like lead and Legionnaires in your water, fire your City Council, stop voting for Democrats, and go buy your own bottled water. I'm not buying it for you. I'm buying stock in bottled water companies and profiting from your stupidity. Thank you Flint!

DON'T LET MUSLIM ATTACK ON BRUSSELS BECOME A HO-HUMMER!

POSTED MARCH 23, 2016

Who didn't see this coming? Not the when or the where, but the "again." Over and over islam continues to murder in the name of their fake god, Allah. I have already shown that Allah is actually Satan.[144] Over and over we are told that islam is the religion of peace and that we don't have a problem with islam, so we must allow millions of them to invade Western countries and occupy our home towns. Muslims hate the West. They admit it and we don't listen. The closest anyone in the media will come to calling out islam as the problem is if they throw the word "radical" in front of it. There is nothing radical about a muslim murdering innocent people. It's time to face the music.

It's normal for a muslim to murder indiscriminately. It's normal for a muslim to kill infidels when the Koran says, "(Koran 2:191) And kill them wherever you find them, and turn them out from where they have turned you out. And Al-Fitnah [disbelief or unrest] is worse than killing... but if they desist, then lo! Allah is forgiving and merciful. And fight them until there is no more Fitnah [disbelief and worshipping of others along with Allah] and worship is for Allah alone."

Until there is no worship for anyone but Allah, **muslims** *will kill everyone else.* That is what they are commanded to do. The Koran says that fighting infidels is virtuous. It's Allah approved. It's Allah commanded. "(Koran 2:216) Fighting is prescribed for you, and ye dislike it. But it is possible that ye dislike a thing which is good for you, and that ye love a thing which is bad for you. But Allah knoweth, and ye know not." Anyone who thinks you can appease the violence by bringing more savages into your homeland is asking for their own life to be put at risk. Political correctness is not worth your life. It's time to start facing reality.

---

[144] See page 69 - Islam: The Religion of Peace

At least 34 people were killed in two attacks by muslims on innocent civilians in Brussels. 14 were killed in an air terminal at the check in desks and 20 at a Metro station. This goes to show how useless any government security is. They'll merely attack people before you enter security or while you are bottle-necked like sheep trying to get through security. Airport security has created easier targets for jihadists. It doesn't matter how much security is added. Those who want to kill large numbers of people can do it. The TSA is the most unconstitutional and dangerous agency we have ever set up in the United States and although it may have taken a while for savage muslims to figure this out, they caught on now.

While our government tries to convince Apple to give them back doors into our privacy, these muslims were way ahead of that idea. Law enforcement alleges that these terrorists used disposable phones for communications, perhaps never using a phone more than once. You can't track that.

ISIS claimed responsibility for the Brussels attacks, as if it matters which group of muslims screamed, "allahu akbar," before blowing people up. They're all muslims. They all have the same end game. Kill infidels. How do so many people act surprised every time this happens? People will lay flowers on the ground with signs that say "Je Suis Brussels." This doesn't even address the problem, let alone fix it. They will post things on social media for a week or two saying, "Pray for Brussels," or "I stand with Brussels." No you don't. You aren't standing for anything. You're going to make a statement for a little while, then move on as if nothing happened and in a few weeks start all over again in shock and amazement when muslims attack the next group of innocent people.

It's time to actually do something. Start in your home town and work your way up. Gather friends and family and show up at your next town hall or city council meeting. Put an absolute stop to any migration of so called muslim refugees into your city. Make yourselves heard loud and clear that you know who the enemy is and it's not blue haired old ladies going through airport security, it's muslims coming under the guise of refugees. It's muslim migration by and large that must stop. Muslim refugees aren't running from anyone, they are running to you. They have a plan. Wake up and recognize it, because they admit it. ISIS and other Islamic terrorist organizations do not hide their intentions. From your city, move on to your state and then to your Congressmen and Senators. Insist that new laws stop enemies without infringing on our rights. When we stand in line at airport security, terrorism has won. If four people would had been armed while flying on 9/11, there might have been a more heroic tale to tell of that day.

If you are in Europe, you are already doomed. You have done yourselves in and you will continue to see more and more of this before there is ever hope of it getting better. Europeans may have become far too politically correct to ever be able to recognize their enemy. In America we have a better chance of stopping a more massive migration numbers before it's too late, especially with elections upon us. It's not a migration, it's an invasion. Now is the time to make yourselves heard loud and clear!

Exercise your right to bear arms. Naysayers claim that guns are no good against bombs. Perhaps not if you are caught in the blast, but not every bomb works as intended and not every muslim kills using a bomb. Muslims have been shot dead in the act of attacking with knives, machetes, and guns. Muslims can't be shot dead if victims are unarmed. If you don't own a gun, go buy one. If you already own a gun, go buy another. Train to use your weapon defensively and with better accuracy. Training is never a bad thing and it's always fun for the whole family!

Become active to put a stop to islam coming to your home town. Don't let your town be the next one everyone is shocked to see victimized by muslim violence. If you put off acting for too long, people may no longer be shocked to see you as a victim. You may just end up as a ho-hummer.

CLIMATE CHANGE HOAX – A COMMIE PLOT

POSTED APRIL 21, 2016

Happy Earth Day! Right?

We're told that there are fun, exciting ways to celebrate Earth Day, such as planting a tree, recycling, turning off lights, or riding a bike! What we're not told is what Earth Day is really all about. It has nothing to do with the environment at all. That's a ruse to make you feel good about getting into lock step with those who want to control you while you pay them to control you.

The entire man made global warming hoax is all about gaining control over you, your property, and your wealth. We're told that there is a consensus in science that man made global warming is real and that we the people need to curtail our behavior and constrain our lives in order to make it all better. We're never given any honest reason to believe that global warming would even be a bad thing. That is a premise we must accept, because it sounds dire and we're shown pictures of polar bears floating on icebergs. Polar bears on icebergs look marooned, so of course global warming must be bad. We're not supposed to look back through history to all the times when the globe was warmer and the entire Earth and human race thrived because of it. I submit that global warming would be a fantastic thing and I will be the first to stake a gold mining claim in Antarctica when the ice melts!

There is plenty of information already out there about all of the proven benefits that global warming would have for mankind and the Earth in general. Thomas Gale Moore, a Senior Fellow at the Hoover Institution sums it up very well here: Why Global Warming Would be Good For you.[145]

In the 1970's we were warned of global cooling and an impending ice age! It sure sounded scary! Unfortunately, facts got in the way of this myth, so those who wanted to scare us into

---

[145] http://stanford.edu/%7Emoore/Boon_To_Man.html

submission had to change tactics. By the 1990's we were being warned about global warming, as if global cooling had never been mentioned. Warming sounds scary too! As with all propaganda, it was assumed we'd forget what we were told in the past and accept the current drum beat. Now, increasing availability of information that refutes global warming alarmism, the name of the crisis has changed to an all-encompassing explanation that covers any looming climate catastrophe. Instead of global cooling or warming, now we're just warned of generic Climate Change. Ooooh! Very scary! We're told that 97% of scientists agree and that the science is settled. No one can agree on whether the Earth is warming or cooling, but only 3% of scientists, who must be dolts, don't agree that the science is settled. Luckily there are people who question such preposterous claims, such as Andrew Montford, who completely debunks any notion of this 97% Consensus in his paper, "Fraud, Bias, and Public Relations – The 97% 'Consensus' and its Critics."[146] It is also noteworthy that 31,000 scientists have signed a petition disagreeing with the so called climate change consensus.

So, why are we fed all this garbage? If man made climate change is not real, why would so many people be so motivated to convince us that it is? Short answer: Your money. Long answer: Control over your life, your property, and your money. People in government want more control. They don't have the power to take control unless they can convince you to relinquish your liberty to them willingly. In small steps they want to ween you into a submissive state. It begins with making you feel good about yourself if you volunteer to save a little energy or separate recyclable materials from your trash to cut green house gases and do your part to save the planet. Because no one wants the planet to die! The next steps are to begin mandating that you do your part. Forced labor. In the United States, a clear violation of the 13th Amendment[147] to the U.S. Constitution. The masses look past this, because they have been dumbed down and don't know their rights. Those who have volunteered "to do their

---

[146] http://www.thegwpf.org/content/uploads/2014/09/Warming-consensus-and-it-critics1.pdf

[147] See page 253

part" find it justifiable and fair to force you to do your part too. If you don't, you'll end up paying fees, fines, and taxes. They don't even have to pass laws to create the fines. Congress has no such power enumerated in the Constitution anyway. So they let unconstitutional agencies such as the EPA do the legislation by creating regulations. The EPA then acts as the judiciary by finding you guilty of violating these regulations and charging you fines.

Why don't scientists who disagree give their evidence showing that the Climate Change models are wrong? Well, they do, but fear sells better than being told "all's well." Crisis makes headlines. The governments who want control over you and your money are far more willing to approve grants for studies that support their agenda. Let's face it, a scientist whose studies constantly show no results is less likely to receive grant money than the scientist who can predict doom and gloom that the government can extort the public over.

It's a vicious cycle. Those in government want to gain and maintain power. Power costs money. Buying votes with entitlements costs money. Paying for grants costs money. The only grants worth paying for are those which suggest that there is something to fear. Who better to get the money from than those they can't buy votes from, the productive members of society? With a combination of controlling the education system with the Department of Education and funding research that supports their propaganda, those in power can control what you know and how you react to it. What they want you to know is that we're doomed and how they want you to react to that is to fork over your money. They call stealing your money with fines, fees, carbon taxes, and even international taxes, "investment." Wording is important.

The tentacles of control they are weaving into our lives are too numerous to count, but can be found in all of the leftist agendas. From various taxes on your activities, to incentives for you to "go green." Incentives become mandates, as we see with the automobile and oil industries. Tax credits were given for buying electric cars. Limiting your movement is a major goal of those in power. What government really wants is to get you onto public transportation where your movement is more controlled and confined. Convincing you to buy vehicles that only have a 50 mile range is a big step in that direction. Subsidies were given to corn farmers to produce expensive ethanol. Neither electric cars nor ethanol save fuel. Your electric car's exhaust just comes out at the power plant instead of your tail pipe. Ethanol uses more fuel to produce than it produces and now has gone from an option to a mandate. David Pimentel, PhD, Professor Emeritus of Ecology and Evolutionary Biology at Cornell University concluded that the manufacture of ethanol uses 46% more fossil fuel than it produces. Yes, you have to burn approximately a gallon and a half of gasoline to produce a gallon of equivalent ethanol. No wonder the government has to subsidize it. It would never sell on the open market. No tree hugger wants to discuss how many toxins and pollutants they put into the environment with all of the discarded batteries. Mandated use of mercury filled compact fluorescent light bulbs rather than incandescent bulbs causes a similar environmental disaster. It's never about a cleaner environment. It's always about control.

Man made climate change is nothing but a hoax, perpetrated by those in power, to stay in power and increase their power. Their goal is nothing short of complete control over your lives. It is no coincidence that Earth Day began on April 22, 1970, Vladimir Lenin's 100th Birthday. Lenin is a hero of those who want to control people under leftist regimes. Of course, they deny this by claiming that Lenin was anti-environmentalist. This is a lie of course. The modern environmentalist movement didn't start until the 1960's, long after Lenin was dead. Lenin knew nothing of the environmentalist movement. Had he known how easily such a movement could be used to gain control over the masses, with their complete consent, Lenin would have embraced the hoax like modern communists do. The environmentalist movement has nothing to do with the environment. Environmentalists do more to destroy the environment than anyone else. It's about control. That's it.

If you kill an eagle or its egg, you're a felon! Windmills kill 10's of millions of birds and bats every year. Nothing is more dangerous to an eagle than a tree hugger and their wind farm. No one even knows how many are actually killed, because the corpses can't even all be found and laws prevent you from counting them all if you do find them. If you actually care about the Earth and the environment then you will be horrified by the statistics on bird deaths here at Save the Eagles International.[148]

It's time to stand up against the climate change commies. If you feel like planting a tree, plant one. If you don't, don't! Maybe you like riding bikes. Great! Ride one. But don't fool yourself into thinking you're saving the planet by doing so. This Earth Day, celebrate by turning your air conditioner on full blast, so you can light up your fire place and sit by the cozy fire! Turn on all your lights and take an extra long shower. Fill your recycle bin with coffee grounds and dirty diapers! You pay your city to pick up and sort the garbage. They don't pay you to sort it. Enjoy your life today and every day!

---

[148] http://savetheeaglesinternational.org/new/us-windfarms-kill-10-20-times-more-than-previously-thought.html

PERVERTS HAVE NO RIGHT TO CHOOSE BATHROOMS!

POSTED MAY 14, 2016

The push for normal people to accept and embrace transsexual deviancy has gone completely insane! A few towns in North Carolina passed laws trying to force the vast majority of people to bend to the twisted, sick will of a super minority of trannies who want to share bathrooms with your children. The state legislature put a halt to that madness and liberals went nuts. It's as if drag queens always had the right to share a bathroom with your 4 year old daughter and evil Christians just stole that God given right away from them!

Now we have Obama giving decrees to all schools in America, ordering them to allow people to use the bathroom of their choice. Our country has officially gone mad! The President of the United States has no such power. The Constitution enumerates presidential powers in Article 2[149] and handing down decrees or executive orders to the American People is not there. Determining where people can urinate is also not a federally enumerated power.

The Decree Obama issued is long winded and tyrannical. Obama says, *"Every child deserves to attend school in a safe, supportive environment that allows them to thrive and grow."* Of course this only means sexually deviant children with deplorable, liberal parents, not Christian children. They deserve no support. Support for the religious freedom of Christians is banned from school. Obama goes on by saying, *"The guidance explains that when students or their parents, as appropriate, notify a school that a student is transgender, the school **must** treat the student consistent with the student's gender identity."* Must? Who is Obama to tell anyone what they must do? Obama is not a king. The only thing anyone must do is ignore the tyrant. Visit the website for

---

[149] See page 239

the full decree issued by Obama via the Department of Justice: Obama Tranny Decree.[150]

The Family Leader web site[151] did a wonderful job of putting bullet points to some of mandates Obama is unilaterally demanding of our schools. Please visit their site to help them organize a response!

- Dictates that boys who self-identify as female be allowed to use girls' locker rooms and **shower facilities**, and vice versa.

- Specifically states that making a gender-neutral, single-stall bathroom available to transgender students is **insufficient**. If a girls' bathroom or locker room exists, boys and men who identify as female must be allowed entry, and vice versa.

- Dictates that students must be allowed to play the **sport** of the gender they self-identify.

- Specifically states that a student may self-identify his or her gender to the school **without parental permission** or knowledge.

- Forbids any medical requirements as a prerequisite of new gender identity.

- Dictates that on **school field trips**, boys who self-identify as female must be allowed to sleep in the same hotel rooms as female students, and vice versa. Providing a private hotel room for a transgender student is not allowed unless all students are lodged in private rooms.

The Founding Fathers did not enumerate any power to the federal government to control who we associate with. The Civil Rights Act of 1964 was completely unconstitutional. The people were lulled into giving up rights under the guise of civility, because

[150] https://www.justice.gov/opa/pr/us-departments-justice-and-education-release-joint-guidance-help-schools-ensure-civil-rights

[151] http://www.thefamilyleader.com/obamas-transgender-bathroom-mandate-is-worse-than-you-think/

racism was seen as cruel. In the name of fairness, the Constitution was ignored and Congress passed the Civil Rights Act, which affected the entire country to address the actions of people in a few towns. The premise behind the Civil Rights Act wasn't necessarily a bad one. The point is that it wasn't the Federal Government's business. Controlling our behavior is not the role of the Federal Government. The 10th Amendment[152] leaves these powers to the States. If you don't like how you are treated in your state, you can vote with your feet by moving to another state. For the Civil Rights Act to have been legitimate, it would have to have been an Amendment to the Constitution, ratified by 75% of the states. Violating the Constitution to legislate it in Congress, said one thing: it didn't have enough support to be legitimately ratified as a Constitutional Amendment.

Does anyone believe that without The Civil Rights Act, anyone could open a business today and ban black people or give them a designated seating area and still stay in business? If they did, would it really hurt anyone? We don't have to patronize any business we don't agree with. We can always go somewhere else or even open our own business. Congress addressed a temporary and localized problem with an overarching law that has caused far more problems than it ever solved. We are not one country with one set of rules, problems, and economic situations, as most countries are. We are 50 states with hundreds of cultures and this is why most legislation of domestic laws was left to states and localities.

The Civil Rights Act was intended to mandate racial fairness. Now it's intent is being twisted in the attempt to include any form of behavior that the vast majority of Americans are uncomfortable with. The Civil Rights Act is being used to compel immorality. The left uses the it to force Christian bakers to bake gay wedding cakes against their religious beliefs, even though homosexuals are not protected by the act. Now we're told that we've been guilty all along of violating the rights of perverts by keeping men out of the girls bathroom, so we need to fix it!

---

[152] See page 251

If you own a business and you want to allow bathroom choice to perverts or spend your own money to build a third bathroom just for degenerates, then you are free to do so. Any government mandate on a business to accommodate behavior the owner and customers find abhorrent, is a violation of the rights of normal people. Mandates such as these coming from a federal level are completely unconstitutional, more so if it is by Presidential decree.

President Obama has threatened to revoke federal funding from schools that don't comply with his decree. Great! This federal funding is unconstitutional. Finally we have some motivation to reject it! States should refuse the funding and completely opt out of Department of Education control. There is no need for the federal funding. The carrot the federal government dangles is poisoned. Federal funding doesn't make up for the harm caused by Department of Education regulations and the liberal curriculum forced on our children. Our states and local communities are much better suited to control our school systems.

Religion, which is constitutionally protected, has been banned from our schools. Children wearing clothing that celebrates constitutional rights like the 2nd Amendment[153] or showing support for military heroes, have been sent home to change clothes. We have seen growing intolerance from liberals for anything patriotic and American being taught or displayed in our public schools. If anything should be banned in our schools it is transvestitism and transgenderism. There is no reason that our children should be subjected to this filth when we are paying for them to learn. The 99% of children who are normal, don't need their education disrupted by the abnormal who are immoral. The Anti-Bully Agenda[154] is designed to force LGBT tolerance. The last place children should have their expectation of normalcy and privacy violated is in the bathroom and locker room of their schools.

Shame on Barack Hussein Obama! He has no right to be involved with this. This unconstitutional blackmail of public schools by decree, which forces privacy violations on your children, is

---

[153] See page 250

[154] See page 193 - The Anti-Bully Campaign is the Bully

grounds for immediate impeachment. States need to refuse to acknowledge Obama or better yet, voice stalwart refusal to obey and public condemnation of him. Some states are getting tired of his abuse of power.

Texas Lt. Governor Dan Patrick said, *"Obama can keep his 30 pieces of silver."* Kentucky Governor Matt Bevin said, *"It is difficult to imagine a more absurd federal overreach into a local issue. Under the Tenth Amendment to the United States Constitution, the federal government has no authority to interfere in local school districts' bathroom policies."*

Every state should follow the examples of Texas and Kentucky. We don't have to tolerate perverted behavior pushed in our faces anymore. It's time for states to start outlawing perversion again.

TIME TO SHUT DOWN THE TSA!

POSTED MAY 17, 2016

Everyone is complaining about the long lines and missed flights that are being caused by the TSA (Transportation Security Administration), but no one is mentioning the root issue. The TSA is an unconstitutional agency. The TSA creates a bigger risk to our lives and prevents nothing.

When you go through the TSA check point, what you leave behind are your 1st Amendment, 2nd Amendment, 4th Amendment, 5th Amendment, and 10th Amendment rights[155], just to name a few. The Federal Government has no enumerated authority to create an agency like the TSA in the first place. The powers listed that Congress can legislate on, in Article 1, Section 8[156] of the Constitution, do not include policing the people, providing security for travel, or violating our rights for any reason. Let's examine each right they violate and how they do it.

When it comes to the 1st Amendment, it is the most minor of the violations of your rights, but a violation nonetheless. It will become obvious to you that you've lost the right to free speech if you crack a joke about a bomb in the TSA line. Congress can make no law abridging the freedom of speech. The TSA can't make any laws. The TSA is an agency that Congress created though unconstitutional legislation. Congress is not allowed to create agencies that wield Congressional powers let alone agencies that wield powers Congress doesn't have. Almost every federal agency is unconstitutional in this way. They effectively legislate by regulation and then act as the judiciary by policing and judging you on the spot.

Your 2nd Amendment right to bear arms is obviously violated when you pass through a TSA checkpoint. The 2nd Amendment doesn't say, *"the right of the people to keep and bear arms, shall not be infringed unless you travel."* No level of government has authority to

---

[155] See pages 249-251

[156] See page 237

infringe upon your right to keep and bear arms for any reason. Had at least four passengers been exercising their 2nd Amendment rights on 9/11/2001, the Twin Towers may still be standing and 3000 people may still be alive.

Liberals and ill informed people claim that being on a plane is a good reason to revoke your 2nd amendment rights for two reasons. Firstly, what if someone goes crazy and starts shooting everyone? Well, what if someone goes crazy and starts shooting everyone in a theater? What if someone goes crazy and starts shooting everyone in a Walmart? Answer: Shoot back. Being in a plane doesn't change anything. Secondly, they claim that if you shoot a hole in the fuselage of an airplane, it will depressurize and everyone will die. This is scientifically impossible as shown on Myth Busters. The pumps which pressurize the plane more than compensate for pressure lost through tiny bullet holes. Sure, air goes out the holes, but at a relatively small rate compared with the size of the cabin. Conduct your own experiment. Shake a 2 liter soda bottle. Poke it with a pin. Does it explode? No. It sprays out a thin jet of soda and depressurizes at a very slow rate. The answer to terrorism isn't to disarm ourselves, it is to arm ourselves better.

Government shouldn't be disarming us for any reason, especially to travel domestically. If you are traveling internationally, it's a different story and should depend on foreign agents or private companies to screen you. When you enter the gate to board a plane to a different country, you're crossing jurisdictional boundaries. The same is true when entering the gate in a foreign airport to travel back to the United States. Domestic travelers should never face a government agent for any reason, let alone to violate your 2nd Amendment rights.

When the TSA agents force you to show your ID and travel documents, you have just lost your 4th Amendment rights. The government has no warrant with your name on it, and no probable cause. Ask the TSA agent for a warrant and see what happens. You are treated as if you are a Jew in NAZI Germany and must show your papers. Keeping this from happening is precisely why the 4th Amendment was ratified. No one in government has any reason to know who you are, where you are going, or why you are going there. They have no right to X-Ray you, search you, frisk you, or seize your property. The 4th Amendment says that your right to be secure in your persons, houses, papers, and effects against unreasonable searches and seizures, shall NOT be violated, and no Warrants shall issue, but upon probable cause supported by Oath or affirmation and particularly describing the **place** to be searched, and the **persons** or **things** to be seized. It doesn't say, *"Federal government has a right to set up agencies with blanket search and seizure power if you travel."* We the People of the United States have been so dumbed down that we allow this without questioning the Constitutionality of it. We complain when the lines are too long, but don't seem to care what the line is for. We didn't need the TSA for over 200 years and we don't need them now.

If you have been through a TSA check point, then you are probably familiar with being questioned about things that are not the government's business. This is a violation of your 5th Amendment rights. You are being made a witness against yourself and you aren't even charged with a crime. They want to know where you are going, why you are going, and even if you packed your own bags. They have a lot more questions when you are traveling back to the United States from a foreign country when you are at the boarding gate. You are considered to be back in U.S. jurisdiction to some degree. At that point in a foreign airport where you are back under American jurisdiction, once they see your passport and verify that you are American, that should end all future discussion and you should be on your way. You have the right not to incriminate yourself, whether you're guilty of something or not. When you go through the TSA checkpoint, try pleading the 5th and see what happens. It is your right!

One other way that your 5th Amendment rights are violated at the TSA checkpoint is that you are never compensated when they steal your property. The 5th Amendment is clear that private property shall not be taken for public use without just compensation. It doesn't matter if that private property is a pocket knife or a bottle of water and the public use is to fill up a garbage can.

The 10th Amendment says that the powers not delegated to the United States by the Constitution, nor prohibited by it to the States, are reserved to the States respectively, or to the people. What does this mean at the TSA check point? Not a single power the TSA wields is delegated to the United States by the Constitution. Not violation of freedom of speech, infringing on the right to bear arms, searching you, seizing your property, or forcing you incriminate yourself. Every moment of every working day for every TSA agent, they are in direct violation of the Constitution, since not one thing they do is a power delegated to them by the Constitution. In fact, the rights they violate *are* delegated to *you* by the Constitution.

What should really concern you about the TSA, just as much as your constitutional rights being violated, is the fact that they put your life in danger. It's not just that they don't allow you to defend yourself by disarming you. Unlike the past, when you could see your family off at the gate in airports and people could wander freely throughout, now we have TSA check points creating bottlenecks of soft targets packed in like sardines. Several hundred people, packed in as tightly as possible, not in a long straight line, but in a winding, back and forth line, designed to get as many people into as small a space as possible. When it comes to mass casualties, there is no target for a terrorist that is quite as easy to take advantage of as the TSA line. Face it, you're corralled into a tight space with several hundred people before the checkpoint. No one you are standing with has been checked yet. The muslim in front of you in line could have *anything* under his jacket. You don't know and neither does the TSA. Ask the people of Brussels, Belgium[157] how well airport security protects people in airports.

We need to demand the TSA be shut down! Not because the lines are long. Because the lines exist. The TSA is unconstitutional!

---

[157] See page 202 - Don't Let Muslim Attack On Brussels Become a Ho Hummer

UCLA GUN FREE ZONE FAILS!

POSTED JUNE 2, 2016

LAPD says UCLA Campus is now safe! The Gun Free Zone sign is hung back up! The wind must have knocked it down.

After a murder/suicide on the campus while it apparently wasn't safe, the LAPD showed up in a massive show of force to put all of the innocent Americans on their knees with their hands up, so they could be frisked. Once it was determined that none of these Americans had the means to protect themselves by exercising their 2nd Amendment[158] rights, LAPD Chief Beck said, "The campus is now safe. There are no suspects outstanding and no continuing threat to the UCLA campus " Really? What is making it safe? The Gun Free Zone sign?

Reports were that three gun shots were heard. Not much has been released about the crime scene, but it appears as though a student murdered a professor and then committed suicide. A suicide note was left, but has not been released to the public.

Not letting the opportunity for a school shooting to go to waste, UCLA was immediately swamped with media and what appeared to be 100s of police in SWAT gear. No official count of how many police were there is readily available. Barricades were created out of the Fire Trucks from 11 Fire Companies. 17 Ambulances were on the scene. Even the FBI and ATF made their unconstitutional appearances. Not only do these agencies violate the Constitution by existing, they also ignored what little jurisdiction Congress illegally gave them. Federal agencies have no business showing up to police anyone, not even in a murder case.

For two hours police swept the school, building by building. First an initial sweep followed by a secondary sweep. Finally, after violating the 2nd and 4th Amendment[159] rights of the staff and

---

[158] See page 250

[159] See page 250

students by detaining them on their knees and frisking them, they had to call off the search for additional suspects.

For the most part, police are great people and do a great job. It's when elected officials forget what that job is and create a police state that things go bad. It's not the job of police to replace our personal right and responsibility to protect ourselves. No crime was stopped at UCLA today. The people of Los Angeles, especially in the Gun Free Zone of The University of California, Los Angeles (UCLA) were not protected. UCLA is a Gun Free Zone, so wasn't everyone supposed to be safe? LAPD Chief Beck says everyone is safe again now. How well did that work out for the two who are dead?

You can never count on the police to keep you safe. Keep yourself safe. If you replace your right to bear arms with a massive police state that illegally frisks and searches innocent people after a crime is already committed, then you're not safe. Protect yourself and let the police do what they do best, catch bad guys that are on the run. The police didn't exactly fail today. No one paid them to prevent murder/suicides. They did what police are supposed to do, even if they did so in a massive, costly spectacle. They showed up after a crime and drew chalk lines. What failed today was yet another Gun Free Zone.

Do yourself and your family a favor. Go gun shopping. Spend some time at a range learning to use your guns proficiently. Take self-defense classes. It's fun for the whole family!

UPDATED 3 JUNE 2016:

The name of the professor who was murdered has been released along with a statement from his family via the UCLA Newsroom[160].

The identity of the shooter has also been released. The shooter was named Mainak Sarkar and not surprisingly, was a muslim. This Everipedia social media image was grabbed by Pardes Seleh[161] before

---

[160] https://twitter.com/UCLAnewsroom/status/738524574560591872

[161]

https://twitter.com/PardesSeleh/status/738394854443515908/photo/1

his religion was changed to Hindu on the Everipedia. Why are they changing a muslim's religion on his social media page after he murdered someone and committed suicide?

UPDATED 4 JUNE 2016:

Pardes Seleh and others have since reported that Mainak Sarkar's religion is unknown, because it was edited on Everipedia at least once. No one appears to be coming forward to clear it up one way or the other.

MUSLIM MURDERS 50 IN GUN FREE, GAY CLUB.

POSTED JUNE 13, 2016

How was muslim, Omar Saddiqui Mateen able to slaughter 50+ people in a mass shooting? Easy, choose a gun free zone that is packed full of unarmed people. Pulse Night Club was a gun free zone by unconstitutional Florida State Law[162]. How could he be sure there would be no one disobeying this law to shoot back? Choose a club full of liberals. How could he possibly know the club would be full of unarmed, gun hating liberals? Choose a gay club. It wasn't rocket science that lead Mateen away from choosing a biker bar to shoot up.

It seems logical that liberals and especially the homosexuals among them face a conundrum. They have openly supported islam while simultaneously waging war against Christianity for years now. The more violent muslims get, the more people they murder, the more vehemently liberals and gays support them, even so far as pushing to import more and more of them into the United States at tax payer expense. So who do liberals side with after Mateen shot up the Pulse Night Club in Orlando, Florida? Gays or muslims?

This isn't a complicated issue for liberals. They will continue to support both. They will most certainly claim that islam had nothing to do with Mateen's attack, even though he pledged allegiance to ISIS. We'll be reading media stories about him being mentally ill or some other excuses will be made, but islam won't be blamed. Without any doubt, guns will be blamed and we'll see more calls from liberals and the LGBT community for gun control.

Omar Saddiqui Mateen was a security agent for G4S Secure Solutions. You see them all of the time in airports, allegedly protecting us from all of the Omar Saddiqui Mateens. He was even background checked several times and interviewed by the FBI on

---

[162] http://www.ammoland.com/2016/06/florida-pulse-gay-bar-mass-shooting-was-in-a-gun-free-zone/#axzz4BRBeuhR5

undisclosed suspicions. We didn't need security in airports before our rights weren't illegally stripped from us.

50 people are dead now and there are two major lessons to be learned from this. First, islam is evil. There is no excuse for it. The Koran demands muslims act just as Mateen did and kill infidels, those of us who aren't muslim. There are no crowds of muslims condemning Mateen's actions. It's time to crack down on islam. It's not a legitimate religion. If the muslim cult were started today with its same teachings and actions, it would be put down, as other religious startups have been, whether it was legitimate to put them down or not, such as The Branch Davidians in Waco, Texas. Even if islam is considered a religion, it is not protected by the 1st Amendment[163] from States. States could ban it, even if Congress cannot. Don't take my word for it, read the 1st Amendment. See if it says "States shall make no law respecting an establishment of religion." It does not.

The 2nd lesson to be taken from this massacre is to arm yourself. Don't be another statistic who can't shoot back if a muslim starts shooting up a place you happen to be. If you don't already own a gun, now is the time to buy one. Practice with it. Get to know your gun well and carry it with you. Take some basic self defense classes and make it a family affair! Finally, get your unconstitutional gun control laws repealed! No state has the authority to infringe on your Right to Bear Arms. A lot of people who were at the Pulse Night Club probably wish they had broken the law and carried a gun when Mateen showed up.

UPDATED 14 JUNE 2016:

After the FBI interviewed the wife of Mateen, Noor ZahiSalmon, from Uzbekistan, it appears she was aware of Mateen's plans and even participated by taking him to scout out locations for his attack. Under conspiracy laws this could make her legally just as guilty as Mateen and face the death penalty. Mateen had regularly visited the Pulse Night Club and other gay clubs and was reportedly gay himself.

---

[163] See page 249

It is very common in the muslim culture to sexually abuse boys, so that they grow up confused sexually. Homosexuality is accepted among young men among muslims, but then condemned later in life after marriage, adding to the psychological confusion. Add muslim preaching of hatred and calls for the murder of homosexuals, and muslims like Mateen are ticking time bombs. If this sounds confusing, that's the point. There is nothing consistent in islam other than hate for infidels.

Don't fall for the false premise being bandied about that Mateen, his dad, or his wife should have been banned from buying guns because of being on terrorist watch lists. This is the slippery slope liberals want us to fall for and slide down. We can't punish people for being suspicious. We can't create a 2nd class citizen that doesn't have rights. Liberals want to turn this into an anti-gun crusade. No law will prevent someone from getting a gun who wishes to use it in a criminal act. Laws only affect the law abiding. All gun control laws are unconstitutional. No new laws are needed. Americans are tired of more and more laws infringing on our rights. We need to address the source of the problem, allowing the enemy into our country. The Obama Administration and Congress are spending billions in taxpayer dollars to import more and put them in publicly funded housing in your neighborhood!

A crime has to be committed before you can be charged. No fly lists are unconstitutional, because they violate 5th Amendment[164] due process. A terrorist watch list is fine. Watch them. Better yet, don't let muslims in the country in the first place. There is no benefit to the United States for allowing them in.

Correction: Mateen murdered 49. The number 50 that was reported by the media includes his own death.

---

[164] See page 250

TRUMP MUST UNITE THE RIGHT, NOT ATTACK RIGHTS!

POSTED JUNE 16, 2016

Donald Trump is the GOP nominee in the 2016 Presidential election. It would be disastrous for Hillary to move back into the White House. Yet as of today, Hillary Clinton has taken a double digit lead over Donald Trump in a new Bloomberg Poll[165]. Complain about the source of the poll all you want, it still doesn't change the fact that Donald Trump will have a very hard time winning against Hillary. This election will not be a walk in the park for him.

Many conservatives, especially those who are part of the #NeverTrump movement, which I am not, really want to see something from Donald Trump that gives us a good reason to jump on board the proverbial Trump Train. We want to actually support him in the general election rather than hold our nose to vote for the lesser of two evils or simply stay home. Day after day, we look for something... anything. Then he goes and says something like, "No Fly, No Buy," meaning that if you are on the No Fly List, you can't buy a gun. This is patently absurd considering that anyone with evil intent can buy a gun faster than they can get a pizza delivered. No law will change that.

For all of you who are Trump supporters, this message goes to you and is not intended as something to be taken negatively. This is an important, maybe slightly bitter reality pill that you need to swallow. You really need to have conservatives and others on the right who oppose Trump on your side if you expect Trump to win the election. You have to stop the infighting and start working toward getting those you taunted for months, to show up to the polls and pull the lever for Donald Trump. You can't do that if you continue to allow your candidate to stick his foot in his mouth. I am

---

[165] http://insider.foxnews.com/2016/06/15/hillary-clinton-opens-double-digit-lead-trump-new-poll

not talking about bad mouthing the media or bashing illegals, feminists and muslims. He should double down on that.

Trump can't get away with claims of being pro 2nd Amendment[166] if he comes out and says that he is willing to violate the rights of Americans on the sole basis of their being added to a list. The No Fly List is a violation of 5th Amendment[167] right of due process. People are barred from flying simply because they have the same name as someone who is under suspicion. Being under suspicion is never grounds for sentencing. You can't be jailed for being suspicious. You can't have rights taken for being suspicious. The No Fly List doesn't even require you to be suspicious, just have the wrong name.

The Federal Government has no authority to determine who can travel or where they travel to domestically. Article 1 Section 8[168] of the Constitution does not enumerate such a power, so this violates the 10th Amendment[169]. If it can't be legislated by Congress, The TSA, an unconstitutional agency[170], certainly can't wield that power. Federal authority regarding travel stops at the U.S. border. A No Fly List for foreigners entering our country is fine and a great idea. We don't have to allow anyone entry to the United States. The government has no such authority over Americans, especially when used as a stepping stone to infringe on other rights. If someone is actually involved with Islamic terrorism groups then they should be on the Mandatory Fly List and sent back where they belong or thrown in prison if they are found guilty of a crime.

It is up to you Trump supporters to advise Donald Trump to get an adviser! Yes, he has plenty of advisers, but he is missing one. He needs a Constitutional Adviser. Someone needs to explain to Trump

---

[166] See page 250

[167] See page 250

[168] See page 237

[169] See page 251

[170] See page 215 – Time to Shut Down TSA!

what he can't say if he wants to unite the right. He earns no credible claim to being pro 2nd Amendment if he goes out there and proposes stripping 2nd Amendment rights from certain groups of his choosing. Rein in your guy, Trump supporters. You have to. This isn't about sticking it to Cruz supporters any longer, it's about winning them over. You can't do that if Trump doesn't show knowledge of and respect for the Constitution. True knowledge and respect, not just saying, "believe me." Supporting Trump by repeating that "Trump is Right" can't work if Trump is wrong. Help him! I understand that the divisiveness goes both ways, but I am only appealing to Trump supporters here. Please help others want to join you.

We have a justice system in America which requires that innocence is assumed until guilt is proven in a court of law. Until such time as your guilt is proven, you enjoy every right that all Americans do. It doesn't matter who you are. That's what American liberty is founded on. That's what true "equal rights" means. Due process is an absolute, unalienable, God given right. Bearing arms is an absolute, unalienable, God given right. Trump supporters, it doesn't matter how you do it. Do it in private if you like. But straighten out your guy if you want him to be ***our*** guy. Do you want to see Hillary win in November and have the #NeverTrump crowd saying, "I told you so?" It's up to Trump's supporters to keep that from happening.

If Trump is who we have nominated, then he must win and can only do so if the right is united. Please don't let Hillary choose Scalia's replacement, because we don't want to help our nominee improve a little!

GAYS ARM UP! RIGHTFULLY SO!

POSTED JUNE 17, 2016

This is an open letter to the entire gay community from someone with whom you don't see eye to eye on with everything. I am as conservative as someone can get. As a devout Christian myself, we will probably never see eye to eye on everything, but I am setting that aside for something far more important: your safety and your lives. Never let our disagreement on a single issue be confused with hatred, because I certainly don't hate people over their sexual preference.

In light of the tragic event at the Pulse Night Club in Orlando, Florida where 49 Americans were viciously murdered in an act of Muslim Jihad, a reality presented itself to the gay community. **Muslims hate you!** This isn't a radical Islamic idea, this is written in the Koran. In muslim countries, gays are executed by hanging and being thrown from the rooftops of tall buildings. This is normal islam, not radical.

The left has tried to turn this tragedy into another one of their grave dancing, propaganda campaigns against guns. However, the gay community, who normally associate with the left, came to the intelligent conclusion that no one is going to protect them, so they must protect themselves. Self reliance is wonderful, but you have to discover you need it on your own. The homosexual community just made this discovery on its own! Gun sales spiked, as normally happens after a mass shooting or terrorist attack, but the difference this time, according to news reports and gun shop owners, is that the LGBT community is buying up all the guns!

I want to take this opportunity to welcome the gay community into the fold of freedom loving patriots, who deserve the right to keep and bear arms like anyone else. We on the right actually care about your lives and safety and aren't using this opportunity to advance a political agenda. Your rights aren't a political agenda. Your safety is not a political agenda. These are your birthright, but come with the responsibility for you to protect them. The leftist political agenda aims to revoke these rights at the risk of your lives. While they blame guns, they import more muslim terrorists from

Syria by the 100's of thousands. The gun control lobbyists spend millions trying to disarm Americans, because a defenseless citizen isn't a citizen at all, he or she is a subject. Straight, bi, gay, whatever, we are all Americans and our lives are valuable. Not one person from the gun control lobby will ever be there to save your life from a nut job with murder on his mind. Not one gun control law they propose will ever keep nut jobs from getting guns. These laws only prevent you from protecting yourself, because only law abiding citizens follow the law.

Many in the homosexual community may have never taken the time to learn about your right to bear arms, because other issues were more important to you at the time. I am here to tell you that this is a topic that you will find millions of conservatives who are willing and eager to help you with. Please begin by reading my article on the 2nd Amendment.[171] From there, join discussions online where patriots defend our rights. On Twitter, if you visit the hashtag #GunSense[172] you will be welcomed with open arms by thousands of patriotic conservatives you have been conditioned into believing hate you. You will soon discover that this has been a lie. Your interest in your right to bear arms and protect yourself has introduced you to the most welcoming group of people you can ever meet.

American Patriots care about your freedom, your liberty, and your life. We are always willing to offer advice. Maybe you want to learn more about your rights. This isn't a subject taught very well in schools any longer, so we are forced to do our own research. Perhaps you want advice on the type of gun to buy for different reasons. There are as many types and styles of guns are there are people who want one and yes, they do come in pink!

Make buying a gun and learning to use it your number one priority! Do not be afraid that you will look stupid if you ask questions at a gun store! I have owned a gun my entire life and still ask questions every time I buy a new gun or different ammunition. You can never ask too many questions. People who work in gun stores are thrilled to answer them. Giving advice on firearms is what

---

[171] See page 139 – The 2nd Amendment: Shall Not Be Infringed!

[172] https://twitter.com/search?q=%23GunSense&src=typd

they love to do! You do not want to walk out of a gun store with a new firearm without knowing everything you can about it. **Safety always comes first!** It's much safer to know everything about your gun. Getting advice will also help you choose the gun that is best for you! You will never look stupid for asking questions. You'll look stupid if you don't.

Practice! When you buy a gun, find out where you can go shoot it. Visit a range and practice! Try to bring a friend who knows guns well or ask the people working at the range for assistance if you are new to shooting. They are there to help! It's better to ask for help than to hurt yourself! Once you learn, you will want to pass on your knowledge to others. There are many courses available that are both fun and educational. Some are offered through the NRA and some from other organizations or from private instructors. Whether you want to learn to be a better marksman or how to confidently and safely use your gun in self defense, there is a course for you and your family!

There are many gun clubs you can join as well including one that has opened dozens of new chapters since the Orlando shooting, called The Pink Pistols[173], a gay and lesbian gun club.

Don't allow the left wing to use you as pawns any longer! They pander to a single issue that you care about in order to get your vote. The right may disagree with gays on a single issue, but will always defend your rights to life, liberty and pursuit of happiness. So to all of the homosexual community, even if you are just dipping your toe into the water of the Pool of Liberty, the water is warm and you are welcome to jump into the deep end at any time! We have lifeguards! We support you where it really counts.

---

[173] http://www.pinkpistols.org/

ADDENDUM

THE U.S. CONSTITUTION, BILL OF RIGHTS AND OTHER CONSTITUTIONAL AMENDMENTS

The Constitution of the United States

SEVEN ARTICLES

We the People of the United States, in Order to form a more perfect Union, establish Justice, insure domestic Tranquility, provide for the common defence, promote the general Welfare, and secure the Blessings of Liberty to ourselves and our Posterity, do ordain and establish this Constitution for the United States of America.

ARTICLE I.

Section. 1.

All legislative Powers herein granted shall be vested in a Congress of the United States, which shall consist of a Senate and House of Representatives.

Section. 2.

The House of Representatives shall be composed of Members chosen every second Year by the People of the several States, and the Electors in each State shall have the Qualifications requisite for Electors of the most numerous Branch of the State Legislature.

No Person shall be a Representative who shall not have attained to the Age of twenty five Years, and been seven Years a Citizen of the United States, and who shall not, when elected, be an Inhabitant of that State in which he shall be chosen.

Representatives and direct Taxes shall be apportioned among the several States which may be included within this Union, according to their respective Numbers, which shall be determined by adding to the whole Number of free Persons, including those bound to Service for a Term of Years, and excluding Indians not taxed, three fifths of all other Persons. The actual Enumeration shall be made within three Years after the first Meeting of the Congress of the United States, and within every subsequent Term of ten Years, in such Manner as they shall by Law direct. The Number of Representatives shall not exceed one for every thirty Thousand, but each State shall have at Least one Representative; and until such enumeration shall be made, the State of New Hampshire shall be entitled to chuse three, Massachusetts eight, Rhode-Island and Providence Plantations one, Connecticut five, New-York six, New Jersey four, Pennsylvania eight, Delaware one, Maryland six, Virginia ten, North Carolina five, South Carolina five, and Georgia three.

When vacancies happen in the Representation from any State, the Executive Authority thereof shall issue Writs of Election to fill such Vacancies.

The House of Representatives shall chuse their Speaker and other Officers; and shall have the sole Power of Impeachment.

Section. 3.

The Senate of the United States shall be composed of two Senators from each State, chosen by the Legislature thereof, for six Years; and each Senator shall have one Vote.

Immediately after they shall be assembled in Consequence of the first Election, they shall be divided as equally as may be into three Classes. The Seats of the Senators of the first Class shall be vacated at the Expiration of the second Year, of the second Class at the Expiration of the fourth Year, and of the third Class at the Expiration of the sixth Year, so that one third may be chosen every second Year; and if Vacancies happen by Resignation, or otherwise, during the Recess of the Legislature of any State, the Executive thereof may make temporary Appointments until the next Meeting of the Legislature, which shall then fill such Vacancies.

No Person shall be a Senator who shall not have attained to the Age of thirty Years, and been nine Years a Citizen of the United States, and who shall not, when elected, be an Inhabitant of that State for which he shall be chosen.

The Vice President of the United States shall be President of the Senate, but shall have no Vote, unless they be equally divided.

The Senate shall chuse their other Officers, and also a President pro tempore, in the Absence of the Vice President, or when he shall exercise the Office of President of the United States.

The Senate shall have the sole Power to try all Impeachments. When sitting for that Purpose, they shall be on Oath or Affirmation. When the President of the United States is tried, the Chief Justice shall preside: And no Person shall be convicted without the Concurrence of two thirds of the Members present.

Judgment in Cases of Impeachment shall not extend further than to removal from Office, and disqualification to hold and enjoy any Office of honor, Trust or Profit under the United States: but the Party convicted shall nevertheless be liable and subject to Indictment, Trial, Judgment and Punishment, according to Law.

Section. 4.

The Times, Places and Manner of holding Elections for Senators and Representatives, shall be prescribed in each State by the Legislature thereof; but the Congress may at any time by Law make or alter such Regulations, except as to the Places of chusing Senators.

The Congress shall assemble at least once in every Year, and such Meeting shall be on the first Monday in December, unless they shall by Law appoint a different Day.

Section. 5.

Each House shall be the Judge of the Elections, Returns and Qualifications of its own Members, and a Majority of each shall constitute a Quorum to do Business; but a smaller Number may adjourn from day to day, and may be authorized to compel the Attendance of absent Members, in such Manner, and under such Penalties as each House may provide.

Each House may determine the Rules of its Proceedings, punish its Members for disorderly Behaviour, and, with the Concurrence of two thirds, expel a Member.

Each House shall keep a Journal of its Proceedings, and from time to time publish the same, excepting such Parts as may in their Judgment require Secrecy; and the Yeas and Nays of the Members of either House on any question shall, at the Desire of one fifth of those Present, be entered on the Journal.

Neither House, during the Session of Congress, shall, without the Consent of the other, adjourn for more than three days, nor to any other Place than that in which the two Houses shall be sitting.

Section. 6.

The Senators and Representatives shall receive a Compensation for their Services, to be ascertained by Law, and paid out of the Treasury of the United States. They shall in all Cases, except Treason, Felony and Breach of the Peace, be privileged from Arrest during their Attendance at the Session of their respective Houses, and in going to and returning from the same; and for any Speech or Debate in either House, they shall not be questioned in any other Place.

No Senator or Representative shall, during the Time for which he was elected, be appointed to any civil Office under the Authority of the United States, which shall have been created, or the Emoluments whereof shall have been encreased during such time; and no Person holding any Office under the United States, shall be a Member of either House during his Continuance in Office.

Section. 7.

All Bills for raising Revenue shall originate in the House of Representatives; but the Senate may propose or concur with Amendments as on other Bills.

Every Bill which shall have passed the House of Representatives and the Senate, shall, before it become a Law, be presented to the President of the United States; If he approve he shall sign it, but if not he shall return it, with his Objections to that House in which it shall have originated, who shall enter the Objections at large on their Journal, and proceed to reconsider it. If after such Reconsideration two thirds of that House shall agree to pass the Bill, it shall be sent, together with the Objections, to the other House, by which it shall likewise be reconsidered, and if approved by two thirds of that House, it shall become a Law. But in all such Cases the Votes of both Houses shall be determined by yeas and Nays, and the Names of the Persons voting for and against the Bill shall be entered on the Journal of each House respectively. If any Bill shall not be returned by the President within ten Days (Sundays excepted) after it shall have been presented to him, the Same shall be a Law, in like Manner as if he had signed it, unless the Congress by their Adjournment prevent its Return, in which Case it shall not be a Law.

Every Order, Resolution, or Vote to which the Concurrence of the Senate and House of Representatives may be necessary (except on a question of Adjournment) shall be presented to the President of the United States; and before the Same shall take Effect, shall be approved by him, or being disapproved by him, shall be repassed by two thirds of the Senate and House of Representatives, according to the Rules and Limitations prescribed in the Case of a Bill.

Section. 8.

The Congress shall have Power To lay and collect Taxes, Duties, Imposts and Excises, to pay the Debts and provide for the common Defence and general Welfare of the United States; but all Duties, Imposts and Excises shall be uniform throughout the United States;

To borrow money on the credit of the United States;

To regulate Commerce with foreign Nations, and among the several States, and with the Indian Tribes;

To establish an uniform Rule of Naturalization, and uniform Laws on the subject of Bankruptcies throughout the United States;

To coin Money, regulate the Value thereof, and of foreign Coin, and fix the Standard of Weights and Measures;

To provide for the Punishment of counterfeiting the Securities and current Coin of the United States;

To establish Post Offices and Post Roads;

To promote the Progress of Science and useful Arts, by securing for limited Times to Authors and Inventors the exclusive Right to their respective Writings and Discoveries;

To constitute Tribunals inferior to the supreme Court;

To define and punish Piracies and Felonies committed on the high Seas, and Offenses against the Law of Nations;

To declare War, grant Letters of Marque and Reprisal, and make Rules concerning Captures on Land and Water;

To raise and support Armies, but no Appropriation of Money to that Use shall be for a longer Term than two Years;

To provide and maintain a Navy;

To make Rules for the Government and Regulation of the land and naval Forces;

To provide for calling forth the Militia to execute the Laws of the Union, suppress Insurrections and repel Invasions;

To provide for organizing, arming, and disciplining, the Militia, and for governing such Part of them as may be employed in the Service of the United States, reserving to the States respectively, the Appointment of the Officers, and the Authority of training the Militia according to the discipline prescribed by Congress;

To exercise exclusive Legislation in all Cases whatsoever, over such District (not exceeding ten Miles square) as may, by Cession of particular States, and the acceptance of Congress, become the Seat of the Government of the United States, and to exercise like Authority over all Places purchased by the Consent of the Legislature of the State in which the Same shall be, for the Erection of Forts, Magazines, Arsenals, dock-Yards, and other needful Buildings; And

To make all Laws which shall be necessary and proper for carrying into Execution the foregoing Powers, and all other Powers vested by this Constitution in the Government of the United States, or in any Department or Officer thereof.

Section. 9.

The Migration or Importation of such Persons as any of the States now existing shall think proper to admit, shall not be prohibited by the Congress prior to the Year one thousand eight hundred and eight, but a Tax or duty may be imposed on such Importation, not exceeding ten dollars for each Person.

The Privilege of the Writ of Habeas Corpus shall not be suspended, unless when in Cases of Rebellion or Invasion the public Safety may require it.

No Bill of Attainder or ex post facto Law shall be passed.

No Capitation, or other direct, Tax shall be laid, unless in Proportion to the Census or enumeration herein before directed to be taken.

No Tax or Duty shall be laid on Articles exported from any State.

No Preference shall be given by any Regulation of Commerce or Revenue to the Ports of one State over those of another: nor shall Vessels bound to, or from, one State, be obliged to enter, clear, or pay Duties in another.

No Money shall be drawn from the Treasury, but in Consequence of Appropriations made by Law; and a regular Statement and Account of the Receipts and Expenditures of all public Money shall be published from time to time.

No Title of Nobility shall be granted by the United States: And no Person holding any Office of Profit or Trust under them, shall, without the Consent of the Congress, accept of any present, Emolument, Office, or Title, of any kind whatever, from any King, Prince, or foreign State.

Section. 10.

No State shall enter into any Treaty, Alliance, or Confederation; grant Letters of Marque and Reprisal; coin Money; emit Bills of Credit; make any Thing but gold and silver Coin a Tender in Payment of Debts; pass any Bill of Attainder, ex post facto Law, or Law impairing the Obligation of Contracts, or grant any Title of Nobility.

No State shall, without the Consent of the Congress, lay any Imposts or Duties on Imports or Exports, except what may be absolutely necessary for executing it's inspection Laws: and the net Produce of all Duties and Imposts, laid by any State on Imports or Exports, shall be for the Use of the Treasury of the United States; and all such Laws shall be subject to the Revision and Controul of the Congress.

No State shall, without the Consent of Congress, lay any Duty of Tonnage, keep Troops, or Ships of War in time of Peace, enter into any Agreement or Compact with another State, or with a foreign Power, or engage in War, unless actually invaded, or in such imminent Danger as will not admit of delay.

ARTICLE. II.

Section. 1.

The executive Power shall be vested in a President of the United States of America. He shall hold his Office during the Term of four Years, and, together with the Vice President, chosen for the same Term, be elected, as follows

Each State shall appoint, in such Manner as the Legislature thereof may direct, a Number of Electors, equal to the whole Number of Senators and Representatives to which the State may be entitled in the Congress: but no Senator or Representative, or Person holding an Office of Trust or Profit under the United States, shall be appointed an Elector.

The Electors shall meet in their respective States, and vote by Ballot for two Persons, of whom one at least shall not be an Inhabitant of the same State with themselves. And they shall make a List of all the Persons voted for, and of the Number of Votes for each; which List they shall sign and certify, and transmit sealed to the Seat of the Government of the United States, directed to the President of the Senate. The President of the Senate shall, in the Presence of the Senate and House of Representatives, open all the Certificates, and the Votes shall then be counted. The Person having the greatest Number of Votes shall be the President, if such Number be a Majority of the whole Number of Electors appointed; and if there be more than one who have such Majority, and have an equal Number of Votes, then the House of Representatives shall immediately chuse by Ballot one of them for President; and if no Person have a Majority, then from the five highest on the List the said House shall in like Manner chuse the President. But in chusing the President, the Votes shall be taken by States, the Representation from each State having one Vote; A quorum for this Purpose shall consist of a Member or Members from two thirds of the States, and a Majority of all the States shall be necessary to a Choice. In every Case, after the Choice of the President, the Person having the greatest Number of Votes of the Electors shall be the Vice President. But if there should remain two or more who have equal Votes, the Senate shall chuse from them by Ballot the Vice President.

The Congress may determine the Time of chusing the Electors, and the Day on which they shall give their Votes; which Day shall be the same throughout the United States.

No Person except a natural born Citizen, or a Citizen of the United States, at the time of the Adoption of this Constitution, shall be eligible to the Office of President; neither shall any Person be eligible to that Office who shall not have attained to the Age of thirty five Years, and been fourteen Years a Resident within the United States.

In Case of the Removal of the President from Office, or of his Death, Resignation, or Inability to discharge the Powers and Duties of the said Office, the Same shall devolve on the Vice President, and the Congress may by Law provide for the Case of Removal, Death, Resignation or Inability, both of the President and Vice President, declaring what Officer shall then act as President, and such Officer shall act accordingly, until the Disability be removed, or a President shall be elected.

The President shall, at stated Times, receive for his Services, a Compensation, which shall neither be encreased nor diminished during the Period for which he shall have been elected, and he shall not receive within that Period any other Emolument from the United States, or any of them.

Before he enter on the Execution of his Office, he shall take the following Oath or Affirmation:—"I do solemnly swear (or affirm) that I will faithfully execute the Office of President of the United States, and will to the best of my Ability, preserve, protect and defend the Constitution of the United States."

Section. 2.

The President shall be Commander in Chief of the Army and Navy of the United States, and of the Militia of the several States, when called into the actual Service of the United States; he may require the Opinion, in writing, of the principal Officer in each of the executive Departments, upon any Subject relating to the Duties of their respective Offices, and he shall have Power to grant Reprieves and Pardons for Offences against the United States, except in Cases of Impeachment.

He shall have Power, by and with the Advice and Consent of the Senate, to make Treaties, provided two thirds of the Senators present concur; and he shall nominate, and by and with the Advice and Consent of the Senate, shall appoint Ambassadors, other public Ministers and Consuls, Judges of the supreme Court, and all other Officers of the United States, whose Appointments are not herein otherwise provided for, and which shall be established by Law: but the Congress may by Law vest the Appointment of such inferior Officers, as they think proper, in the President alone, in the Courts of Law, or in the Heads of Departments.

The President shall have Power to fill up all Vacancies that may happen during the Recess of the Senate, by granting Commissions which shall expire at the End of their next Session.

Section. 3.

He shall from time to time give to the Congress Information of the State of the Union, and recommend to their Consideration such Measures as he shall judge necessary and expedient; he may, on extraordinary Occasions, convene both Houses, or either of them, and in Case of Disagreement between them, with Respect to the Time of Adjournment, he may adjourn them to such Time as he shall think proper; he shall receive Ambassadors and other public Ministers; he shall take Care that the Laws be faithfully executed, and shall Commission all the Officers of the United States.

Section. 4.

The President, Vice President and all civil Officers of the United States, shall be removed from Office on Impeachment for, and Conviction of, Treason, Bribery, or other high Crimes and Misdemeanors.

Article III.

Section. 1.

The judicial Power of the United States, shall be vested in one supreme Court, and in such inferior Courts as the Congress may from time to time ordain and establish. The Judges, both of the supreme and inferior Courts, shall hold their Offices during good Behaviour, and shall, at stated Times, receive for their Services, a Compensation, which shall not be diminished during their Continuance in Office.

Section. 2.

The judicial Power shall extend to all Cases, in Law and Equity, arising under this Constitution, the Laws of the United States, and Treaties made, or which shall be made, under their Authority;—to all

Cases affecting Ambassadors, other public Ministers and Consuls;—to all Cases of admiralty and maritime Jurisdiction;—to Controversies to which the United States shall be a Party,—to Controversies between two or more States;— between a State and Citizens of another State,—between Citizens of different States,—between Citizens of the same State claiming Lands under Grants of different States, and between a State, or the Citizens thereof, and foreign States, Citizens or Subjects.

In all Cases affecting Ambassadors, other public Ministers and Consuls, and those in which a State shall be Party, the supreme Court shall have original Jurisdiction. In all the other Cases before mentioned, the supreme Court shall have appellate Jurisdiction, both as to Law and Fact, with such Exceptions, and under such Regulations as the Congress shall make.

The Trial of all Crimes, except in Cases of Impeachment, shall be by Jury; and such Trial shall be held in the State where the said Crimes shall have been committed; but when not committed within any State, the Trial shall be at such Place or Places as the Congress may by Law have directed.

Section. 3.

Treason against the United States, shall consist only in levying War against them, or in adhering to their Enemies, giving them Aid and Comfort. No Person shall be convicted of Treason unless on the Testimony of two Witnesses to the same overt Act, or on Confession in open Court.

The Congress shall have Power to declare the Punishment of Treason, but no Attainder of Treason shall work Corruption of Blood, or Forfeiture except during the Life of the Person attainted.

ARTICLE. IV.

Section. 1.

Full Faith and Credit shall be given in each State to the public Acts, Records, and judicial Proceedings of every other State. And the Congress may by general Laws prescribe the Manner in which such

Acts, Records and Proceedings shall be proved, and the Effect thereof.

Section. 2.

The Citizens of each State shall be entitled to all Privileges and Immunities of Citizens in the several States.

A Person charged in any State with Treason, Felony, or other Crime, who shall flee from Justice, and be found in another State, shall on Demand of the executive Authority of the State from which he fled, be delivered up, to be removed to the State having Jurisdiction of the Crime.

No Person held to Service or Labour in one State, under the Laws thereof, escaping into another, shall, in Consequence of any Law or Regulation therein, be discharged from such Service or Labour, but shall be delivered up on Claim of the Party to whom such Service or Labour may be due.

Section. 3.

New States may be admitted by the Congress into this Union; but no new State shall be formed or erected within the Jurisdiction of any other State; nor any State be formed by the Junction of two or more States, or Parts of States, without the Consent of the Legislatures of the States concerned as well as of the Congress.

The Congress shall have Power to dispose of and make all needful Rules and Regulations respecting the Territory or other Property belonging to the United States; and nothing in this Constitution shall be so construed as to Prejudice any Claims of the United States, or of any particular State.

Section. 4.

The United States shall guarantee to every State in this Union a Republican Form of Government, and shall protect each of them against Invasion; and on Application of the Legislature, or of the Executive (when the Legislature cannot be convened), against domestic Violence.

ARTICLE. V.

The Congress, whenever two thirds of both Houses shall deem it necessary, shall propose Amendments to this Constitution, or, on the Application of the Legislatures of two thirds of the several States, shall call a Convention for proposing Amendments, which, in either Case, shall be valid to all Intents and Purposes, as Part of this Constitution, when ratified by the Legislatures of three fourths of the several States, or by Conventions in three fourths thereof, as the one or the other Mode of Ratification may be proposed by the Congress; Provided that no Amendment which may be made prior to the Year One thousand eight hundred and eight shall in any Manner affect the first and fourth Clauses in the Ninth Section of the first Article; and that no State, without its Consent, shall be deprived of its equal Suffrage in the Senate.

ARTICLE. VI.

All Debts contracted and Engagements entered into, before the Adoption of this Constitution, shall be as valid against the United States under this Constitution, as under the Confederation.

This Constitution, and the Laws of the United States which shall be made in Pursuance thereof; and all Treaties made, or which shall be made, under the Authority of the United States, shall be the supreme Law of the Land; and the Judges in every State shall be bound thereby, any Thing in the Constitution or Laws of any State to the Contrary notwithstanding.

The Senators and Representatives before mentioned, and the Members of the several State Legislatures, and all executive and judicial Officers, both of the United States and of the several States, shall be bound by Oath or Affirmation, to support this Constitution; but no religious Test shall ever be required as a Qualification to any Office or public Trust under the United States.

ARTICLE. VII.

The Ratification of the Conventions of nine States, shall be sufficient for the Establishment of this Constitution between the States so ratifying the Same.

The Word, "the," being interlined between the seventh and eighth Lines of the first Page, The Word "Thirty" being partly written on an Erazure in the fifteenth Line of the first Page, The Words "is tried" being interlined between the thirty second and thirty third Lines of the first Page and the Word "the" being interlined between the forty third and forty fourth Lines of the second Page.

Attest William Jackson Secretary

done in Convention by the Unanimous Consent of the States present the Seventeenth Day of September in the Year of our Lord one thousand seven hundred and Eighty seven and of the Independance of the United States of America the Twelfth In witness whereof We have hereunto subscribed our Names,

G°. Washington
Presidt and deputy from Virginia

Delaware
Geo: Read
Gunning Bedford jun
John Dickinson
Richard Bassett
Jaco: Broom

Maryland
James McHenry
Dan of St Thos. Jenifer
Danl. Carroll

Virginia
John Blair
James Madison Jr.

North Carolina
Wm. Blount
Richd. Dobbs Spaight
Hu Williamson

South Carolina
J. Rutledge
Charles Cotesworth Pinckney
Charles Pinckney
Pierce Butler

Georgia
William Few
Abr Baldwin

New Hampshire
John Langdon
Nicholas Gilman

Massachusetts
Nathaniel Gorham
Rufus King

Connecticut
Wm. Saml. Johnson
Roger Sherman

New York
Alexander Hamilton

New Jersey
Wil: Livingston
David Brearley
Wm. Paterson
Jona: Dayton

Pensylvania
B Franklin
Thomas Mifflin
Robt. Morris
Geo. Clymer
Thos. FitzSimons
Jared Ingersoll
James Wilson
Gouv Morris

Bill of Rights and Amendments

AMENDING THE CONSTITUTION

- The Bill of Rights, made up of the first ten amendments to the Constitution of the United States was ratified on December 15th, 1971.
- Each subsequent amendment was proposed by the consent of two thirds of both houses and ratified by consent of three fourths of the State Legislatures.
- States may also propose amendments by calling for a Constitutional Convention with the application of two thirds of the State Legislatures, but this has never been done.

AMENDMENT I

Congress shall make no law respecting an establishment of religion, or prohibiting the free exercise thereof; or abridging the freedom of speech, or of the press; or the right of the people peaceably to assemble, and to petition the Government for a redress of grievances.

AMENDMENT II

A well regulated Militia, being necessary to the security of a free State, the right of the people to keep and bear Arms, shall not be infringed.

AMENDMENT III

No Soldier shall, in time of peace be quartered in any house, without the consent of the Owner, nor in time of war, but in a manner to be prescribed by law.

AMENDMENT IV

The right of the people to be secure in their persons, houses, papers, and effects, against unreasonable searches and seizures, shall not be violated, and no Warrants shall issue, but upon probable cause, supported by Oath or affirmation, and particularly describing the place to be searched, and the persons or things to be seized.

AMENDMENT V

No person shall be held to answer for a capital, or otherwise infamous crime, unless on a presentment or indictment of a Grand Jury, except in cases arising in the land or naval forces, or in the Militia, when in actual service in time of War or public danger; nor shall any person be subject for the same offence to be twice put in jeopardy of life or limb; nor shall be compelled in any criminal case to be a witness against himself, nor be deprived of life, liberty, or property, without due process of law; nor shall private property be taken for public use, without just compensation.

AMENDMENT VI

In all criminal prosecutions, the accused shall enjoy the right to a speedy and public trial, by an impartial jury of the State and district wherein the crime shall have been committed, which district shall have been previously ascertained by law, and to be informed of the nature and cause of the accusation; to be confronted with the witnesses against him; to have compulsory process for obtaining witnesses in his favor, and to have the Assistance of Counsel for his defence.

AMENDMENT VII

In Suits at common law, where the value in controversy shall exceed twenty dollars, the right of trial by jury shall be preserved, and no fact tried by a jury, shall be otherwise re-examined in any Court of the United States, than according to the rules of the common law.

AMENDMENT VIII

Excessive bail shall not be required, nor excessive fines imposed, nor cruel and unusual punishments inflicted.

AMENDMENT IX

The enumeration in the Constitution, of certain rights, shall not be construed to deny or disparage others retained by the people.

AMENDMENT X

The powers not delegated to the United States by the Constitution, nor prohibited by it to the States, are reserved to the States respectively, or to the people.

AMENDMENT XI

The Judicial power of the United States shall not be construed to extend to any suit in law or equity, commenced or prosecuted against one of the United States by Citizens of another State, or by Citizens or Subjects of any Foreign State.

Ratified February 7, 1795

Amendment XII

The Electors shall meet in their respective states and vote by ballot for President and Vice-President, one of whom, at least, shall not be an inhabitant of the same state with themselves; they shall name in their ballots the person voted for as President, and in distinct ballots the person voted for as Vice-President, and they shall make distinct lists of all persons voted for as President, and of all persons voted for as Vice-President, and of the number of votes for each, which lists they shall sign and certify, and transmit sealed to the seat of the government of the United States, directed to the President of the Senate; -- the President of the Senate shall, in the presence of the Senate and House of Representatives, open all the certificates and the votes shall then be counted; -- The person having the greatest number of votes for President, shall be the President, if such number be a majority of the whole number of Electors appointed; and if no person have such majority, then from the persons having the highest numbers not exceeding three on the list of those voted for as President, the House of Representatives shall choose immediately, by ballot, the President. But in choosing the President, the votes shall be taken by states, the representation from each state having one vote; a quorum for this purpose shall consist of a member or members from two-thirds of the states, and a majority of all the states shall be necessary to a choice. [And if the House of Representatives shall not choose a President whenever the right of choice shall devolve upon them, before the fourth day of March next following, then the Vice-President shall act as President, as in case of the death or other constitutional disability of the President. --]* The person having the greatest number of votes as Vice-President, shall be the Vice-President, if such number be a majority of the whole number of Electors appointed, and if no person have a majority, then from the two highest numbers on the list, the Senate shall choose the Vice-President; a quorum for the purpose shall consist of two-thirds of the whole number of Senators, and a majority of the whole number shall be necessary to a choice. But no person constitutionally ineligible to the office of President shall be eligible to that of Vice-President of the United States.

Ratified June 15, 1804

AMENDMENT XIII

Section 1.

Neither slavery nor involuntary servitude, except as a punishment for crime whereof the party shall have been duly convicted, shall exist within the United States, or any place subject to their jurisdiction.

Section 2.

Congress shall have power to enforce this article by appropriate legislation.

Ratified December 6, 1865

AMENDMENT XIV

Section 1.

All persons born or naturalized in the United States, and subject to the jurisdiction thereof, are citizens of the United States and of the State wherein they reside. No State shall make or enforce any law which shall abridge the privileges or immunities of citizens of the United States; nor shall any State deprive any person of life, liberty, or property, without due process of law; nor deny to any person within its jurisdiction the equal protection of the laws.

Section 2.

Representatives shall be apportioned among the several States according to their respective numbers, counting the whole number of persons in each State, excluding Indians not taxed. But when the right to vote at any election for the choice of electors for President and Vice-President of the United States, Representatives in Congress, the Executive and Judicial officers of a State, or the members of the Legislature thereof, is denied to any of the male inhabitants of such State, being twenty-one years of age,* and citizens of the United States, or in any way abridged, except for participation in rebellion, or other crime, the basis of representation therein shall be reduced in the proportion which the number of such male citizens shall bear to the whole number of male citizens twenty-one years of age in such State.

Section 3.

No person shall be a Senator or Representative in Congress, or elector of President and Vice-President, or hold any office, civil or military, under the United States, or under any State, who, having previously taken an oath, as a member of Congress, or as an officer of the United States, or as a member of any State legislature, or as an executive or judicial officer of any State, to support the Constitution of the United States, shall have engaged in insurrection or rebellion against the same, or given aid or comfort to the enemies thereof. But Congress may by a vote of two-thirds of each House, remove such disability.

Section 4.

The validity of the public debt of the United States, authorized by law, including debts incurred for payment of pensions and bounties for services in suppressing insurrection or rebellion, shall not be questioned. But neither the United States nor any State shall assume or pay any debt or obligation incurred in aid of insurrection or rebellion against the United States, or any claim for the loss or emancipation of any slave; but all such debts, obligations and claims shall be held illegal and void.

Section 5.

The Congress shall have the power to enforce, by appropriate legislation, the provisions of this article.

Ratified July 9, 1868

AMENDMENT XV

Section 1.

The right of citizens of the United States to vote shall not be denied or abridged by the United States or by any State on account of race, color, or previous condition of servitude.

Section 2.

The Congress shall have the power to enforce this article by appropriate legislation.

Ratified February 3, 1870

Amendment XVI

The Congress shall have power to lay and collect taxes on incomes, from whatever source derived, without apportionment among the several States, and without regard to any census or enumeration.

Ratified February 3, 1913

Amendment XVII

The Senate of the United States shall be composed of two Senators from each State, elected by the people thereof, for six years; and each Senator shall have one vote. The electors in each State shall have the qualifications requisite for electors of the most numerous branch of the State legislatures.

When vacancies happen in the representation of any State in the Senate, the executive authority of such State shall issue writs of election to fill such vacancies: Provided, That the legislature of any State may empower the executive thereof to make temporary appointments until the people fill the vacancies by election as the legislature may direct.

This amendment shall not be so construed as to affect the election or term of any Senator chosen before it becomes valid as part of the Constitution.

Ratified April 8, 1913

Amendment XVIII

Section 1.

After one year from the ratification of this article the manufacture, sale, or transportation of intoxicating liquors within, the importation thereof into, or the exportation thereof from the United States and all territory subject to the jurisdiction thereof for beverage purposes is hereby prohibited.

Section 2.

The Congress and the several States shall have concurrent power to enforce this article by appropriate legislation.

Section 3.

This article shall be inoperative unless it shall have been ratified as an amendment to the Constitution by the legislatures of the several States, as provided in the Constitution, within seven years from the date of the submission hereof to the States by the Congress.

Ratified January 16, 1919

Repealed December 5th, 1933 By Amendment 21

Amendment XIX

The right of citizens of the United States to vote shall not be denied or abridged by the United States or by any State on account of sex.

Congress shall have power to enforce this article by appropriate legislation.

Ratified August 18, 1920

AMENDMENT XX

Section 1.

The terms of the President and the Vice President shall end at noon on the 20th day of January, and the terms of Senators and Representatives at noon on the 3d day of January, of the years in which such terms would have ended if this article had not been ratified; and the terms of their successors shall then begin.

Section 2.

The Congress shall assemble at least once in every year, and such meeting shall begin at noon on the 3d day of January, unless they shall by law appoint a different day.

Section 3.

If, at the time fixed for the beginning of the term of the President, the President elect shall have died, the Vice President elect shall become President. If a President shall not have been chosen before the time fixed for the beginning of his term, or if the President elect shall have failed to qualify, then the Vice President elect shall act as President until a President shall have qualified; and the Congress may by law provide for the case wherein neither a President elect nor a Vice President elect shall have qualified, declaring who shall then act as President, or the manner in which one who is to act shall be selected, and such person shall act accordingly until a President or Vice President shall have qualified.

Section 4.

The Congress may by law provide for the case of the death of any of the persons from whom the House of Representatives may choose a President whenever the right of choice shall have devolved upon them, and for the case of the death of any of the persons from whom the Senate may choose a Vice President whenever the right of choice shall have devolved upon them.

Section 5.

Sections 1 and 2 shall take effect on the 15th day of October following the ratification of this article.

Section 6.

This article shall be inoperative unless it shall have been ratified as an amendment to the Constitution by the legislatures of three-fourths of the several States within seven years from the date of its submission.

Ratified January 23, 1933

AMENDMENT XXI

Section 1.

The eighteenth article of amendment to the Constitution of the United States is hereby repealed.

Section 2.

The transportation or importation into any State, Territory, or possession of the United States for delivery or use therein of intoxicating liquors, in violation of the laws thereof, is hereby prohibited.

Section 3.

This article shall be inoperative unless it shall have been ratified as an amendment to the Constitution by conventions in the several States, as provided in the Constitution, within seven years from the date of the submission hereof to the States by the Congress.

Ratified December 5, 1933

AMENDMENT XXII

Section 1.

No person shall be elected to the office of the President more than twice, and no person who has held the office of President, or acted as President, for more than two years of a term to which some other person was elected President shall be elected to the office of the President more than once. But this Article shall not apply to any person holding the office of President wher_ this Article was proposed by the Congress, and shall not prevent any person who may be holding the office of President, or acting as President, during the term within which this Article becomes operative from holding the office of President or acting as President during the remainder of such term.

Section 2.

This article shall be inoperative unless it shall have been ratified as an amendment to the Constitution by the legislatures of three-fourths of the several States within seven years from the date of its submission to the States by the Congress.

Ratified February 27, 1951

AMENDMENT XXIII

Section 1.

The District constituting the seat of Government of the United States shall appoint in such manner as the Congress may direct:

A number of electors of President and Vice President equal to the whole number of Senators and Representatives in Congress to which the District would be entitled if it were a State, but in no event more than the least populous State; they shall be in addition to those appointed by the States, but they shall be considered, for the purposes of the election of President and Vice President, to be electors appointed by a State; and they shall meet in the District and perform such duties as provided by the twelfth article of amendment.

Section 2.

The Congress shall have power to enforce this article by appropriate legislation.

Ratified March 29, 1961

AMENDMENT XXIV

Section 1.

The right of citizens of the United States to vote in any primary or other election for President or Vice President, for electors for President or Vice President, or for Senator or Representative in Congress, shall not be denied or abridged by the United States or any State by reason of failure to pay any poll tax or other tax.

Section 2.

The Congress shall have power to enforce this article by appropriate legislation.

Ratified January 23, 1964

AMENDMENT XXV

Note: Article II, section 1, of the Constitution was affected by the 25th amendment.

Section 1.

In case of the removal of the President from office or of his death or resignation, the Vice President shall become President.

Section 2.

Whenever there is a vacancy in the office of the Vice President, the President shall nominate a Vice President who shall take office upon confirmation by a majority vote of both Houses of Congress.

Section 3.

Whenever the President transmits to the President pro tempore of the Senate and the Speaker of the House of Representatives his written declaration that he is unable to discharge the powers and duties of his office, and until he transmits to them a written declaration to the contrary, such powers and duties shall be discharged by the Vice President as Acting President.

Section 4.

Whenever the Vice President and a majority of either the principal officers of the executive departments or of such other body as Congress may by law provide, transmit to the President pro tempore of the Senate and the Speaker of the House of Representatives their written declaration that the President is unable to discharge the powers and duties of his office, the Vice President shall immediately assume the powers and duties of the office as Acting President.

Thereafter, when the President transmits to the President pro tempore of the Senate and the Speaker of the House of Representatives his written declaration that no inability exists, he shall resume the powers and duties of his office unless the Vice President and a majority of either the principal officers of the executive department or of such other body as Congress may by law provide, transmit within four days to the President pro tempore of the Senate and the Speaker of the House of Representatives their written declaration that the President is unable to discharge the powers and duties of his office. Thereupon Congress shall decide the issue, assembling within forty-eight hours for that purpose if not in session. If the Congress, within twenty-one days after receipt of the latter written declaration, or, if Congress is not in session, within twenty-one days after Congress is required to assemble, determines by two-thirds vote of both Houses that the President is unable to discharge the powers and duties of his office, the Vice President shall continue to discharge the same as Acting President; otherwise, the President shall resume the powers and duties of his office.

Ratified February 10, 1967

Amendment XXVI

Section 1.

The right of citizens of the United States, who are eighteen years of age or older, to vote shall not be denied or abridged by the United States or by any State on account of age.

Section 2.

The Congress shall have power to enforce this article by appropriate legislation.

Ratified July 1, 1971

Amendment XXVII

No law, varying the compensation for the services of the Senators and Representatives, shall take effect, until an election of Representatives shall have intervened.

Ratified May 7, 1992

Thanks to http://www.usconstitution.net for providing a very nice online version of the U.S. Constitution.

www.ingramcontent.com/pod-product-compliance
Lightning Source LLC
Chambersburg PA
CBHW071328310526
45789CB00017B/1932